MARITIME HISTORY

VOLUME 2:

The Eighteenth Century
and
The Classic Age of Sail

Vaisseau du premier rang portant pavillon d'Amiral

An Eighteenth-century French ship from *Le Neptune François ou Atlas Nouveau des Cartes Marines* (Paris, 1703). Courtesy of the John Carter Brown Library at Brown University.

MARITIME HISTORY

VOLUME 2:

The Eighteenth Century
and
The Classic Age of Sail

Edited by
John B. Hattendorf
Ernest J. King Professor of Maritime History
Naval War College, Newport, RI

KRIEGER PUBLISHING COMPANY
MALABAR, FLORIDA
1997

Original Edition 1997

Printed and Published by
KRIEGER PUBLISHING COMPANY
KRIEGER DRIVE
MALABAR, FLORIDA 32950

Library of Congress Cataloging-in-Publication Data

Maritime history volume 1: the Age of Discovery/edited by John B. Hattendorf.
     p.   cm.—(Open forum series)
   "A selection from the lectures delivered . . . at the John Carter Brown Library's
month-long Summer Institute in Early Modern Maritime History held during
August 1992"—Foreword.
   Includes bibliographical references and index.
   ISBN 0-89464-834-9 (V. 1 paperback) (alk. paper)
   ISBN 1-57524-010-6 (V. 1 cloth) (alk. paper)
   ISBN 0-89464-944-2 (V. 2 paperback (alk. paper)
   ISBN 1-57524-007-6 (V. 2 cloth) (alk. paper)
   ISBN 1-57524-013-0 (set cloth) (alk. paper)

   1. Navigation—Europe—History 15th century. 2. Navigation- Europe—
History 16th century. 3. Europe—History, Naval
  I. Hattendorf, John B. II. Series.
VK55.M373 1996
387'.0094'09024–dc20   94-24805
                                          CIP

10 9 8 7 6 5 4 3 2

TABLE OF CONTENTS

LIST OF ILLUSTRATIONS

ABOUT THE CONTRIBUTORS

Daniel A. Baugh is Professor of Modern British History at Cornell University. His principal works are *British Naval Administration in the Age of Walpole* (1965) and *Naval Administration, 1715–1750* (1977). He has written on government and society in England, 1660–1830, especially on relief of the poor. During the past dozen years his articles and essays have been chiefly concerned with the maritime, financial, and imperial aspects of British defense policy from the sixteenth to the early twentieth century.

Karel Davids is Professor of Economic and Social History at the Vrije Universiteit Amsterdam, The Netherlands. He is the author of *Zeewezen en wetenschap: De wetenschap en de ontwikkeling van de navigatietechniek in Nederland tussen 1585 en 1815 [Seafaring and Science: Science and the Development of Navigation Technology in the Netherlands between 1585 and 1815]*(1986) and numerous articles on the history of navigation technology in the early modern period.

John B. Hattendorf, is the Ernest J. King Professor of Maritime History and Director of the Advanced Research Department at the U.S. Naval War College, Newport, Rhode Island. A member of the faculty of the Munson Institute of American Maritime History at Mystic Seaport, Connecticut, he was the academic director of the NEH Summer Institutes on Early Maritime History held at the John Carter Brown Library in the summers of 1992 and 1993, where these essays were first presented as lectures. He is the general editor of the John Carter Brown Library's series of facsimiles of rare books in maritime history.

R. J. B. Knight is the Deputy Director of the National Maritime Museum, Greenwich, and Director of the Museum's Information Division. He has worked at the Museum since 1974 in a number of roles, including collection management, computerization and displays. As Custodian of Manuscripts, he compiled the two volume *Guide to the Manuscripts in the National Maritime Museum*

(1977–80). A specialist in late eighteenth-century naval administration, he has edited a volume in the Portsmouth Record Series, *Portsmouth Dockyard Papers, 1774–1783* (1987). He was the editor for the eighteenth-century section of the Navy Records Society's *British Naval Documents, 1204–1960* (1993), and in the same year was the Alexander O. Vietor Fellow at the John Carter Brown Library.

Benjamin W. Labaree is Director of the Munson Institute of American Maritime Studies at Mystic Seaport; Professor of History and Environmental Studies, *Emeritus,* Williams College, and co-author of the forthcoming American maritime history to be published by Mystic Seaport Museum in 1997.

Willem F. J. Mörzer Bruyns is Senior Curator (navigation) at the Nederlands Scheepvaartmuseum, Amsterdam, The Netherlands. His is a Fellow of the Royal Institute of Navigation in London, and in 1995 the Huntington Fellow at The Mariners' Museum, Newport News, Virginia.

Thomas Philbrick, Emeritus Professor of English at the University of Pittsburgh, is the author of *James Fenimore Cooper and the Development of American Sea Fiction* and editor of several works of nineteenth-century American maritime literature, including Cooper's *The Red Rover* and Dana's *Two Years before the Mast.*

N. A. M. Rodger, is a former Assistant Keeper in the Public Record Office, and now Anderson Research Fellow of the National Maritime Museum, where he is working on a new naval history of Britain. He has already published *The Wooden World, An Anatomy of the Georgian Navy* (1986) and *The Insatiable Earl: A Life of John Montagu, Fourth Earl of Sandwich, 1718–1792* (1993.)

Glyndwr Williams is Professor of History at Queen Mary and Westfield College, University of London, and a former President of the Hakluyt Society. His books include *The British Search for the Northwest Passage in the Eighteenth Century* (1962); *The Expansion of Europe in the Eighteenth Century* (1966); *The Great Map of Mankind* (with P.J. Marshall, 1982); *Terra Australis to Australia* (with Alan Frost, 1988). His most recent publication is a two-volume edition of *Voyages in Search of a Northwest Passage, 1741–1747* (with William Barr, 1994, 1995).

PREFACE

This volume is a selection from the lectures delivered in Providence, Rhode Island, at the John Carter Brown Library's month long, Summer Institute in Early Modern Maritime History held during August 1993. This was the second of three such summer institutes, supported by the National Endowment for the Humanities, recognizing a national need for academic support of the maritime humanities. The first institute focused on European oceanic voyages in the fifteenth and sixteenth centuries; the second focused on the seventeenth and eighteenth centuries, and the third, held at Mystic Seaport in 1996, on America and the sea.

As the 1993 Institute's program director, I designed the month's course of study as a broad outline of maritime history from the early seventeenth century through the end of the Napoleonic Wars and with a glance toward the end of the age of sail. The Institute was held at the John Carter Brown Library in order to utilize its rich collection of maps and charts and other published materials emphasizing the discovery, exploration, settlement, and development of the Americas, with its associated collection of navigation treatises, voyage and battle narratives, trade reports, seamen's trading manuals, works on naval architecture and rigging, accounts of shipwrecks, and sailing guides.

In addition, the Library's location on the campus of Brown University placed it close to the major maritime museums and related activities in the New England area, including a walking tour of Boston as an eighteenth-century port, and visits to Mystic Seaport, the Peabody Museum, and Kendall Whaling Museum. During the course of the Institute, the participants viewed these museum collections and were able to examine closely the replica of the *Mayflower* at Plymouth and spend a day at sea on board the Sea Education Association's sail training and research vessel, *Corwith Cramer*.

Complementing seminar discussions and the examination of original materials, they heard more than 30 lectures that were intended to illuminate the full scope of issues relating to nautical and oceanic affairs, embracing technology, economics, sociology, art and literature, politics, ideas, ship design, navigation, and cartography. Of this wide range, it has been possible to publish only 21, concentrating primarily on the eighteenth century.

The Summer Institute educated 20 university and college-level faculty members in the rudiments of maritime history. Since 1993, nearly all members have put the results of the Summer Institute to work on their home campuses by integrating it into their own courses in such disciplines as history, literature, and political science. This volume is an attempt to capture the work of the Summer Institute and to create from it a basic text at the high school or undergraduate level, leading new students into a deeper appreciation of a topic that has become widely neglected in university curricula.

As the product of the Summer Institute in Early Modern Maritime History at the John Carter Brown Library, this volume owes much to the many people who supported and encouraged the Institute, in a wide variety of ways. Among these I would like to acknowledge foremost among my colleagues on the staff of the Institute: the director of the John Carter Brown Library, Dr. Norman Fiering, who was the administrator in charge of the Institute; Dr. Mary Malloy, a member of the teaching staff at the Sea Education Association of Woods Hole, Massachusetts, who was the energetic and knowledgeable assistant director of the institute; and Edward Gray, at the time a graduate student in the History Department at Brown, who was our student assistant for the project. (He has since completed work for the Ph.D.) Together, the four of us worked effectively and cooperatively as a team, learning from our previous experience together in the preceding year, to make the Institute a success.

A number of others contributed to the origins and the successful functioning of different facets of the of the Institute: Elizabeth Welles from the National Endowment for the Humanities; staff members of the John Carter Brown Library, in particular, Susan Danforth, Susan Newbury, Daniel Slive, Vivian Tetreault, Karen DeMaria, Richard Hurley, and Lynne Harrell; and members of the Ad Hoc Maritime Studies Committee at Brown University, chaired by Richard Gould. In addition, all institute members benefited from the participation of lecturers, whose work, for one reason or another, could not be included in this volume: Professor Jonathan Israel of the University of London; Professor Lionel Casson of New York University; Professor Joachim Stieber of Smith College; Paul Johnston of the Smithsonian Institution; Thomas R. Adams and Susan Danforth of the John Carter Brown Library; Dr. Jeffrey Bolster of the University of New Hampshire; William H. Andrewes of Harvard University and Dr. James Welu of the Worcester Art Museum.

Newport, Rhode Island   John B. Hattendorf

INTRODUCTION
John B. Hattendorf

The study of maritime history is a broad theme within general historical studies that, by its very nature, cuts across standard disciplinary boundaries. A student who pursues the theme may choose from a variety of vantage points, and at the same time, touch upon many perspectives and approaches, ranging from the histories of science, technology, industry, economics, trade, and politics to art, literature, ideas, sociology, military and naval affairs, international relations, institutional and organizational development, communications, migration, intercultural relations, and the exploitation and protection of natural resources. In short, maritime history is a humanistic study that includes all the dimensions of man's multifaceted relationship with the sea.

Maritime history focuses on ships and the sailors who operated them, relating an identifiable segment of society to a specific range of technological development and to the hostile geographical environment that covers seven-tenths of the globe's surface. The relative importance of maritime affairs has varied from one period to another in general history. It stands out in some periods and in some cultures and not in others. For example, maritime affairs were an essential aspect of general European and European colonial history from the fifteenth century to the twentieth century. Only in the twentieth century have alternative means of communication and transport developed to displace much of the technological, social, economic and industrial fabric that surrounded maritime affairs, although a number of these aspects have survived and continue to flourish. In addition to these concerns, maritime affairs have come to play a role in the identity and ideology of some countries and this has found expression in their arts, literature, leisure-time activities and popular culture.

While the subject may seem to brighten and fade for the general historian, a specialist in the subject of maritime history must keep in mind the continuity of maritime development through all periods. Maritime affairs are rarely, if ever, absent in history. At the same time, ships and sailors are not isolated phenomena. They are very much a part of larger developments. In order to understand what happened at sea and to analyze those events, one needs to relate them and interpret them in the context of broad issues occurring on land. Maritime history is, in many respects, only an extension of events on land, but it does involve a variety of very technical and specialist issues, such as shipbuilding, navigation, naval gunnery and tactics, marine engineering, hydrography, and so on. In order to understand the elements, which are key factors in maritime history, maritime historians must explain them in terms of the broadest context, while at the same time, they must come to grips with the details and make sense of the specific developments within that special area.

One of the main problems for maritime historians is the need to see events at sea in terms of many perspectives and levels of understanding. For example, a ship that was built in a particular country was the product of a certain national political, economic, social, technological and industrial factors. When the same ship sailed at sea, it entered a different realm with an international dimension that might have involved such additional factors as wars, cross-cultural relations, imperial competition, scientific research, the exchange of goods or the accumulation of capital through international trade.

Additionally, when ships left land and the network of activities that created and prepared them, they spent long isolated periods at sea. This human experience created a social dimension that, itself, became a new factor, creating microcosms and permutations of land-based societies while bringing the seamen into various new environments and experiences. These experiences, in turn, were reflected in land-based societies when sailors returned from the sea. In this area, as in others, maritime affairs typically acted as both a conduit as well as a separate channel of development.

Although focusing on ships and sailors, maritime historians treat the interrelationship of events at land and sea, dealing simultaneously with the integrated, parallel, and unique aspects involved. As maritime historians move forward in their researches, they must also strive to compare and to contrast maritime events at different times, in different circumstances, and in different contexts. As a theme in general history, maritime history is not separate from other aspects of historical study. Nevertheless, it involves a wide range of specialized learning and knowledge that justifies the identification of maritime history as one of the many legitimate fields for historical research and writing. Identifying the field in this way, however, neither removes it from the accepted standards of the best historical scholarship nor creates any unique standards or exclusive prerogatives for those who follow it. It merely recognizes that the topic is broad enough to identify fully a range of specialization and that it is complicated enough to sustain the wide-ranging work of a number of different scholars devoting their scholarly careers to working on different aspects within the theme.

The extended eighteenth century, from the mid-1600s to the early 1800s, has some characteristics that define it as one of the major periods within the broad topic of maritime history. In the first place, it lies chronologically at the end of the Early Modern period. As such, it is part of a whole range of earlier trends that culminate at this period and that first developed in the Age of Discovery. The eighteenth century encompasses a second Age of Discovery. Like the earlier period, there is strong a Eurocentric component to it, but at the same time, this factor diminishes considerably. Through the catalyst of maritime affairs, more sustained overseas cultural interactions and colonial developments result in important and powerful new forces.

In terms of science and technology, the eighteenth century saw important refinements. Above all for the maritime historian, it may be seen as the classic age of the sailing ship along with the technologies and skills surrounding it. But, these refinements extended beyond the ship, itself, to the science and practice of navigation, the industrial basis that produced the ships, the social system surrounding them and the economic system to which they contributed.

This period also saw important developments and refinements in the nation-state. The development of bureaucratic structures and state financing and state control were particularly important factors in maritime affairs during this period. A key expression of this can be seen in a wide range of factors connected with the development of navies in the eighteenth century. As a follow-on from the predominant emphasis on maritime exploration in the earlier age, the eighteenth-century maritime world saw commercial, economic, imperial, and colonial rivalry develop in its stead. The military and naval aspects for this were important in the period. The continuing legacy of all this found expression in a variety of ways, one of the most important being in art and literature.

Like any good piece of historical analysis on a specific theme, historians working in maritime history strive to make a positive contribution to knowledge on a small, but not isolated sector of that front. While they may limit themselves in scope to maritime affairs, the questions they answer have a discernible relationship with problems of more general interest. The essays that follow in this volume outline many such broad themes, providing an introduction and an overview to some aspects involved in both the specific subject of maritime history and the general history of the eighteenth century.

Part I
The Second Age of Discovery:
The Opening of the Pacific

1

PRECURSORS AND PREDATORS

Glyndwr Williams

The 70 years between the voyages of Narborough (1670–1) and Anson (1740–44) were part of the long interval between the hesitant Spanish incursions of the sixteenth century into the Mar del Zur and the systematic explorations of the later eighteenth century. From Magellan onward Europeans of several nations had ventured into, and sometimes across, the Pacific, but their explorations were for the most part inconclusive if not downright confusing. After Tasman's voyages in the 1640s the slow-moving course of European seaborne discovery expeditions almost came to a halt. If the geography of the Pacific was uncertain and fanciful, so was knowledge of its inhabitants. Among the island groups the explorers found a bewildering and unpredictable variety of appearance and behavior. Their observations were usually hasty and superficial, often the result of only a few days', or sometimes even a few hours' stay. Encounters varied from friendly to violent, but misunderstanding was more common than comprehension, and contact often ended with a blast of cannon and musket on one side and a shower of stones and arrows on the other. It was characteristic somehow that the difficult eastern entrance into the Pacific through the Strait of Magellan was supposedly guarded by a race of giants, symbolic of the fact that Europeans were entering an alien world where conventional standards did not apply.

When English interest in the Pacific revived in the later seventeenth century, the motives were the same as those which had prompted Drake and Cavendish a century before: trade and plunder. The Pacific caught the imagination not as a vast, trackless ocean but as the western rim of Spain's American empire. The "South Sea" which now began to exercise its fascination over distant enterprises was limited, in English eyes, to the waters which lapped the shores of Chile, Peru and Mexico. Along that remote Pacific seaboard English buccaneers and traders hoped to find a way of tapping the silver lifeline of Spanish America. The first English expedition to enter the Pacific in the seventeenth century differed from most of its successors in that it was an official one, fitted out by the Admiralty under the command of John Narborough. In 1670, he passed through the Strait of Magellan in an attempt to open trade with the Spaniards of Chile. The folly of this mission was exposed when the local garrison seized four of Narborough's men, and he could do nothing but return home, again by way of the Strait of Magellan. Narborough's detailed map of the Strait was published in 1673, and became a standard guide to that difficult navigation. If he had done nothing else, his return voyage had shown the fallacy of the Spanish reports which insisted that wind and current made a Pacific to the Atlantic passage of the Strait impossible.

After Narborough's unsuccessful venture, little more was heard in government circles about the South Sea. Instead, it attracted the attention of unofficial forces in the disreputable shape of the buccaneers. Although the center of their operations remained the Caribbean, Henry Morgan's attack on Panama in 1671 was followed in the next decade by forays across the Isthmus, or round Cape Horn, and into the South Sea. Neither trade nor exploration featured high on the buccaneers' list of priorities. As one of them wrote, "Gold was the bait that tempted a pack of Merry Boys of us." Violent, disputatious, anarchic, they pillaged and burnt their way along the Pacific coasts of Spanish America from Valparaiso to Acapulco. Their first irruption across the Isthmus and on to "the fair South-Sea" was led by Bartholomew Sharp. With him were those assiduous recorders of events—Basil Ringrose, Lionel Wafer, William Dampier—whose journals, like Sharp's, were to be published to intrigue and excite the reading public at home. Too small to attack the main Spanish citadels along the coast, Sharp's force pillaged smaller ports and ships before retiring to Juan Fernández at the end of 1680. Uninhabited, but with water and goats the island was, Sharp wrote, "a very refreshing Place to us," and it soon became a favorite haunt of the buccaneers.

By 1684, many of Sharp's old shipmates were back in the South Sea, and at least two expeditions (Eaton's in 1684 and Swan's in 1685) sailed northwest across the Pacific heading for the Marianas or the Philippines. At eight thousand miles, this was the longest unbroken sea passage in the world. With Swan on the buccaneer vessel *Cygnet* was Dampier, whose remarkable story of his wanderings was to be published in 1697 as *A New Voyage Round the World*. In late 1687, *Cygnet* was south of Timor, farthest south of the Dutch East Indies, and Dampier was on the fringe of one of his most important geographical discoveries. With the winds unfavorable for a return north, Dampier wrote, "we stood off South, intending to touch at New-Holland, a part of Terra Australis Incognita, to see what that Country would afford us." On 5 January 1688, the *Cygnet* anchored in a bay in latitude 16°50′S where, according to Dampier's book, the vessel remained until 12 March. However, a shorter manuscript account of the voyage gives 12 February as the departure date; even so, it still represents the longest known stay by Europeans on the Australian mainland. Tasman's visit to Van Diemen's Land, by contrast, had lasted only three days, and he himself had not gone ashore.

Dampier's description of the area around Cygnet Bay was uninspiring: dry, sandy soil; no surface water; some thin grass and stunted trees; little animal or bird life. But it was Dampier's description of the Aborigines encountered there which was to live long in the European memory: naked, black, without covering or habitation, "The Inhabitants of this Country are the miserablest People in the World . . . setting aside their Humane Shape, they differ but little from Brutes." It is one of the several puzzles of Dampier's peregrinations that his section on the Aborigines in his manuscript account, if shorter, is more dispassionate, and with none of the derogatory language which was to influence Cook and Banks on the east coast of Australia more than eighty years later.

It was the longer version which was to be printed, and become standard, for *A New Voyage* was a best-seller, and by 1699 it was in its fourth edition, and Dampier was a minor celebrity. Herman Moll's maps in the *New Voyage* made the outline of New Holland familiar in England for the first time, and seem to reflect Dampier's geographical notions. Both on the world map and the map of the East Indies, there is a hint of continental rather than insular dimensions about New Holland, and in the latter map the identification is made, "New Holland or Terra Australis Incognita." All this has its bearing on Dampier's second voyage to the region in 1699. Letters from him to the First Lord of the Admiralty, the Earl of Orford, reveal the genesis of the naval discovery expedition (a rarity in itself) whose fortunes were recounted by Dampier in his *Voyage to New Holland*. Although 1699 marked the moment when the long-impending crisis over the Spanish Succession, and the future of Spain's overseas empire, broke over Europe, there is no evidence

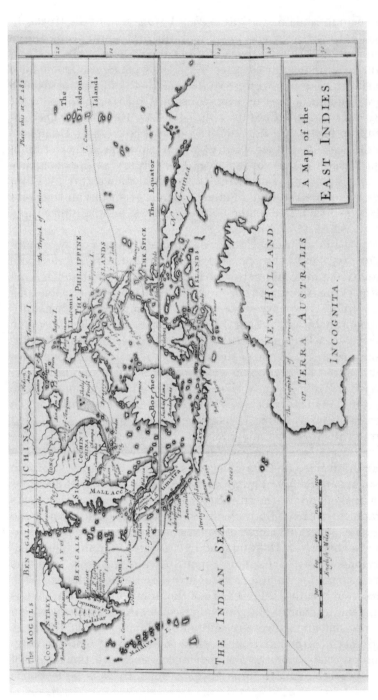

Figure I. Herman Moll, "A Map of the East Indies" from William Dampier, A New Voyage round the World (London, 1697). Courtesy of the John Carter Brown Library at Brown University

that Dampier's voyage of that year represented any serious thrust of national policy. The choice of area to be explored seems to have been Dampier's rather than the government's as he responded to an official request "to make a proposal of some voyage wherein I might be serviceable to My Nation." Nor is there any evidence of knowledge of the explorations of de Vlamingh's Dutch expedition on the west coast of Australia in 1696–7. The motives were sternly practical and commercial, as Dampier explained how the unknown vastness of Terra Australis must have "very valuable commodities."

As preparations for the voyage slowly proceeded the initial emphasis on Terra Australis, to be reached from the east by way of Cape Horn, changed to a plan for a voyage around the Cape of Good Hope into the Indian Ocean, touching on New Holland, and then searching for spice islands. In as far as one can detect any systematic geography in all this, it seems to rest on an interpretation of Tasman's voyage (and Dampier carried with him an English map of Tasman's track) which identified the stretch of the New Zealand coast reached by the Dutch as the edge of the great southern continent, Terra Australis, so that his track north from there to New Guinea had the unknown east coast of New Holland lying to port, and the equally unknown shoreline of the southern continent to starboard. Certainly, Dampier seems to have viewed New Holland as an obstacle, a barrier concealing more promising lands to the east—hence the original plan for a direct approach from Cape Horn. Dampier's letters to the Admiralty, it must be said, may have concealed as much as they revealed—a trading venture to islands just outside the Dutch sphere was possibly more appealing than a risky voyage to totally unknown shores.

In the event, the voyage was a troubled and contentious one, and Dampier was court-martialed on his return. In a shabby little vessel, the *Roebuck*, Dampier reached Shark Bay in western Australia in August 1699 (visited twice by the Dutch), and then sailed northeast. At a landing at Roebuck Bay in latitude 18°S., he had his only encounter with the Aborigines, a brief and violent scuffle. In Dampier's published account, there is little doubt but that the Aborigines were the aggressors—"menacing and threatening of us" until Dampier, reluctantly, was forced to open fire—but the manuscript journal of the *Roebuck*'s master gives a rather different account in which the Aborigines were depicted as "very shy," and were chased by Dampier's men until a scuffle took place during which one of Dampier's men was wounded by what he feared was a poisoned weapon, and Dampier shot one of the Aborigines seeking to pick up a wounded comrade. Dampier then pulled is men back, "being very sorry for what had happened already," to quote his own words. The natives, he described as being the much the same as those he had seen in 1688 with "the most unpleasant Looks and the worst Features of any people that ever I saw" though among them he identified what "seem'd to be the chief of them, a kind of Prince or Captain."

From New Holland, Dampier worked his way around the northern coast of New Guinea, and to the east discovered a large island (later found to be two adjoining islands) which he named New Britain. Contact with the inhabitants was fleeting. Some trade was carried on from the ship, but landing for wood and water was a tense business, accompanied by much firing of cannon to warn off possible attackers. Attempts at Montagu Harbour to trade for pigs ended in musket fire, though if Dampier's account is to be trusted, no one was killed. It stands as a stereotype for many confrontations between Europeans and Melanesians in this early contact period.

Apart from the valuable, if limited, charting of previously unknown areas, Dampier's voyage set a precedent of a sort. It was an Admiralty venture of Pacific exploration in which Dampier was instructed to make careful observations, collect specimens, and bring back "some of the Natives, provided they shall be willing to come along." On board he had "a Person skilled in Drawing," who managed some rather clumsy coastal profiles and illustrations of flora and fauna. Unless such drawings perished in the sinking of the *Roebuck* at Ascension Island, no attempts were made to draw either views or human figures. Dampier was no Cook, and his unknown artist no Parkinson; but at least some attempt was being made to meet the criticism of a writer a few years earlier that "This to be lamented, that the English Nation have not sent along with their Navigators some skilful Painters, Naturalists and Mechanists."[1] Dampier's main contribution came through his writings. So vivid were his word-pictures of the Aborigines of the west and northwest coasts, and what the West Countryman saw as their arid, fly-blown habitat, that 70 years later and a continent's span away, Cook and Banks looked at the Aborigines of Botany Bay through his eyes.

A more exact precursor of the expeditions of the second half of the eighteenth century were the contemporaneous voyages of Edmond Halley in the *Paramore* (1698–1701). They were concerned with new navigational methods rather than with new lands, and above all were intended "to improve the knowledge of the Longitude and variations of the Compasse." They stand as a landmark in English oceanic enterprise, not least in the burgeoning relationship they revealed between the Admiralty and the Royal Society. Although there was originally some intention of reaching "the East Indies or South Seas," Halley's voyages took him no farther than the South Atlantic, and the largest blank spaces on his magnificent world map of 1702 was the Pacific. As he explained, "I durst not presume to describe the like Curves in the South Sea wanting accounts thereof."

In 1703, Dampier was heading for the Pacific once more, this time on a disastrous privateering venture which ended in mutiny and recrimination. The track of the *St. George* was the standard one: Cape Horn, Juan Fernández, Galapagos Islands, Chile, Peru and Mexico. Dampier returned with reports of French trading vessels along the Pacific coast—a reminder that in the years between 1695 and 1726 no fewer than 168 French merchant ships were fitted out for the South Sea, though not all got there, and only about a half-dozen went on to cross the Pacific. Because of Spanish concern, French trading ships sometimes sailed, as a French minister put it, as if "going on exploration, or some other pretext." Among those who had read French accounts of the profits to be made in the South Sea was a young privateering captain, Woodes Rogers, who fitted out a new expedition. Dampier, who had been a friend of Rogers's father, this time sailed in the less arduous capacity as—"pilot to the South Seas." The venture was conducted efficiently and profitably, and within a year of its return to an England where the foundation of the South Sea Company had caused a great stir, accounts of the voyage had been published by Rogers and by Captain Edward Cooke. The voyage was marked by two events which caused, in their different ways, excitement at home: the capture of a galleon off Lower California in late 1709, and the finding on Juan Fernández of the most celebrated of all castaways, Alexander Selkirk. Daniel Defoe, it so happens, was connected with both events. As early as 1701 he had put forward proposals for South Sea trade and bases, though the Company established in 1711 seemed to him designed to waste rather than exploit the opportunities. The captured Acapulco galleon anchored in the Thames must have seemed the very incarnation of the wealth of the South Sea. Selkirk's story was to have an even more lasting impact, for it formed the inspiration for Defoe's *Robinson Crusoe* (1719). Woodes Rogers himself had no doubt about the interest of Selkirk's story. In vivid, direct language he described the first sighting of Selkirk, "a Man clothed in Goat-Skins, who looked wilder than the first Owners of them." Inevitably it seemed, Selkirk was an old shipmate of Dampier's, the "best man" on the ship Dampier claimed, but he had been marooned on the island for four years and four months. Rogers gave a careful detailed account of Selkirk's experiences and how "At his first coming on board us, he had so much forgot his language for want of use, that we could scarcely understand him, for he seem'd to speak his words by halves."

Ten years later there were two European expeditions in the Pacific, one English, one Dutch—and it was the latter which was the more important from the point of view of geographical discovery. This was the expedition of Jacob Roggeveen, whose objective was to find the great Southland or Terra Australis. Sailing west from Juan Fernández the expedition found, not continental shores, but Easter Island. For the first time Europeans saw the great statues, and wondered—for the first but not the last time—how they had been erected. Keeping west, Roggeveen ran along the edges of two island groups not previously known to Europeans—the Society Islands and Samoa. In general terms, the track of the expedition set a limit to the northward extension of a possible great continent, but its sightings of land seemed to make the existence of such a continent more likely.

The English expedition was that of George Shelvocke (1719–21), the last of the series of privateering voyages to enter the Pacific. The attempt to emulate Woodes Rogers was a failure, but there were features of interest about it, including a shipwreck on Juan Fernández, and in Lower California an enthusiastic panegyric on the lifestyle of the local inhabitants. At the opposite edge of the Pacific rim to Dampier's landing places in New Holland, Shelvocke or his editor had come up with a very different representation of a primitive lifestyle. The contrast is too ephemeral to bear any weighty generalizations, but there is here a hint that writers, and their readers, could cope with either of those artificial categories, noble or ignoble savages, but nothing in between.

The survivors of the expedition returned to an England where for years to come mention of the South Sea raised a specter—that of the collapse of the South Sea Company stock in the infamous "Bubble" of 1720. The financial speculations and chicanery which led to the crisis had little to do with the overseas trade, actual or potential, of the South Sea Company, but the catastrophe had a chastening effect on promoters and investors alike. The Pacific dropped out of reckoning as a sphere of British activity for almost 20 years, though it retained its attraction for compilers of travel accounts and for writers looking for a safe haven in which to pitch their satires and fantasies. This raises the question of the links, if any, between literary activity and practical interest. The outpouring of travel accounts about the South Sea from the 1690s onward might be expected to provide a test case, but the evidence is inconclusive. It is possible to argue the issue in two quite different ways. There is a temptation to see the Pacific locations of, say, *Gulliver's Travels* (1720) as evidence both of continuing interest in the area, and a channel through which that interest was enhanced because of the wide popularity of Swift's work. A contrary view might argue that Swift's choice of the Pacific for Gulliver's exploits firmly categorized it as a region outside the sphere of reality, a never-never land approachable only in fiction and satire.

In other ways Swift seemed determined to pit those natural allies, Dampier and Defoe, against each other in *Gulliver's Travels*. On his fourth and final voyage Gulliver appears to be attempting to emulate Crusoe as he explains that on leaving the land of the Houyhnhnms, "my design was, if possible, to discover some small island uninhabited, yet sufficient by my labour to furnish me with the necessaries of life." What follows owes much to Dampier as Gulliver pointed his canoe eastward and after two days paddling reached "the south-west point of New Holland." "The maps and charts placed this country at least three degrees more to the east than it really is," his account ran—a gloss on Dampier's note that the west coast of New Holland "is less by 195 Leagues [from the Cape of Good Hope] than is usually laid down in our common Draughts." On the fourth day after landing Gulliver, "venturing out early in a little too far" encountered twenty or thirty natives. In Swift's account there is more than an echo of Dampier's brush with the Aborigines in 1699—the nakedness, the hostility, the fear of poisoned weapons. The move to a solitary life had ended in pain and despair. Only a few pages later, in the last chapter of the book, Swift launches his attack on travel accounts and, more somberly, on discovery and its consequences, in which Europeans appeared as nothing more than "a crew of pirates."

During the brief bout of Anglo-Spanish hostilities in 1727 Defoe and a few other memorialists resurrected plans for conquest in the South Sea, but these efforts lacked conviction. Not until the imminence of war with Spain in 1739 were new schemes put forward, and these resulted in the naval expedition of George Anson to the Pacific. The four-year voyage was a drama of hardship and endurance, catastrophe and death, and its sole success was the taking of the Acapulco treasure galleon off Manila. The expedition followed the old route of the buccaneers, losing men and ships as it did. In June 1741 the surviving vessels and their scurvy-stricken crews arrived off Juan Fernández. Previous accounts of the island as a haven and refuge reached new heights in the official account of the voyage (published in 1748), where the narrator wrote, "I despair of conveying an adequate idea of its beauty," before leaving it to the drawing by Lieutenant Peircy Brett. An ocean's width away and a year later, the island of Tinian in the Ladrone or Mariana Islands led to similar effusions. This "little paradise," appeared in an engraving, breadfruit tree well to the fore. There is an anticipation here of Tahiti, William Hodges, and much else. The imaginative framework of a different, more spacious South Sea, one of islands rather than continents, is beginning to take shape. For Europeans Polynesia is still to come, but already Gavan Daws's "Dream of Islands" is taking its hold of the European consciousness."[1] Near the island, Anson's men seized a flying proa—often described before, but never in such careful detail. The craft was taken to pieces, so that Brett could make accurate drawings of it. The fact that similar boats had been encountered in other parts of the Pacific (by Schouten and Le Maire, for example, in 1615 more than three thousand miles to the southeast), led the writer to speculate "that the Ladrones are only a part of an extensive chain of Islands, spreading themselves to the southward, towards the unknown boundaries of the Pacific Ocean . . . only one small portion of a range of Islands reaching from Japan, perhaps to the unknown southern Continent."

Anson's capture of the Acapulco galleon the next year resulted in a colossal haul of treasure. It took 32 wagons to carry the silver from Portsmouth to London after the return of Anson's ship in 1744, and the reading public was eager for accounts of the expedition. Newspaper accounts, serial publications and individual books quickly appeared, while other writers considered the wider implications of Anson's expedition. In his revised edition of Harris's collection of voyages, first published in 1705, that prolific writer on maritime affairs, John Campbell, concluded his roll call of Pacific voyages with Anson's. The first volume of his mammoth revision, published in 1744, contained accounts of the main Pacific voyages from Quiros, Schouten and Le Maire in the early seventeenth century to those of Tasman, the English buccaneers, and Roggeveen's of 1722 which, with its sighting of Easter Island, had touched on the eastern edge of Polynesia. The abbreviated narratives of the voyages were accompanied by generous dollops of Campbell's own comments and exhortations. He advocated the establishment of two British bases in the Pacific: one at Juan Fernández, the other on New Britain. From these islands, expeditions could be sent toward the southern continent, of which the accompanying map said, "It is impossible to conceive of a Country that promises fairer."

Anson's expedition forms an appropriate climax to an analysis of English interest in the South Sea in the late Stuart and early Hanoverian period. If, in its origins, it summed up the aspirations of generations of projectors and predators, its grim experiences revealed the difference between the easy theories of the armchair strategists and the realities of a Pacific voyage under stress. Navigational difficulties, contrary wind systems, the threat of scurvy, hostile Spaniards on one side of the Pacific, unfriendly Dutch on the other—the obstacles seemed not to have lessened over the centuries. But there is another dimension to the central issue of why the period did not see more in the way of methodical exploration. Before this could happen, British thinking had to win clear of its obsession with Spanish America, and with the old South Sea of the buccaneers, privateers and illicit traders. From Narborough to Anson the expeditions discussed here aimed to exploit the Spanish-American empire. They were predatory and parasitic; and as long as Spanish-American trade was the target, then English vessels would cling to the known routes of the Spanish trading and bullion ships. Discoveries would be incidental and accidental.

NOTE

1. Gavan Daws, *A Dream of Islands: Voyages of Self-Discovery in the South Seas.* (New York, 1980).

SUGGESTIONS FOR FURTHER READING

O. H. K. Spate, *The Pacific Since Magellan,* volume II, *Monopolists and Freebooters.* (Canberra, 1983).

Glyndwr Williams and Alan Frost, eds., *Terra Australis to Australia.* (Melbourne, 1988).

William Dampier, *A New Voyage Round the World,* ed. Albert Gray. (London, 1937).

Woodes Rogers, *A Cruising Voyage Round the World,* ed. G. E. Manwaring. (London, 1928).

George Shelvocke, *A Voyage Round the World,* ed. W. G. Perrin. (London, 1928).

Richard Walter and Benjamin Robins, *A Voyage Round the World by George Anson,* ed. Glyndwr Williams. (London, 1974).

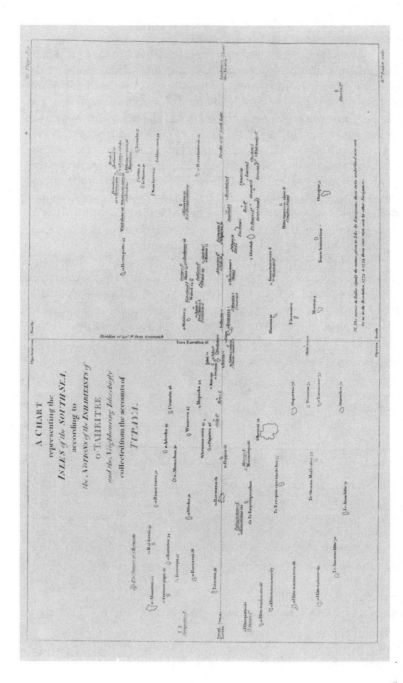

Figure II. A Polynesian Chart of the South Pacific Islands from J. R. Forster, *Observations made during a Voyage round the World* (London, 1778). *Courtesy of the John Carter Brown Library at Brown University.*

2

EXPLORERS AND GEOGRAPHERS

Glyndwr Williams

As late as the middle of the eighteenth century Europe's knowledge of the Pacific basin, covering almost one-third of the earth's surface, was sketchy and incomplete. The situation was transformed in the last 40 years of the century, when a spectacular surge of seaborne exploration, associated above all with the voyages of James Cook, resulted in the discovery and mapping of the previously unknown areas of the great ocean. Left unqualified, this statement would give a misleading impression of the nature of that "discovery." Long before Magellan's ships entered the Pacific in 1520, its 25,000 or so islands had been subject to a steady process of exploration, migration and settlement. To its own inhabitants the Pacific was known, and some indication of the extent of their "local" knowledge is suggested by the map drawn for Cook in 1769 by Tupaia, a priest or *arii* from Raiatea (one of the Society Islands). With its center at Tahiti, the map showed 74 islands in all, scattered across an area of ocean measuring about 3,000 miles from east to west, and a thousand miles from north to south. Although to European eyes some of the map is difficult to interpret, it remains, in the words of one of Cook's scientists, "a monument of the ingenuity and geographical knowledge of the people of the Society Islands."

If we turn to a European map of the Pacific in the early eighteenth century, the uncertainties far outnumbered the certainties. Although from Magellan onward Spaniards, French, Dutch and English had ventured into the great ocean their explorations were for the most part inconclusive if not downright confusing. The immensity of the ocean, problems with longitude, the threat of scurvy and mutiny, and the constraints of wind and current, posed formidable problems. In the North Pacific stretched the one regular European trade route across the ocean, that of the annual galleon between

Acapulco and Manila which touched at Guam in the Marianas. Japan was roughly charted, but the ocean to the north and east remained unexplored. The Pacific coast of America was known only as far north as California; what lay beyond was a matter of guesswork. How far east Asia stretched was equally problematical; and what lay in the colossal void, five thousand miles or so, between Kamchatka and California, was a mystery. The emptiness might contain ocean or land, islands or continent, a land-bridge between Asia and America, or the entrances to the Northwest and Northeast Passages.

In the South Pacific, some knowledge had been obtained of the islands on the diagonal sailing course between the tip of South America and New Guinea—the Tuamotus, the Marquesas, the Solomons, Espiritu Santo—but their location shifted from voyage to voyage. "There are in the South-Sea many Islands, which may be called Wandering-Islands," an English geographer remarked in the 1750s. The coastline of New Guinea, the western half of New Holland, and stretches of the coastline of Van Diemen's Land (Tasmania) and New Zealand were known from Dutch and Spanish explorations; but it remained an open question whether any of these lands formed part of a mighty southern continent, *Terra Australis Incognita*. The concept of such a continent was as old as geographical science, for Ptolemy in the second century A.D. had argued that there was a huge counterbalancing landmass in the Southern Hemisphere, and later advocates were not unduly depressed by the failure of explorers to bring back conclusive evidence. Since the prevailing winds tended to push vessels onto a track which slanted away from high latitudes as they left Cape Horn mapmakers merely had to shift the continent a degree or two farther south. Maps of the mid-eighteenth century tended to show New Holland joined to New Guinea and Van Diemen's Land, and incorporating Espiritu Santo (New Hebrides, now Vanuatu) to the northeast. New Zealand was indicated as the outlying fringe of a great continental landmass. Its looming presence was there in the instructions of the British and French explorers of the 1760s.

The end of the global conflict of the Seven Years War in 1763 brought discovery expeditions into the Pacific from both Britain and France. The great ocean and the hoped-for southern continent promised resources of such potential that its discovery and control might tip the commercial balance of power in Europe—for Britain confirm the overseas superiority brought by the wartime conquests, for France redress the humiliations of an unsuccessful war. Byron's expedition of 1764 was the first—a false start because he followed the customary route west-northwest from the Strait of Magellan and made no discoveries of note. This was followed by the two-vessel expedition of Wallis and Carteret in 1766, and the more glamorous French one of Bougainville. Carteret proved an enterprising commander and crossed the Pacific farther south than any of his predecessors, so making considerable inroads into the conjectural southern continent. Wallis, by contrast, showed little initiative in his track across the Pacific, but his voyage was marked by a chance discovery whose emotional impact was out of all proportion to its geographical significance, for in June 1767 he sighted Tahiti. It was an encounter between Europe and Polynesia which stamped an erotic imprint upon western images of the South Seas. To the breaking surf, the palm-fringed beaches and gentle climate were added sensual overtones—of welcoming, garlanded women. When Bougainville's ships reached Tahiti the following year reactions were even more enthusiastic and extravagant. For long Tahiti remained a symbol of the romance of the Pacific islands in defiance of those cautionary voices which pointed to the darker side of life there.

Despite these additions by British and French explorers to knowledge, little progress had been made toward solving the crucial issue of the southern continent. Bougainville had managed to separate Espiritu Santo from the Australian coast; but Wallis had introduced a further error with the supposed sighting just south of Tahiti of "the tops of several mountains and Extreems bearing from South to S.W. upwards of twenty Leags." Yet within a few years there was no longer any doubt. The South Pacific took shape on the maps in much the same form as it does today, and the man responsible for this leap in knowledge was James Cook. His three voyages, following each other in quick succession, revealed the Pacific to Europe in a way no previous explorations had done. As the books, maps and views came off the presses—not only in England, but also in France, Holland, Germany and Italy—Cook became a figure of European renown. Other explorers were in the Pacific during the years that Cook's ships were out, but public attention was dominated by the methodical, comprehensive explorations of the Englishman. Supported by an Admiralty willing to allow detailed publication of the voyagers' findings, Cook and his officers were able to give a fuller picture than had emerged during the previous two centuries of sporadic, often secretive exploration.

In 1768 Cook left England in the *Endeavour* for his first Pacific voyage. His vessel was not the usual naval sloop or frigate, but a bluff-bowed Whitby collier chosen for strength, shallow draught,

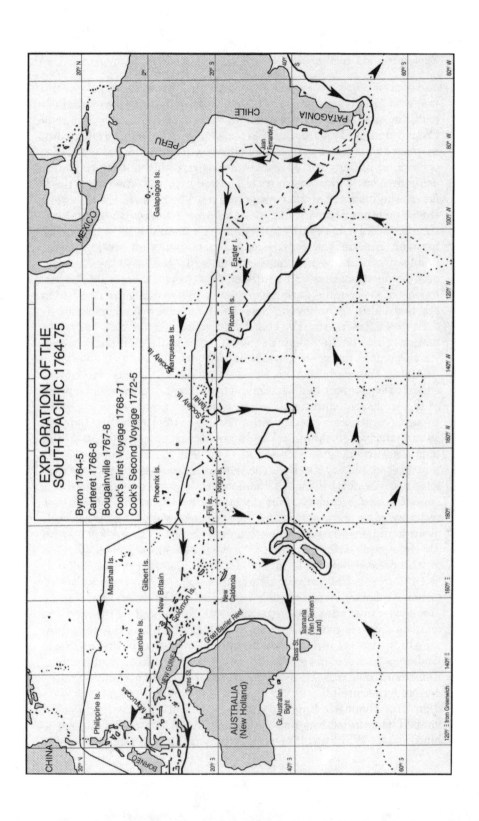

EXPLORATION OF THE
SOUTH PACIFIC 1764-75

Byron 1764-5
Carteret 1766-8
Bougainville 1767-8
Cook's First Voyage 1768-71
Cook's Second Voyage 1772-5

and storage capacity. Although Cook's ship was to change, the type was not. The *Resolution* of the second and third voyages even came from the same shipyard as the *Endeavour*. He was to test the case argued most fully by the geographer Alexander Dalrymple for the existence of a southern continent, visualized in his writings as a great landmass with a population, possibly, of fifty million inhabitants. Cook and Dalrymple have been seen as antagonists: the difference of approach is there early in the first voyage as Cook charted the Cape Horn region—"In this Chart I have laid down no land nor figur'd out any shore but what I saw my self, and thus far the chart may be depented upon." It was Bougainville, though, who denounced speculative geography and its practitioners most vigorously—"Geography is a science of facts; one cannot make systems in one's study without risking errors which can only be corrected at the expense of the navigators."

In 1768 Cook sailed first to Tahiti to carry out those astronomical observations for the Royal Society which were the ostensible reason for the voyage before he turned south where, his secret instructions told him, "there is reason to imagine a Continent or Land of great extent may be found." But he reached lat. 40°S. without sighting land, and he noted that the long rolling swell coming from the south argued against the existence of any landmass in that direction. He then turned west to New Zealand whose coasts he charted in a little over six months by means of a superb running survey from the sea which showed that the two islands were not part of any continent. From there Cook pointed the *Endeavour* toward that region of mystery, the unexplored eastern parts of New Holland. Cook coasted northward, stopping at Botany Bay and then at Endeavour River after the vessel was almost wrecked on the Great Barrier Reef. From there he sailed through Torres Strait, a passage first made by the Spaniards in 1606 and then lost to sight, though Spanish documents he had acquired enabled Dalrymple to mark the route on a map which Cook had on board. There was no acknowledgment of this by Cook, who instead at this point broke out into one of his longest complaints about the inaccuracy of existing maps. He blamed navigators, geographers and publishers in turn—"so that between the one and the other we can hardly tell when we are possessed of a good sea Chart until we our selves have proved it." With only one ship, and without the loss of a single man from scurvy, Cook had put more than five thousand miles of previously unknown coastline on the map. The twin islands of New Zealand, the east coast of Australia, and Torres Strait, had at last emerged from the mists of uncertainty.

On the great southern continent Cook was emphatic—"I do not believe that any such thing exists unless in a high latitude . . . hanging Clowds and a thick horizon are certainly no known Signs of a Continent."

On his first voyage, Cook had lopped a considerable slice off the supposed continent to the south, but there remained vast unexplored stretches in the high latitudes of the Atlantic, Pacific and Indian Oceans where land might yet be found. Cook's second Pacific expedition (1772–5) was arguably the greatest, most perfect, of all seaborne voyages of discovery. In his three years away he disposed of the imagined southern continent, reached closer to the South Pole than any man before him, and touched on a multitude of lands— New Zealand and Tahiti again, and for the first time Easter Island, the Marquesas, Tonga, New Caledonia, the New Hebrides, and South Georgia. In doing so Cook connected many of the uncertain discoveries of earlier explorers which had brought so much confusion to the map of the Pacific. In high latitudes he crossed and recrossed the Antarctic Circle in long, methodical sweeps. At his farthest south he reached lat. 71°S. before being stopped by the ice barrier which encircles the immense continent of the south. This was not the fertile land of the geographers' dreams, but the frozen Antarctic—in Cook's words, "a Country doomed by Nature never once to feel the warmth of the suns rays, but to lie for ever buried under everlasting snow and ice." There was, thought Cook, little more to do in the South Pacific as he wrote of "the Southern Hemisphere sufficiently explored and a final end put to the searching after a Southern Continent, which has at times ingrossed the attention of some of the Maritime Powers for near two Centuries past and the Geographers of all ages." From the safety of his Thames-side home, Horace Walpole was dismissive: "They fetched blood of a great whale called Terra Australis *incognita,* but saw nothing but its tail." But it would be wrong to think of Cook's achievement as a negative one. In his first two voyages he had established the framework of the modern map of the South Pacific: Polynesia and southern Melanesia; New Zealand and New South Wales; Torres Strait and the southern extremities of the great ocean.

Cook's third and final voyage (1776–80) had its own logic in that it took him to the North Pacific in an effort to solve that other longstanding geographical mystery—the existence of a Northwest Passage. The contemporary obsession with South Sea islands makes it easy to overlook the fact that the first major increase in Europe's knowledge of the Pacific in the eighteenth century had come from

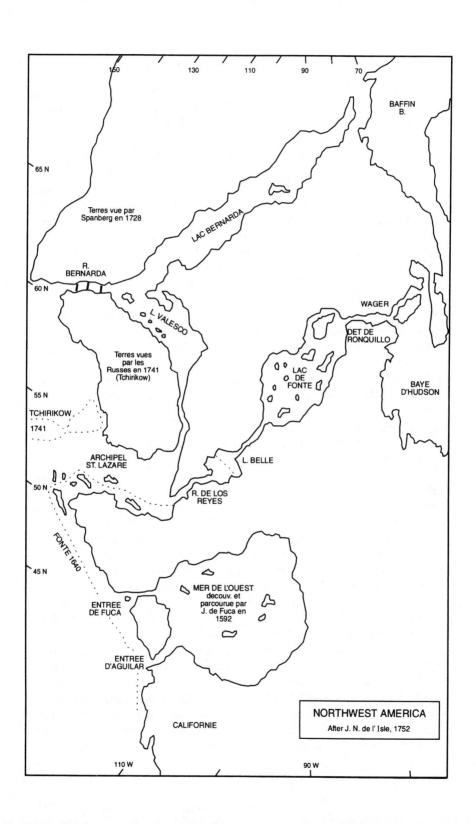

NORTHWEST AMERICA

After J. N. de l' Isle, 1752

Russia, where Bering's two voyages of 1728 and 1741, followed by other navigators sailing east from Kamchatka, had thrown a flickering light on the geography of the North Pacific. Although there were scientists with Bering, the failure to publish the working charts of the Russian explorers, and the eagerness of speculative geographers to fill the spaces with their own eccentric creations, brought mystification rather than illumination to the scene. The French geographers J. N. de l'Isle (who had helped plan the second Bering expedition) and the celebrated Philippe Buache, issued maps which showed northwest America split by the inland seas and straits supposed to have been found on the voyages of Juan de Fuca (1592) and Bartholomew de Fonte (1640). The Spaniards too, sailed north from Lower California in the 1760s and 1770s, and reached Alaska; but again little was known of these voyages at the time, and their maps remained unpublished. Cook sternly rejected the speculations of de l'Isle and Buache, but—quite out of character—was beguiled by the equally bizarre map published in Russia (and in English translation) under the name of Jacob von Stählin in 1774. This claimed to show the explorations of a Russian naval officer, Ivan Synd, in the 1760s, and showed Alaska, not as a peninsula, but as a large island. Between it and the American continent opened a wide strait, in latitude 65°N., leading into a polar sea which geographers such as Samuel Engel and Daines Barrington had assured Cook would be ice-free.

So, by way of Tahiti and Tonga, Cook sailed into the South Pacific once again, before heading north into the unknown. In taking the unfrequented route from the Society Islands to the northwest coast of America, Cook made the major discovery of the Sandwich or Hawaiian Islands before turning to the main task. The summer of 1778 he spent in hazardous exploration along the Northwest Coast from Nootka Sound on Vancouver Island to Bering Strait, searching in vain for a way through to the polar sea. So adamant was he that no strait existed south of latitude 65°N. that he sailed past the entrance of today's Juan de Fuca Strait in the night. No passage was found before Bering Strait was reached, and from there Cook's ships were forced to retreat as a wall of ice bore down upon them in August 1778. Cook's surprising reliance on theoretical geography had led him into major errors. He seems to have lacked the professional detachment which had always been one of his strengths. His ships were not strengthened to meet ice, he took no Russian-speaking crew members with him (and so had to converse in sign language with those Russians he met), and he relied on a map (Von Stählin's)

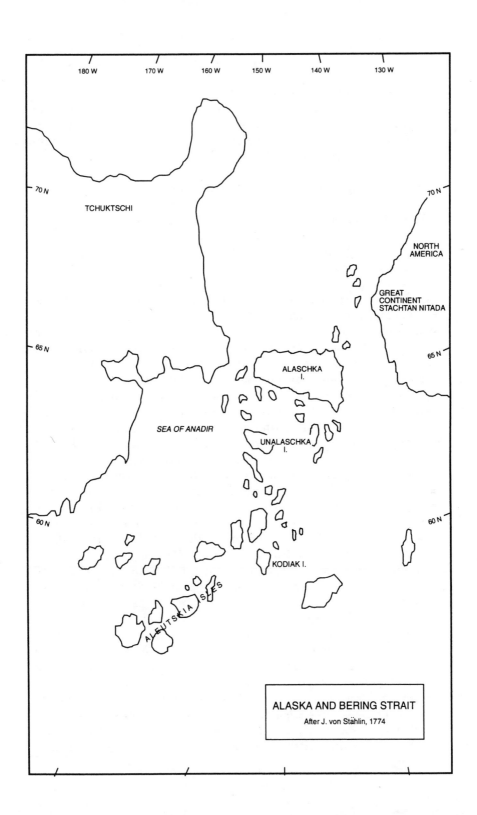

180 W 170 W 160 W 150 W 140 W 130 W

70 N

TCHUKTSCHI

NORTH
AMERICA

GREAT
CONTINENT
STACHTAN NITADA

70 N

65 N

ALASCHKA
I.

65 N

SEA OF ANADIR

UNALASCHKA
I.

60 N

60 N

KODIAK I.

ALEUTSKIA I·S·LES

ALASKA AND BERING STRAIT

After J. von Stählin, 1774

which—after the event—he described as one which "the most illiterate of his illiterate Sea-faring men would have been ashamed to put his name to." Cook had been imposed upon to the world's advantage, his biographer John Beaglehole has written;[1] and the results of his single season of exploration were impressive. Although unaware of the insular nature of much of the coastline along which he was sailing, Cook charted the main outline of America's northwest shores from Mount St. Elias to Bering Strait, determined the shape of the Alaskan peninsula, and touched on the coast of modern British Columbia. He closed the gap between the Russian and Spanish explorations, and for the first time the region takes recognizable form on the maps.

If Cook's voyage seemed to have ended hopes of a navigable passage between the Pacific and Atlantic, it also drew attention to the commercial possibilities of the Northwest Coast. The quest for beaver had drawn men across the North American continent from east to west, and the maritime traders were quick to respond to the reports of the sea-otter pelts traded by Cook's men, and sold at high prices on the Canton market. Some of the trading commanders had sailed with Cook, and as their trading vessels pushed into inlets and sailed through channels never seen by Cook, they realized that what Cook had assumed was mainland was a screen of islands. It was not long before they began to query his dismissal of the Fuca and Fonte accounts, and new maps appeared which incorporated Cook's landfalls into the apocryphal accounts. By 1787 several traders were convinced they had found some part or other of the Fonte channels and rivers on the coast, while William Barkley discovered what he took to be Juan de Fuca's strait. Familiar names among the geographical fraternity took up the torch once more: Alexander Dalrymple in England, now Hydrographer to the East India Company, and in France, Buache de la Neuville (nephew of Philippe Buache), Geographer to the King. Between them they were responsible for the instructions given to the French expedition of the Comte de la Pérouse (on the coast in 1786), the Spanish expedition of Malaspina (1791), and the British one of George Vancouver (1792–4), to search for the entrance of a strait which they hoped would lead into or at least toward the Atlantic. None of the three commanders showed much belief in the task they were set. After spending three months on the Alaskan coast, La Pérouse concluded that Fonte had never existed, that the idea of a passage was "absurd" and was like the "pious frauds" of an earlier age. Malaspina was more detached, and thought that the problem lay in the splitting of geography between academic scholars and practical navigators—"between the branch that reasons and the branch that experiments . . . the first does not interfere in the experiments and the second is not authorized to contradict the reasoners . . . this chaos of mistaken ideas rather retards than favours progress." But it was George Vancouver who saw himself as the self-conscious opponent of theoretical geography and its practitioners. He spent three grueling seasons on the Northwest Coast proving that there was no opening along it which led into the interior.

In this process of exact surveys and empirical observations the speculative geographers found little place. If the explorers, the Cooks and the Bougainvilles, were the heroes, the geographers were the antiheroes. Their role in stimulating interest in distant regions was ignored in the face of complaints about their uncritical approach, their lack of practical experience, their casual misdirection of explorers. There is a sharp edge to the satisfaction with which the Pacific explorers controverted the geographers of their day—the "closet navigators," the "speculative fabricators of geography," the "purveyors of vague and improbable stories" (the words are George Vancouver's). Cook's editor Dr. Douglas was another of those who saw explorers and geographers as natural adversaries. "The fictions of speculative geographers in the Southern Hemisphere have been continents; in the Northern Hemisphere, they have been seas. It may be observed, therefore, that if Captain Cook in his first voyages annihilated imaginary southern lands, he had made amends for the havoc, in his third voyage, by annihilating imaginary Northern Seas."

Such strictures underestimated both the importance of promotional geography in securing support for discovery ventures, and the difficulties under which cartographers labored as they strove to make sense of the journals and maps in front of them. It was the common complaint of navigators that they were the victims of armchair scholars and their speculative theories. Equally well might the scholars retort that they were at the mercy of navigators and their muddled, inaccurate observations. Cook himself wrote of fellow seamen who "lay down the line of a Coast they never have seen and put down soundings where they have never sounded, and after all are so fond of their performances as to pass'd the whole off as sterling under the Title of A *Survey Plan* &c." Emphasis on conflict between explorers and geographers has obscured the links of dependence and collaboration which existed between them. Rather there should be more recognition that the relationship between explorers and geographers—whether one of collaboration or antagonism, acknowledgment or mutual suspicion—was always important, and sometimes crucial.

NOTE

1. J. C. Beaglehole, *The Life of Captain James Cook* (London, 1974), p. 633.

SUGGESTIONS FOR FURTHER READING

Lynne Withey, *Voyages of Discovery: Captain Cook and the Exploration of the Pacific.* (New York, 1987).

O. H. K. Spate, *The Pacific since Magellan,* volume III, *Paradise Found and Lost.* (Canberra, 1988).

Robin Fisher and Hugh Johnston, eds., *Captain Cook and His Times* (Vancouver, 1979).

J. C. Beaglehole, ed., *The Journals of Captain James Cook on His Voyages of Discovery.* (Cambridge, The Hakluyt Society, 1955–1967).

3

SCIENCE AND PHILOSOPHY
Glyndwr Williams

To see the importance of the Pacific voyages of the later eighteenth century in terms only of maps and mapping would be to underestimate their broader significance. There was more to the achievement than the accumulation of geographical knowledge; for the voyages had revealed a second New World to Europe. There was, if it is not too grand a term, a new methodology. It was European rather than narrowly English in scope, but the clearest manifestation came by way of Cook's voyages. The observations made by Cook and his contemporaries played an important role in hydrography, oceanography, meteorology, astronomy—and much else. On his first voyage Cook was accompanied by the young and wealthy botanist, Joseph Banks, who followed the example set by the French (Bougainville had on board the naturalist Commerson and the astronomer Véron) and took on the voyage a small retinue of artists and scientific assistants, though at his own expense. With Cook on his second voyage was the learned Johann Reinhold Forster, the astronomer William Wales, and the painter William Hodges. These voyages set the precedent, so that by the later years of the century the expeditions of La Pérouse and Malaspina carried on board an imposing array of scientists, observers and artists. Though the scientific equipment seems primitive by modern standards, the ships used on the Pacific voyages were by eighteenth-century standards floating laboratories. On Cook's ships the Admiralty put on board a range of experimental equipment and foodstuffs, ranging from a device for distilling seawater to supplies of antiscorbutics.

For contemporaries one of the most astounding features of Cook's first voyage was that there were no deaths from scurvy, that terrible scourge of the sea caused, we know now, by vitamin C deficiency. Deaths had occurred, but mostly after the homeward call at Batavia. Cook's achievements would not have been possible without healthy crews, and his record in this respect was an impressive one. There were no deaths from scurvy on his second and third voyages, and very few from natural causes generally. Yet, in the 1740s, Anson's expedition around the world had lost three-quarters of its men. Four had died from enemy action, more than 1,300 from disease, mostly from scurvy. Much research had gone into scurvy since Anson's voyage, notably by James Lind at the Haslar Naval Hospital. He had broken the back of the problem with his discovery, or rather rediscovery, of the antiscorbutic properties of lemon juice. The work of specialists has corrected the popular view that it was Cook who discovered the cure for scurvy on long sea voyages. Paradoxically, Cook's success in keeping his crews alive delayed the acceptance of the remedy for scurvy, for although he used lemon juice he attributed no particular importance to it, and preferred sauerkraut and malt wort (which contain no vitamin C). What was unusual about Cook was the thoroughness with which he carried out a whole range of antiscorbutic measures. His crews were given only a small ration of salt meat. Instead, sauerkraut, vinegar, orange and lemon juice, malt wort, and (whenever they could be found) fresh meat and vegetables were substituted. Cook had men flogged for refusing to follow their prescribed diet, and used subterfuges to persuade them to eat sauerkraut and walrus meat. Exacting standards of cleanliness were enforced; dry clothing and bedding were provided; stoves kept the lower decks dry. Uncertain of the causes of scurvy, Cook combined all suggested remedies in a way described by the medical historian, Sir James Watt, as "a blunderbuss approach which confused the issue by failing to differentiate true antiscorbutics from the empirical remedies of longstanding tradition."[1] Even so, as the contributor to a medical journal claimed in 1799, Cook had "proved to the world the possibility of carrying a ship's crew through a variety of climates, for the space of near four years, without losing one man by disease; a circumstance which added more to his fame, and is supposed to have given a more useful lesson to maritime nations, than all the discoveries he ever made."

In the realm of natural history the voyages were among the great collecting expeditions of any era. The specimens, sketches, and data brought back were overwhelming in their profusion. The museums of the world still hold much of this; more still has been lost or remains to be sifted. The amount of material simply could not be assimilated by the older encyclopedic science; the polymaths—the Bankses and the Forsters—were to be superseded by the specialists. Above all, there was the human dimension. Neither Cook nor his scientific companions had any training in anthropological investigation because there was none to be had. It was these voyages which helped to give birth in the nineteenth century to the new disciplines of ethnology and anthropology; for the earnest inquiry by the explorers into the exotic lifestyles which confronted them, and their careful if uninformed collection of data, brought a new urgency to the need for a more systematic study of man.

The surge of Pacific exploration after 1760 coincided with new thinking in Europe about the origins and development of society which in many ways stood opposed to the fashionable ideas expressed by Rousseau in his *Discourse on Inequality* (1755) and *Social Contract* (1762). Scholars in France and Britain were devising an economic scale by which to measure the progress of nations. They selected the mode of subsistence as the essential element by which a society could be identified and established four categories—hunting, pastoral, agricultural, commercial. Each successive stage was an advance on the previous, and societies were expected in time to progress from the rudimentary first stage to the sophisticated fourth stage. This new school of philosophical thought contradicted Rousseau's claim that economic specialization and intellectual development were root causes of human misery. It was totally out of sympathy with the primitivist appeal to the virtues of the simple life, with equality, lack of property, and freedom from formal laws. The progressivist theories of Adam Smith and his followers in Scotland, Buffon and his disciples in France, stressed the immaturity, if not inferiority, of "savage" peoples, intimidated by their environment, and without capacity to improve it. These bleak assumptions did not go altogether unchallenged. In his *Supplément au Voyage de Bougainville* (written in 1772, but not published until 1796), Diderot advocated free love and had his Tahitian sage refer to Bougainville as "chief of the brigands," intent on "the theft of a whole country."

With hindsight, scholars saw the importance of Pacific societies in this debate. Cook's editor, Dr. Douglas, wrote in 1784 that the Pacific offered "untrodden ground . . . the inhabitants unmixed with any different tribe . . . uninformed by science, unimpaired by education; in short, a fit soil from whence a careful observer could collect facts." The young French scholar Dégerando was even more emphatic at the end of the century—in the Pacific, he wrote, "we shall be taken back to the first periods of our own history, and able to set up secure experiments on the origin and generation of ideas"—we shall be "travelling in time," "exploring the past." The actual observations of the explorers in the Pacific formed a mirror image of this philosophical debate, though there is not much evidence that the journal-keepers on the discovery ships had kept up with their philosophical reading. Banks might have, and Commerson, and Forster, but they were the exceptions. There were those who had some idea of Rousseauite concepts, albeit in hazy and insecure fashion. George Robertson, master on the *Dolphin,* the first European vessel to reach Tahiti, was an unsophisticated man if his spelling is any criterion; but he seemed to be making direct reference to Rousseau's doctrines when he pointed out that the fact that nails had to be offered before trees could be cut down "in my oppinion plainly demonstrates that their is both justice, and property in this happy island."

The converse might be expected to be easier to prove—that the scholars of the age relied on the observations of the Pacific explorers to support their own theories, but again care is necessary. The passage by Kames in his *Sketches of the History of Man* (1774) on the effects of climate on society might seem to be a running commentary on Banks's observation on Cook's first voyage that one hour's digging and planting by a Tahitian would produce enough breadfruit for a lifetime. But it should be remembered that Adam Ferguson was saying much the same before Cook's first voyage— "the shade of the barren oak and the pine are more favourable to the genius of mankind, than that of the palm or the tamarind." The example might be taken from a voyager, but the conviction was already there. Underlying the existence of the mirror image was the fact that the observers on the spot, and the scholars in their studies, came from a common cultural background; and their acceptance of similar standards of assessment may have cut across differences of education, status and experience.

In the various accounts of the first dozen years or so of the Pacific voyages some consensus seemed to be emerging. After the first enthusiastic reactions—to Tahiti in particular—a slow disillusionment had set in. At Tahiti the length of Cook's stay for four months in 1769 taught him much about the island that Bougainville had missed in his few days there. The Frenchman wrote of a garden of Eden, full of "hospitality, ease, innocent joy, and every appearance of happiness;" but as they explored the interior Cook's men came across skeletons left from the warfare which had swept the island since the French visit. And they found a darker side to the free love of the *ario'i* with the realization that "the Children who are so unfortunate as to be thus begot are smother'd at the moment of their birth." There was little in the English journals of the carefree equality which the French thought they had found; instead there were references to "the better sort" and the "inferior sort," even (inaccurately) to slaves. It is true that Cook, like Byron and Wallis before him, looked for familiar political forms—for kings, queens, priests and chiefs—but the cultural patterns of Polynesian society refused to conform to European shapes.

New Zealand presented the Englishmen with a different set of challenges: violent clashes and deaths, a political and religious system which seemed quite impenetrable, and above all the issue of cannibalism. The Aborigines of the east coast of Australia presented a different test again, and in some ways an even more searching one. The voyagers' predisposition was a critical one, based on Dampier's account, and first impressions—of a naked, filthy people, lacking clothes, housing or possessions—seemed to confirm this. But it is a sign of Cook's growing confidence in his own judgment that he did not dismiss out of hand the Aborigines, so unprepossessing in conventional European terms. Instead, he wrote of a people living in harmony with their natural environment, enjoying " a tranquility which is not disturbed by the inequality of condition." Whatever the eccentricities of some aspects of primitivist writing, it helped men such as Cook to assess indigenous peoples against their own background, not by the standards of contemporary Europe. His comments show that confidence in the superiority of their own system was no longer necessarily part of the cultural baggage which Europe's explorers took with them.

By the time of Cook's second voyage, there was not much repetition of the more sentimental effusions which had marked the initial reaction of both English and French; and the change can be seen in comparing the first and second editions of Bougainville's *Voyage*. The evidence of a Tahitian taken back to France persuaded Bougainville that the island paradise in fact contained not only "distinction of ranks" but also "tyrannical power of life and death." As George Forster (Johann's son) said on encountering the shivering inhabitants of Tierra del Fuego on Cook's second voyage, "Till it can be proved, that a man in continual pain, from the rigour of the climate, is happy, I shall not give credit to the eloquence of the philosophers." Even so, there was now a whole new series of thoughtful comparisons with Europe, for it was clear that advanced civilizations were not necessarily equated with happiness, simply with technical development. "Felicity" might be more easily attained in Tahiti than in Europe. As societies had moved forward, so they had become perverted. "Our civilized communities," wrote George Forster, "are stained with enormities." The ravages of venereal disease were symbolic of this, but there were vices more insidious than those of the body. In 1774 Kames had argued the "Luxury, the never failing concomitant of wealth is a slow poison that debilitates men;" two years later came the first volume of Gibbon's *Decline and Fall* with its warning of the dangers of decadence.

Both skepticism about the alleged perfection of South Sea islands, and concern about the impact on them of the European arrival—the two coincidental sentiments of the mid-1770s—were strengthened by the events of Cook's third voyage. Cook's death, following as it did the killing of the *Adventure's* boat crew in New Zealand in 1773 on the second voyage, and the deaths of French navigator, Marion du Fresne and two dozen of his men not far away a year earlier, was proof to many of treacherous disposition of the Pacific peoples. Crozet (Marion's second-in-command) bitterly criticized the image of the "affable, humane and hospitable" islander depicted by the philosophers—"there is among all the animals of creation none more ferocious and dangerous for human beings than the primitive and savage man . . . reason without culture is but a brutal instinct." The grim centerpiece of Cook's stay at Tahiti (his third) was his presence at a ceremony of human sacrifice. This same voyage also saw Cook ruminating on the lack of application shown by Omai, the Society Islander brought to England on the *Adventure*. "This kind of indifferency is the true character of his nation. Europeans have visited them for these ten years past, yet we find neither new arts nor improvements in the old."

This had become crucial. Expeditions were sailing from a Europe where the capacity for improvement had become a touchstone by which societies were measured; and whether the discoverers looked at silent, apathetic Fuegans or gregarious, boisterous Tahitians, they found no Pacific peoples which conformed to western ideals of progress and improvement. James King wrote of his first, long-anticipated sight of Tahiti that it "instead of being a delightful garden, is a rich wilderness." As the freshness and novelty of the first discoveries faded, so did the earlier conviction that Europe could learn much from the Pacific. The South Sea retained its allure, but as a remote haven for the few, far removed from the conventions of European society. Tahiti, in particular, still cast its spell, as the *Bounty* mutineers showed. George Hamilton, surgeon of the *Pandora,* wrote of the island in terms as extravagant as those used 30 years earlier— "where the earth without tillage produces both food and clothing, the trees loaded with flowers, and fair ones ever willing to fill your arms with love."

More experienced observers of the Pacific generally held different opinions. George Vancouver in the 1790s noted with foreboding the changes which had overtaken Tahiti where European implements and supplies were taken for granted by the islanders—"regardless of their former tools and manufacturers, which are now growing fast out of use, and, I may add, equally out of remembrance." The editor of Cook's second voyage had expressed similar concern—"It would have been far better for these poor people, never to have known our superiority in the accommodation and arts that make life comfortable, than, after once knowing it, to be again abandoned to their original incapacity." To implications of European material superiority were added darker criticisms. The published account of the La Pérouse expedition of 1785–88 included a sour comment by its commander on the violent nature of the peoples of the Pacific. Man in a state of nature, he wrote, was "cruel, base, and deceitful . . . In vain may philosophers exclaim against this picture. While they are making books by the fireside, I have been traversing the globe for thirty years, and have actually witnessed the cunning and injustice of nations they portray as simple and virtuous." Here the scholar runs head-on into one of the main problems of assessing the concept of a "noble savagery" which to outward appearance was so pervasive in the age of discovery—that by and large it was a theoretical construct more honored in the study than in the field, that there was invariably a tension between the ideal and the reality. We see this in the reaction of the European settlers to the Australian Aborigines in 1788. There was a consensus that the Aborigines, "shivering savages . . . ready to perish for one half of the year with hunger," must "rank very low, even in the scale of savages." The arrival of the Europeans at Botany Bay, wrote Governor Phillip, brought "order and useful arrangement" to a scene of "tumult and confusion." Watkin Tench, captain of marines on the First Fleet, went on to wish "a thousand times" that "those European philosophers, whose closet-speculations exalt a state of nature above a state of civilization, could survey the phantom, which their heated imaginations have raised: possibly they might learn, that a state of nature is, of all others, least adapted to promote the happiness of a being."

To these secular considerations was to be added missionary endeavor—Protestant and Catholic—coming from a Europe which (in Bernard Smith's words) "was slowly but surely ceasing to be diverted, instructed, and amused by savages."[2] In the nineteenth century the missionaries were to give extra impetus to the insistence that disorder must be replaced by order, and that moderate rule, regular cultivation, and conventional morality must be encouraged.

By the end of the eighteenth century there was a general acceptance that to relate primitive and European lifestyles was unscholarly and misleading. This cut deeply into those philosophical notions which had seen in the apparently carefree existence of the savage an implicit condemnation of western society. Institutions and customs at home would still come under critical fire, but were less likely to be seriously compared with those of the Pacific islander or Amerindian. In a Europe torn by revolutionary and counterrevolutionary ideology it was no longer necessary for a late eighteenth-century counterpart of Voltaire or Montesquieu to conceal attacks on established institutions by writing about distant or exotic societies. There is little reference to noble savages or wise Chinese in Thomas Paine. The life of the savage was clearly not an alternative to that of the European—rather it was now seen as enforced backwardness produced by adverse circumstances. The analogy of the savage as an infant was a popular concept in that it explained existing backwardness and allowed for future improvement. There is something of this in Sir James Frazer's phrase a century later—"humanity in the chrysalis stage."

The alarming fragility shown by Pacific societies as they came into contact with Europeans raised doubts about their integrity and brought into prominence the role of the European as guide and teacher. Vancouver saw his Pacific surveys as part of "that expansive arch over which arts and sciences should pass to furthermost corners of the earth, for the instructions and happiness of the most lowly children of nature . . . the untutored parts of the human race." The identity of these tutors might vary from country to country in Europe, but they would find common cause in the insistence of a writer in the *Edinburgh Review* in 1802 that "Europe is the light of the world, and the ark of knowledge; upon the welfare of Europe, hangs the destiny of the most remote and savage peoples."

NOTES

1. James Watt, "Medical Aspects and Consequences of Cook's Voyages', in Robin Fisher and Hugh Johnston, eds., *Captain James Cook and His Times*. (Vancouver, 1979), p. 135.

2. Bernard Smith, *European Vision and the South Pacific 1768–1850*. (Oxford, 1960), p. 100.

SUGGESTIONS FOR FURTHER READING

Bernard Smith, *European Vision and the South Pacific 1768–1850.* 2nd edition. (New Haven, 1985).

P. J. Marshall and Glyndwr Williams, *The Great Map of Mankind: British Perceptions of the World in the Age of Enlightenment.* (London, 1982).

Derek Howse, ed., *Background to Discovery: Pacific Exploration from Dampier to Cook.* (Berkeley and Los Angeles, 1990).

Anne Salmond, *Two Worlds: First Meetings between Maori and Europeans.* (Auckland, 1991).

4

AFTERMATH AND EXPLOITATION

Glyndwr Williams

Dr. Douglas, the editor of the journals of Cook's third voyage, pointed the way forward to the next stage of Pacific enterprise when he wrote in his introduction that "Every nation that sends a ship to sea will partake of the benefit [of the published accounts]; but Great Britain herself, whose commerce is boundless, must take the lead in reaping the full advantage of her own discoveries." By the end of the century there were British settlements in New South Wales; Nootka Sound had taken on a new significance—no longer Cook's former watering place on the northwest coast of America but a center of international dispute; the first missionaries had reached Tahiti, Tonga and the Marquesas; and everywhere the traders and the whalers were following the explorers' tracks. What Alan Moorhead has called "The Fatal Impact" had begun.

Prominent in these ventures was Joseph Banks. The young naturalist of Cook's first voyage was now one of the most influential men in England: President of the Royal Society, virtual "Director" of Kew Gardens, friend of ministers and leading merchants, and patron of scientific enterprises in all parts of the world. The new Pacific voyages were more practical and commercial than scientific, but Banks seemed to be involved at every turn, in both the North and South Pacific. The South Pacific after Cook was reached simultaneously by settlers and whalers. Cook's report of 1770 on Botany Bay that "most sorts of Grain, Fruits, Roots etc. of every kind would flourish here," and that the soil was "a deep black mould" interspersed with "some of the finest meadows in the world," was enhanced by Banks's recollection before a parliamentary committee in 1785 that the land there was "sufficiently fertile to support a considerable number of Europeans," and that its native inhabitants were weak and few in number. Cook had taken possession of New South Wales in 1770 in the name of King

George III, and in default of what seemed to be regular forms of social organization and government the whole region was thought of as "terra nullis." Bank's first-hand evidence may have been sufficient to prompt the government to choose Botany Bay as its new place of transportation for convicts who would previously have been sent to the American colonies. Less publicized reasons may also have played a part: the possibility of developing Botany Bay as a base strategically placed on the south or "blind" side of the Dutch East Indies; the hope of producing naval stores in the form of timber and flax; the necessity of a preventive move to stifle French initiatives in the region.

The First Fleet, as it was called, of forced settlers and their guards arrived at Botany Bay in January 1788 under Governor Phillip. A Second Fleet arrived in 1790, and a Third in 1791. It took years to battle through the early hardships, with a move first of all from Botany Bay to Sydney Cove (set inside a superb harbor) and then a move slightly inland to the fertile soil of Parramatta (Rose Hill). The shock of disillusionment was instant. As Phillip wrote home, the "situation was so very different from what might be expected." Botany Bay was unrecognizable from the area described by Cook; there were huge problems in clearing the land; and the native inhabitants were more numerous than expected. To the tensions and anxieties inevitable in a mixed community of convicts and their guards as it struggled to come to terms with an alien environment was added the unnerving thought that large numbers of possibly hostile natives might be gathering in the bush. "There will not be a soul alive in the course of a year," one officer wrote. A sense of antipodean inversion is too glib an explanation to explain the evident demoralization among many of the First Fleet, but there was a real sense of bewilderment. It is there in the obsessive harking back to Cook's misleading description of the area (made when the May rains had freshened the grass), in the failure of the Second Fleet to arrive in 1789 with provisions, and in the unpredictable behavior of the Aborigines. It was not only, as captain of the marines Tench wrote, that famine was approaching with giant strides. Hardest to bear was the sense of abandonment. To keep discipline, and to instill a sense of common purpose among the officers, marines and convicts, had been difficult from the beginning. Now, the only bond was a chilling sense of isolation and disorientation. "We know of no more of what is happening at home," one officer wrote, "than of what passes in the moon." The great harbor, able to hold a thousand sail, mocked them by its emptiness.

Then in June 1790 the first vessels of the Second Fleet began to arrive. They brought supplies, more convicts, and news. Suddenly there was a surfeit of information, impossible to take in at first hearing—of

the King's madness, the French Revolution, the private events of in-
numerable families. "News burst upon us like the meridian splendour
on a blind man," Tench wrote. If the worst was over, there were still
hardships to endure. Relations with the Aborigines remained brittle,
and Phillip was wounded in one encounter. Much hope was pinned on
the new settlements at Parramatta and nearby. By 1791, one officer
wrote, Sydney was "only a depot for stores; it exhibited nothing but a
few old scattered huts, and some sterile gardens; cultivation of the
ground was abandoned, and all our strength transferred to Rose Hill."
It was, in effect, the third remove—first Botany Bay, then Sydney
Cove, and now Parramatta. It was a slow process, but gradually cultivation and settlement increased at Rose Hill. By the time of Phillip's
departure for home at the end of 1792 there were 1,300 acres under
crops (plus some private farms), and some sheep, cattle, pigs and
horses. When Malaspina's Spanish expedition reached Port Jackson
in March 1793 this is what they saw: "370 troops and 3,000 other per-
sons . . . two townships were taking shape, with the larger one ex-
hibiting a Government House, rows of cottages, streets, barracks and
parade ground, a prefabricated hospital, the beginning of port facilities; and the smaller, built along a mile-long street parallel to the
river . . . with the Governor's house sited on a slight rise ("Rose Hill")
at the eastern end, so that it had views of both village and water, and
already the centre of an agricultural district—and all this after only
five years."[1] The story of Sydney and the young colony of New South
Wales marked the beginnings of a new empire in the South Pacific,
and one directly linked with the discovery voyages.

At one stage during the preparation of the First Fleet there were
plans to use one of its vessels to put into effect a favored scheme of
Banks: the shipping of breadfruit plants from Tahiti to the British
West Indies where their cultivation would provide cheap food for the
slave population. Eventually, Banks decided that it would be better
to send a vessel from England direct to Tahiti, properly adapted to
take the plants, and with a captain appointed for the specific voyage.
The vessel was the *Bounty,* its commander William Bligh, Cook's
master on his third voyage. Half-obscured by the drama of the famous mutiny is the fact that there was a second breadfruit voyage,
again commanded by Bligh, in the *Providence,* which succeeded in its
task, and established breadfruit in the Caribbean. It never quite became the staple food Banks had envisaged, but its transporting and
transplanting across half a world was further evidence of the global
thinking which the Pacific voyages had helped to set in train.

Among the transports both of the First and subsequent fleets were
whalers. Once released from their transportation duties they turned

to the quest for the great sperm whales of the southern seas, whose oil was more highly valued than that of the "right" whales of the traditional Greenland fishery. Soon whalers were sailing direct from Europe and the United States to the whaling grounds. They used the recently mapped Pacific islands for refitting, and paid with firearms and liquor—a lethal combination for the islanders. The demoralizing activities of the whalers were repeated by the European traders, searching for sandalwood, dried sea-slugs and birds' nests for the gourmets of China; and, later, copra and coconut fibre for the manufacturing industries of Europe. Often the whalers and traders were the rejects of society, and their uncontrolled activities wrought havoc among the islands. Since European governments refused to accept responsibility for the region (Vancouver's negotiation of the British acquisition of sovereignty over Hawaii in 1793, for example, was repudiated by the home government), the only resistance came from the missionaries. In 1797 the London Missionary Society sent missions to Tahiti, and American and French societies quickly followed suit. They were self-appointed protectors in one way; in another, their teachings had as great a disintegrating effect on the traditional societies they found as did the whalers and traders.

In the North Pacific the connection between exploration and exploitation involved great power rivalry in its most acute form as Spain made a desperate last effort to preserve its traditional claims over the Pacific seaboard of North America. After Cook's final voyage those claims were threatened by the arrival of traders on the northwest coast in search of sea-otter pelts to trade at Canton. Reconnaissance expeditions from New Spain along the coast in the later 1780s found not only traders from Europe and New England, but farther north, Russians establishing themselves in Alaska and moving south from there. The flash-point in this situation occurred at Nootka Sound, first sighted by the Spaniards in 1774, then Cook's watering place in 1778, and by the late 1780s a regular port of call for the trading vessels. To stop this activity, and to reinforce its claim to the northwest coast, the Viceroy of New Spain decided to send one of his most experienced navigators, Estéban José Martínez, who had been on the first Spanish voyage along the coast in 1774, to Nootka. There he was to establish a "pretended settlement"—activity on shore during the day, return to the ships at night. But this strategy was disrupted by developments at Nootka during the summer of 1788, when two British trading vessels arrived, commanded by John Meares (a half-pay naval lieutenant) and William Douglas.

What exactly happened at Nootka in summer of 1788 is difficult to disentangle from the accounts of the various participants: Meares and his associates; Maquinna, the first-ranking chief among the Nootka or Nuu-chah-nulth people whose power and wealth had greatly increased in the previous two or three years because of his control over the local fur trade; and the American traders, Robert Gray and John Kendrick. Meares claimed that Maquinna sold him "a spot of land" at Friendly Cove for a pair of pistols; another British officer maintained that Maquinna sold the whole cove for eight or ten sheets of copper. Moreover, Meares claimed that Maquinna did "obedience to us as his lords and sovereigns, to acknowledge, in presence of his people, our superiority over him." Later, Maquinna angrily denied much of this. Clearly there was some transaction, some permission, for in a corner of Friendly Cove Meares built what he described as a substantial, two-storied house, and a small vessel, the *Northwest America,* to trade along the coast. The building must have been much flimsier than Meares claimed—it was probably little more than a shelter for the carpenters—for before Meares sailed away it was pulled to pieces, and some given to the Americans. They were wintering at the Cove, for Maquinna's people had gone inland to their traditional wintering quarters at Tahsis, deep in the interior of the Sound.

If the summer of 1788 was the prelude to the drama now beginning to unfold, the summer of 1789 saw the first act proper as rival forces converged on Nootka. Sailing up from San Blas was Martínez with two vessels and two hundred men; heading for the same spot from Hawaii and China were British trading vessels. After preliminary skirmishes in which Martínez had a busy time arresting, half-arresting, detaining, releasing various surprised arrivals—the real crisis occurred in mid-June when the British trader, James Colnett, arrived in the *Argonaut.* On board, he carried Chinese laborers to build ships and a fort to be called "Fort Pitt." His arrest precipitated stormy scenes, for both the leading protagonists were unstable and volatile characters. Martínez was notorious for his temper and his drinking, while the excitable Colnett ran through a whole repertoire of dramatic and extravagant gestures before throwing himself overboard in an apparent suicide attempt. Amid all this, Martínez took formal possession of Nootka—sword in hand he gashed tree trunks, cut off branches, moved stones around. A giant cross was erected carrying the name of the King, (Carlos III), Martínez's initials, and the dates 1774 and 1789. The high drama of the summer ended in anticlimax when orders came from San Blas—which had heard nothing about these events—to evacuate Nootka; so in October a reluctant Martínez, with his prisoners, sailed south.

If the crisis at Nootka, the local crisis, was over, the wider crisis, the international crisis, was only just beginning. The first, rather unspecific, news reached the British government in London in February 1790 via its diplomats in Spain. The immediate British reaction was to demand an apology together with a recognition of the right to trade and settle in areas not actually controlled by Spain. But in April Meares arrived in England, full of sound and fury, claiming that he had already bought land at Nootka, had built there, and obtained recognition of British overlordship from Maquinna. Acting as a "lieutenant in his Majesty's Navy," he had "hoisted British colours," and had taken possession "in the King's name." The government prepared for war, for which there was traditional enthusiasm. "The mines of Mexico and Peru are already in our possession," one newspaper claimed. An American observer listened to the Parliamentary debate, and then dined with M.P.s. "In my life I do not remember to have been among such insolent bullies. They were all for war, talked much of old England and the British Lion, laughed at the Idea of drubbing the Dons, and seemed uneasy lest the Spaniards . . . come immediately to terms." A minister put it thus: "We are not contending for a few miles, but for a large world." Faced with the mobilization of the Royal Navy, Spain had little alternative but to concede the Nootka Sound Convention in October 1790—restitution of the land and buildings seized the previous summer, with free access and trade along all areas of the coast not actually occupied by Spain. A British naval expedition was to be sent to receive the restitution, and to examine the coast to determine, once and for all, whether there was a Northwest Passage. Its commander was yet another of Cook's men, George Vancouver.

The old Spanish claim to exclusive sovereignty was gone forever, but ironically on the coast itself there was intense Spanish activity. The Spanish post at Nootka was reestablished in 1790, and exploring expeditions were sent out. In 1791 the prestigious Malaspina discovery expedition arrived, and its artists show the Spanish establishment at Nootka with its cannon and no fewer than six vessels in sight. The next year, 1792, Vancouver arrived from Britain—to negotiate and to explore. Negotiations broke down on the extent of the land to be restored, and in any case in Europe, now torn by war, the British and Spanish governments had agreed on a mutual abandonment of Nootka as the simplest answer to a tangled situation. The ceremony in March 1795 was brief. The site of Meares's building was restored to Britain; the British flag was hoisted, then lowered—and entrusted to Maquinna. As the ship carrying the two commissioners sailed out of Friendly Cove, Maquinna's people were already demolishing the Spanish buildings in search of nails and other pieces of metal. There was never again to be white settlement at Nootka. Today it is under the jurisdiction of the Nuu-chah-nulth Tribal Council, whose prerogatives include consent to land.

Ironically, the nation that benefitted most from the dispute was the United States, which had not been involved at all. As Britain became more deeply involved in war with France, so her trade decreased on the northwest coast, where sea-otter stocks began to dwindle in the face of ruthless hunting. The region was dominated by American fur-traders, some of whom were now arriving overland as spearheads of the American drive toward the Pacific. After 1815, the race for domination of the northwest coast lay between Britain, the United States and Russia. Spain was out of the reckoning, for its great American empire disappeared in a series of revolutions. Russia, with traders but no settlers, was mainly confined to Alaska, and Britain and the United States came to grips over the region farther south. In 1846, after the threat of war brought the long-standing "Oregon Question" to a head, the dispute was settled peacefully by a treaty between Britain and the United States which fixed the boundary line along the 49th parallel.

NOTE

1. Alan Frost, "Going Away; Coming Home," in John Hardy and Alan Frost, eds. *Studies from Terra Australis to Australia.* (Canberra, 1989), p. 221.

SUGGESTIONS FOR FURTHER READING

David Mackay, *In the Wake of Cook: Exploration, Science and Empire.* (London, 1985).

Ged Martin, ed., *The Founding of Australia. the Argument about Australian Origins.* (Sydney, 1978).

Margaret Steven, *Trade, Tactics and Territory: Britain and the Pacific 1783–1823.* (Melbourne, 1983).

W. L. Cook, *Flood Tide of Empire: Spain and the Pacific Northwest 1543–1819.* (New Haven 1973).

Robin Fisher and Hugh Johnston, ed., *From Maps to Metaphors: The Pacific World of George Vancouver.* (Vancouver, 1993).

Part II
The Science and Practice
of Navigation

Figure VI. Celestial globe by Jodocus Hondius, Amsterdam, 1600. Hondius was the first cartographer to depict constellations on the Southern Hemisphere. *Courtesy Nederlands Scheepvaartmuseum, Amsterdam.*

5

THE DEVELOPMENT OF NAVIGATIONAL TECHNIQUES BEFORE 1740: GENERAL BACKGROUND

Karel Davids

In order to conduct a ship from one position to another three key problems have to be solved: first, find the course and distance to be sailed from the point of departure to the point of destination; given a course steered and a distance sailed, estimate where the ship has arrived; check whether the estimated point is the true one. These problems in navigation have to be solved irrespective of whether a ship sets out for a routine voyage or, as in the case of Hudson, Tasman, Cook or Bougainville, for a voyage of exploration. Finding a solution is not just of direct importance for navigators themselves, however. It is also relevant for cartography. The results of a voyage of exploration can only be entered at the right place in a map if navigators have indeed succeeded in checking whether estimated positions are true ones. This was one of the reasons why Cook made every effort to achieve an exact determination of longitude and time and again censured predecessors for their "sloppy" work, which often made it hard to retrieve places that supposedly had been "discovered" in the past.

The Portuguese and the Spaniards, who took the lead in European expansion overseas, used particular solutions to these key problems in navigation, which were later brought to higher perfection in England, Holland and France. But the Iberian countries, too, built on achievements of their predecessors, notably seafaring peoples in the Mediterranean like the Pisans, the Genoese, or the Venetians. This chapter will deal first with the "state of the art" in navigation technology in the Iberian Peninsula around the middle of the sixteenth century, next discuss the transfer of nautical knowledge to northwest Europe and finally sketch the main advances realized in England and the Dutch Republic in the late sixteenth and seventeenth centuries.

The State of the Art in Portugal and Spain. Rutters and charts were the principal means used by the Portuguese and the Spaniards to solve the first key problem in navigation: find the course and distance to be sailed from the point of departure to the point of destination. The first sailing directions, *roteiros* (rutters), compiled by the Portuguese probably date back to the period just after the rounding of Cape Bojador in 1434. In the sixteenth century, many more *roteiros* were composed both for the route between Portugal and Asia and for sailing in Asian waters. The Spaniards followed suit.

Portuguese seamen used charts, next to rutters, from at least the fifteenth century onward. But the use of charts was in itself no more a Portuguese invention than the employment of rutters. Both had already been known to seafarers in the Mediterranean before they were adopted in ocean shipping by navigators from Portugal and Spain. There was an innovation, however. The charts used in the Mediterranean had shown compass roses and rhumb or direction lines, but no grid of meridians and parallels. What the Portuguese added to nautical charts in the fifteenth century, was a scale of latitude. This enabled the seaman, once he knew the latitude of his position at sea, to determine, by referring to the scale in the chart, the difference of latitude to the place where he came from or where he was heading.

The Mediterranean was also the source from which the Portuguese and the Spaniards borrowed the instrument, the magnetic compass, to determine directions at sea, both for courses and bearings. But again, they went beyond the model of their predecessors. It did not take long before the experience of ocean navigation made them aware of the fact that magnetic meridians generally do not coincide with geographical meridians. In other words, that there is a difference between the directions of magnetic and true meridians. The instruments and techniques they subsequently developed to measure the extent of this "variation" or magnetic declination, and to take account of it in the navigation of the ship, are discussed in Chapter 6. An instrument to measure speed was not yet known. The distance sailed could still only be assessed by estimation. All depended on the ability and experience of the navigator in charge. The data on the course steered and the distance sailed which had thus been obtained were in turn employed to solve the second key problem in navigation: to find the estimated position of the ship. This was done by plotting in a chart or using a traverse table, which gave the distance to be sailed on a given course to raise or lay a degree of latitude.

If a ship sailed in sight of land, or found itself in shallow waters, the third problem of navigation—to find whether the estimated position was the true one—could normally be solved by taking bearings or soundings. But the case was of course different on the high seas. The chief contribution of the Portuguese and the Spaniards to the advance of the art of navigation in the fifteenth and sixteenth centuries lay in the creation of instruments and techniques to determine a ship's position at sea by the aid of celestial bodies. They developed astronomical navigation.

Ideally, seamen should have had the means to check on both latitude and longitude, when they had chosen this grid as a frame of reference. In practice, the Portuguese and Spaniards were not yet able to do both. Finding longitude posed problems which at the time could not be solved; Willem Mörzer Bruyns's contribution to the following chapter makes clear why. But nautical experts in the Iberian Peninsula *did* develop methods to find latitude.

The simplest way was to determine latitude by measuring the altitude of the Pole Star, Polaris, above the horizon and applying a correction to take account of the distance between this star and the celestial North Pole (depending upon the position of the Pole Star in its diurnal circle); the corrected altitude (PnN) equals the geographical latitude (EZ) (see Figure VII). As Polaris is not visible south of the equator, however, the method of finding latitude by the Pole Star could not be applied along the whole length of the overseas shipping routes opened up since the last decades of the fifteenth century. For latitudes south of the equator, the Portuguese developed a comparable method based on measuring the altitude of the Southern Cross.

A third method, which was also worked out at the end of the fifteenth century, could be applied both on northern and southern latitudes: finding latitude by the meridian altitude of the sun (S). The principle can be explained with the help of Figure VIII: The latitude of an observer equals the altitude of the celestial pole above the horizon (PnN). The altitude of the elevated pole equals the angular distance (EZ) between the zenith of the observer (Z) and the plane of the equator (EQ). This angular distance can be determined by measuring the altitude of the sun (a) at noon in the celestial meridian (the great circle through Z, Pn, Na and Ps), which yields the zenith distance of the sun (z), and combining this datum with the declina-

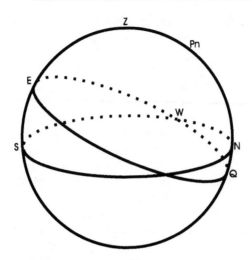

Figure VII. Principles and practice for finding latitude by measuring the altitude of the Pole Star.

circle EWQ	celestial equator
circle SWN	observer's horizon
Z	observer's zenith
Pn	celestial North Pole
arc EZ	geographical latitude of the observer
arc PnN	altitude of the Pole Star

tion of the sun (d) at the time of observation; the declination of the sun is the angular distance along the hour circle between the plane of the equator and the sun. The rules of combination, laid down in navigational textbooks, varied of course according as the declination of the sun was north or south of the equator and as the sun crossed the celestial meridian of the observer to the north or the south of his zenith (depending on the position of the observer). The instruments and tables used in the application of this method are described in the following companion chapter by Mörzer Bruyns.

But even if the Portuguese and the Spaniards had thus significantly advanced the art of navigation, the solutions of the key problems in navigation were by no means perfect. The charts and traverse tables used did not yet take into account the spherical shape of the earth, or had done so only in an imperfect way. Instruments for measuring altitude still showed shortcomings and devices for measuring speed were even completely lacking—to name but a few of the remaining deficiencies. And the problem of finding longitude had not been solved at all.

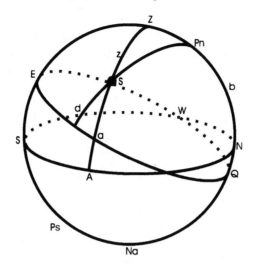

Figure VIII. Principles and practice of finding latitude by the meridian altitude of the sun.

circle EWQ	celestial equator
circle SWN	observer's horizon
circle ZPnNaPs	celestial meridian
Z	observer's zenith
Na	observer's nadir
Pn	celestial North Pole
Ps	celestial South Pole
S	sun
arc EZ	geographical latitude of the observer
arc PnN	altitude of the Pole Star
arc SA (a)	altitude of the sun's center
arc ZS (z)	zenith distance of the sun's center
arc d	sun's declination

The Transfer of Nautical Knowledge to Northwest Europe. When the English, French and Dutch in the sixteenth century joined in the process of European expansion overseas, and thus had to master the art of ocean navigation too, they first followed closely the example of the Spaniards and the Portuguese. The transfer of nautical knowledge between the Iberian Peninsula and north-west Europe occurred in several ways.

First of all, there was a movement of people. Sebastian Cabot, pilot-major in the *Casa de Contratación* in Seville since 1518, moved to England in 1548 and subsequently played a key role in the growth of nautical education and the production of charts for the benefit of the English shipping industry. Stephen Borough, who received an appointment as chief pilot of the Muscovy Company in 1558, had a firsthand knowledge of Spanish practice as well. Portuguese cartographers worked in France, French pilots sailed on Portuguese ships to Brazil and Dutch seamen—like Dirk Gerritsz. Pomp or Jan Huyghen van Linschoten—traveled on Portuguese vessels to Asia. Movement of people could easily shade into acts of espionage. It was in these ways that the Dutch in the 1580s and 1590s managed to lay their hands on charts or *roteiros* composed by the Portuguese. The book published in 1594–1595 by Van Linschoten based on his experience in Portuguese service, the *Itinerario,* "has preserved . . . in contemporary translation, so many Portuguese *roteiros* of the period which would otherwise have been lost," Charles Boxer reminds us. "If all the printed and manuscript copies of Portuguese *roteiros,* which are known to exist were to disappear, leaving only Van Linschoten's *Itinerario,* this would still be more than sufficient to establish the fame and efficiency of those pilots."[1]

Tracts and textbooks composed in Portugal and Spain found in translation their way to seamen in the North or were an important source for newly produced nautical literature published in England, Holland or France. Spanish manuals written by Pedro de Medina (1545), Martín Cortés (1551) and Rodrigo Zamorano (1581) appeared in French, English or Dutch translations before the end of the century. A Portuguese one by Manuel de Figueiredo was rendered into French shortly after 1600. In the period 1580–1610, Dutch, Flemish and English authors such as Michiel Coignet, Simon Stevin and Edward Wright borrowed important insights from the work that Portuguese experts like Francisco Faleiro and Pedro Nunez had done 50 years before. A telling instance of the relevance of the Iberian heritage in the early phase of ocean navigation by seafarers from in northwest Europe is the discovery in 1871 among the objects left on the island of Nova Zembla in 1597 by an unsuccessful Dutch expedition trying to reach the East Indies through a northeastern route, of a copy of the Dutch translation of De Medina's *Arte de Navegar.*

English and Dutch Contributions to the Art of Navigation. Having mastered the technology developed in southern Europe, the seafaring nations in northwest Europe started to make contributions of their own. In the late sixteenth and seventeenth centuries, the leading centers in the development of the art of navigation in Europe were no longer Portugal and Spain, but England and the Dutch Republic; France came to the fore in the course of the eighteenth century. The first peaks in innovative activity in navigation technology in these countries almost exactly coincided with the first phase of their overseas expansion, between c. 1570 and 1630 in England, and between c. 1590 and 1630 in the Dutch Republic. These were times of feverish innovation and experimentation. A great number of new methods and instruments was invented and tried. But many of these were sooner or later discarded. The variety of innovations that eventually became part of the common navigational practice was much smaller than that which had originally been proposed.

Referring to the three key problems in navigation mentioned above, the principal achievements of the English and the Dutch can be summarized as follows. With regard to the problem of finding course and distance to be sailed from the point of departure to the point of destination, the main contribution consisted of improvements in cartographic aids, notably the introduction of printed sea-atlases and the application of the Mercator projection in nautical charts. The Mercator projection resolved the distortions attaching to plane charts, which did not take account of the spherical shape of the earth.

With respect to the second problem: given a course steered and a distance sailed, estimate where the ship has arrived, the English and the Dutch helped to advance the art of navigation by the introduction of improvements in the measurement of magnetic declination, of new techniques for the measurement of speed (the log and line and the Dutchman's log) and a calculation of the value of a common unit of distance employed at sea, the mile. Before the early seventeenth century, seamen used to express speed in terms of leagues or miles sailed (which were assumed to be in a fixed relation to a degree of latitude, for example, 17 1/2 or 15 miles per degree of latitude), but were not able to specify the exact length of these measures, as the length of a degree of latitude was still unknown. The length of a degree was first determined in 1617 by a professor of mathematics at the University of Leiden in Holland, Willebrord Snellius, and, in 1635, by a mathematical practitioner in England, Richard Norwood. Moreover, both the English and the Dutch made significant advances in the development of more accurate methods for the calculation of an estimated position based on data about courses steered and distances sailed. They introduced new kinds of traverse tables (Dutch: *kromstreektafels*) by which, given a course steered and a distance sailed, changes in latitude and longitude could be determined. They also designed techniques by which the result could be found by computation, in part with the aid of logarithms or mathematical instruments. The mathematization of dead reckoning had by the 1620s thus greatly advanced as compared to the state of the art reached in Portugal and Spain around the middle of the sixteenth century.

Regarding the third problem: check whether the estimated point was the true one, the main contributions of the English and the Dutch in the period before 1740 consisted of innovations in techniques and instruments for measuring altitude. New methods for finding latitude were not yet created. The problem of finding longitude at sea was still not resolved. Of the various innovations in the art of navigation that were in fact introduced, the most important ones will be discussed in the following chapter.

NOTE

1. C.R. Boxer, *From Lisbon to Goa, 1500-1750: Studies in Portuguese Maritime Enterprise.* (London, 1984), p.178.

SUGGESTIONS FOR FURTHER READING

L. de Albuquerque, "Instruments for Measuring Altitude and the Art of Navigation," in A. Cortesão, *History of Portuguese Cartography.* (Coimbra, 1971), volume 2, pp. 359–442.

Charles H. Cotter, *A History of Nautical Astronomy.* (London, 1968).

C.A. Davids, "Dutch Contributions to the Development of Navigation Technology in the 17th Century," in Charles Wilson and David Proctor, eds., *1688: The Seaborne Alliance and Diplomatic Revolution.* (London, 1989), pp. 59–74.

H.L. Hitchins and W.E. May, *From Lode-stone to Gyro-scope.* (London, 1955).

Ad Meskens, "Michiel Coignet's Nautical *Instruction,"* The *Mariner's Mirror,* 78 (1992), pp. 257–292.

José Maria Lopez Piñero, *El arte de navegar en la España del Renacimiento.* (Barcelona, 1986).

A. Pannekoek and E. Crone, eds., *Astronomy and Navigation.* Vol. III, *The Principal Works of Simon Stevin.* (Amsterdam, 1961), pp. 419–501.

David W. Waters, *The Art of Navigation in England in Elizabethan and Early Stuart Times.* (London, 1958).

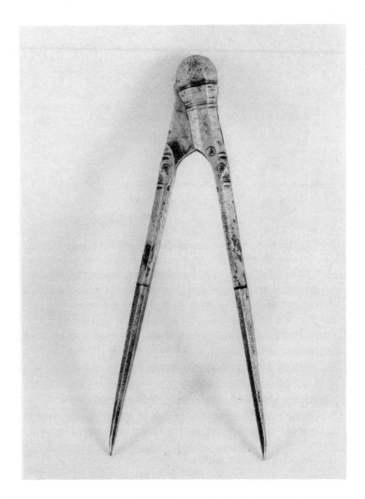

Figure IX. Pair of Dividers from the wreck of the Dutch East Indiaman, *Lastdrager,* which sank near the Shetland Islands in 1653. *Courtesy Nederlands Scheepvaartmuseum, Amsterdam.*

6

TECHNIQUES AND METHODS OF NAVIGATION BEFORE 1740

Willem F. J. Mörzer Bruyns

Portuguese navigators, in the fifteenth century, were capable of calculating their latitude. They could, however, not find their longitude. Also the Portuguese were not capable of accurately ascertaining their speed run through the water. Sailed distances had to be estimated on the basis of experience, thus depending greatly on the experience of the seamen. The combination of the estimated distance run and the observed latitude gave a position. As the world was explored and charted in north-south direction, an increasing number of places were established and charted by latitude. Subsequently, these were used for "sailing down the latitude." This was a method by which a ship would sail along the coast of Europe until reaching the latitude of the place of destination. She would then be sailed due west, checking the latitude daily with quadrant, sea or mariner's astrolabe or cross staff and, if necessary, correcting the position by sailing west-by-north or west-by-south. The latitude was found by measuring the sun's altitude at noon using a quadrant, a mariner's astrolabe or a cross-staff. At night, on the Northern Hemisphere and using these instruments, Polaris could be observed for the same purpose. The earliest known use of a quadrant by a mariner dates from 1460. The mariner's astrolabe was also introduced at sea during the fifteenth century, the earliest mention dating from 1481, during a voyage by Portuguese down the west coast of Africa. The cross-staff too was introduced at sea by the Portuguese, however, not until around 1515. In order to convert the sun's altitude into observer's latitude, it was necessary to know the sun's declination. This is the distance between the equator and the sun's projection on the earth's surface, expressed in arc of circle. Around 1509 the declination, which varies with the date, was available in print for Portuguese navigators titled *Regimento do Estrolabio e do Quadrante*. Using Polaris was easier, as it is situated almost directly above the North Pole making its altitude equivalent to an observers latitude. A small correction titled "Regiment for the North Star" had to be applied to the observation. As navigation by Europeans on the southern hemisphere became more frequent, the Southern Cross was used in a similar way for latitude observations, although a far larger correction had to be made.

Instruments. The oldest navigating instrument is, without doubt, the sounding lead and its line. A weight of lead attached to a long marked line was lowered into the sea. When touching the bottom, the depth could be read from the marks on the line. A hollow in the bottom of the lead was filled with tallow to which particles from the seabottom would stick, a further indication of the position.

The basic appearance of the compass hardly changed over the centuries. The earliest known surviving example, found in the 1545 wreck of the *Mary Rose* is very similar to classic eighteenth-century examples in museum collections. They consist of a brass or wooden bowl mounted on gimbals (in use after ca. 1545) in a second, square wooden box. The inner box, covered with glass, contained a paper card or fly with a magnetized needle fixed underneath. The card was placed on a pin in the center of the inner box so that it could swing around freely and would rest pointing to the north. The card had the "32 compass points" drawn or printed on top. The inside of the inner box contained a lubber's line for use when steering. The whole could be placed in a binnacle, containing a lantern for using the compass when dark. The needle of the compass would have to be remagnetized at regular intervals, for which purpose a loadstone was available.

There were, however, a number of substantial changes concerning the use of the compass, mainly due to the requirement to know the value of variation during a voyage. Variation is the angle between the direction of the true and the magnetic north. The value of variation varies or can be zero according to the place on earth. It increases or decreases annually due to the movement of the magnetic North and South Pole. Steering a magnetic rather than the compass course could lead to disaster. There were several methods to establish the variation. One was by taking a bearing of the sun at rise or set. Comparing the compass bearing with the amplitude, i.e., the angle along the horizon between east or west and the point were the sun rises or sets, gives the variation. Tables containing the sun's amplitude from day to day were published from the early seventeenth century. Another method was to take two such bearings, at sunrise and at sunset. The difference of the average of these bearings and south gave the variation. Similar to this method was to take bearings of the sun before and after culmination when in the same altitude. In order to take a bearing of the sun or star with high altitude adjustments had to be made to the compass. In the late sixteenth and early seventeenth century a quadrant was mounted on the compass. In the seventeenth century one index arm was fitted to the compass bowl, with a thread running from its top across the card to the other side of the bowl. The shadow cast on the card by the thread gave an accurate reading. Thus the azimuth compass was created. Later a horizontal circular brass scale with lines engraved was fixed around the card. Then accuracy with which the shadow could be read was even greater. Around 1730 azimuth compasses were equipped with sights. These were two vertical brass vanes, one with a thread and the other with a narrow slit, placed on either side of the compass bowl. Still later one of the sights was lengthened. The value of the variation could be eliminated in a compass if this was equipped with a card under which the needle could revolve around the center. After ascertaining the value of variation the needle would be moved according to that value, but in contrary direction. Due to the changing position of the ship the angle would regularly have to be corrected. Failing to do so would cause serious mistakes.

Compasses equipped with sights were also used to take bearings of landmarks in order to establish the ship's position when sailing within sight of the coast. The point of intersection of two or more bearings of church towers, hills or capes drawn in the chart would, after correction for variation, give an accurate position.

As mentioned before, for altitude measurement, quadrant's, sea or mariner's astrolabes and cross-staffs were available. All three were derived from existing instruments for astronomical observations. The quadrant was a simple wooden or brass quarter of a circle with two sighting vanes along one edge. A plumb line suspended from the center indicated the altitude along the 0°-90° graduation on the arc. The quadrant was superseded by sea astrolabe and cross-staff. Mariner's astrolabes were manufactured in seafaring European countries like Spain, Portugal, England and the Netherlands. An astrolabe consisted of a heavy cast brass ring with a 0°- 90°- 0° graduation and its complement engraved on the upper half, and suspended on a ring. Around a central pin of the instrument an alidade with two sights revolved. When the imaginary line through the center of the sights was directed at a celestial body, its altitude and zenith distance could be read from the graduation at the end of the alidade. However, the division of the graduation was up to no more than ½°, and often only 1°.

Not only was the astrolabe's reading course, in use it was a heavy and cumbersome instrument and, because of the weight of the brass, expensive. The use of sea astrolabes decreased after 1670 and was abandoned completely after about 1700. Besides the mentioned drawbacks, the back-staff (see below) had become more popular and the cross-staff greatly improved. The latter consisted of a 1½ by 1½ cm. square wooden staff of about 80 cm. length and graduated on each of the four sides. Four crosses, one for each side, could slide along the staff until the observer saw the horizon under the lower end of the cross and the sun or star above the upper end. Altitude and zenith distance could then be read from the staff. The graduation of the cross-staff, at the end of the sixteenth century up to a mere 30', could be as fine as 2' in the early eighteenth century. In the middle of the seventeenth century, brass sights were added to the end of the crosses. In these colored glasses could be fitted to protect the eye when observing facing the sun. The vanes also served to use the cross-staff with the observer's back toward the sun. This innovation not only protected the observer's eye from sunlight, but also eliminated the greatly inaccurate "blinking" between the ends of the cross.

It was not until 1595 that a new instrument for measuring the altitude of celestial bodies was introduced at sea. It was, in fact, the first precision instrument designed solely for navigational purposes. The back-staff or Davis quadrant, was named after its inventor the English mariner John Davis and described in his book, *The Seamens Secrets*. As its name suggests it was used with the observer's back towards the sun, by which the observer could avoid looking directly into the sun. Around 1670 the English Astronomer Royal, John Flamsteed, added a lens to this instrument, enabling it also to be used when the sun was less bright through clouds.

At the beginning of the seventeenth century, seamen had a reasonably accurate instrument to determine the speed of their ship through the water. Although probably invented in the 1570s, it was not until the end of the century that log and line were in general use at sea. The log and line consisted of a reel with rope marked with knots. At the end of the rope a quadrant shaped piece of wood, was attached. The arc was fitted with lead so that when in the water it would float upright. With the wood in that position the knotted rope would, using a sand glass, be unrolled during 15 to 30 seconds. The number of counted knots indicated the number of miles the ship was running per hour.

Longitude. In 1530, a Louvain professor, Gemma Frisius, published a proposal suggesting that the difference in longitude be-

Figure X. Hour Glass for 30 minutes. *Courtesy Nederlands Scheep-vaartmuseum, Amsterdam.*

tween two places (the distance between two meridians measured along the equator and expressed in arc of circle) could be established using an accurate timekeeper measuring the difference in time between the places. In order to measure this an extremely accurate timekeeper is needed. Such an instrument would have to "keep the time" on the meridian of departure during a voyage. It was not until the mid-eighteenth century that such an instrument was constructed with success. This did, however, not stop scholars, scientists and inventors from searching for methods to solve the problem with or without a timekeeper. They were stimulated by monetary rewards offered by the Spanish kings Philip II in 1567 and Philip III in 1598, by the Dutch around 1600 and by British Parliament in 1714. The rewards attracted applicants from all around Europe, among them Galileo Galilei. He suggested observing the eclipses of Jupiter's satellites. This phenomenon, which occurs at the same moment of time where visible on earth, was indeed practical, however, not on a moving ship. Much earlier than Galilei the German astronomer Johann Werner had, in 1514, proposed a solution for the longitude problem. He suggested that, using a cross-staff, the distance between the moon and a fixed star, both with known positions, should be measured. The distance could provide the observer's longitude. This method, later known as lunar distance, described and illustrated by Petrus Apianus in 1524, had to wait until the middle of the eighteenth century before sufficiently accurate instruments and tables were available for its practical use.

Many of the solutions concerned the variation of the compass needle. Although there is indeed a relation between the variation and longitude, it was not directly available to work with. It requires a vast amount of data (variation value in combination with the position). Both Petrus Plancius and Simon Stevin developed, without success due to lack of data, methods to find longitude using the variation. Timekeepers were developed and even tried at sea during the seventeenth century. A well-known attempt at a seaclock, mounted on gimbals and with a pendulum, was by Christiaan Huygens. However, at sea a pendulum is useless. It is deranged by the movement of the ship and the time of oscillation is influenced by gravity as that changes with latitude because the earth does not have a perfect spherical shape.

An important stimulant to solve the problem of finding longitude at sea was the founding of Greenwich Observatory in 1675 by king Charles II. The founding had been initiated by the Royal Society and inspired by the Paris observatory, founded eight years before by the French king. John Flamsteed was appointed Astronomer Royal with the instruction to " . . . rectify[ing] the tables of the motions of the heavens, and the places of the fixed stars, so as to find the so-much-desired longitude of places for perfecting the art of navigation."

In 1698–1701, the astronomer Edmund Halley was given the command of the *Paramore* for the specific purpose of collecting data on magnetic variation. This work resulted in a number of charts with isogens, lines over places on the earth's surface with the same magnetic variation. The first one was of the Atlantic Ocean, published in 1701, a chart of The Channel, and a world chart followed the year after. For the latter, additional observations were taken from journals and logs of other navigators such as William Dampier. Besides in England, the world chart was also published in France and the Netherlands. The Amsterdam cartographers J. Loots published The Channel chart as early as 1705, with an explanation in Dutch and French. The Dutch East India Company, the VOC, adopted the Halley charts and their use for estimating longitude from variation, around 1740.

Dead Reckoning. Dead reckoning is the method of navigation based on estimation and recording the way of a ship, taking into consideration the mean speed and course but also the effect of wind and tide. For this chart, dividers, log and line, Dutchman's log, traverse board, compass and tables were used. The position found through dead reckoning was an estimated one. The true course, found by applying the variation to the magnetic course, is plotted on the chart. The number of miles sailed since the previous position, found by adding the hourly logged speeds, is taken between dividers and marked on the chart in the direction of the steered course. Thus the new estimated position is established, which could be corrected by a true position attained from an astronomical observation or by taking bearings when in sight of the coastline. If neither of these was available a ship would continue to be navigated by dead reckoning. Because of the inaccuracy of logged speeds and the lack of knowledge of ocean currents, the element of mistake would increase day by day. The result could be that, after a prolonged period at sea, the estimated position could differ greatly from the true one. Evidence from Dutch charts indicates that longitudinal errors of several hundreds of miles are no exception.

Over the years, instruments and techniques were developed for dead reckoning. In the early sixteenth century, the traverse board came into use. It consisted of a wind rose painted on wood with eight holes in each of the compass points and separately a table of holes indicating speed. Each half hour a pin would be plugged in the hole corresponding with the steered course and one in the hole corresponding with the logged speed. After four hours course and speed could be "read" from the traverse board. The Dutchman's log was a method of determining the ship's speed which came into use at the end of the sixteenth century. A chip of wood was thrown overboard at the bow and the time the ship took to sail passed the chip was measured, by counting. Knowing both time and the ship's length, the speed could be calculated. The method became popular with Dutch seamen, hence the name.

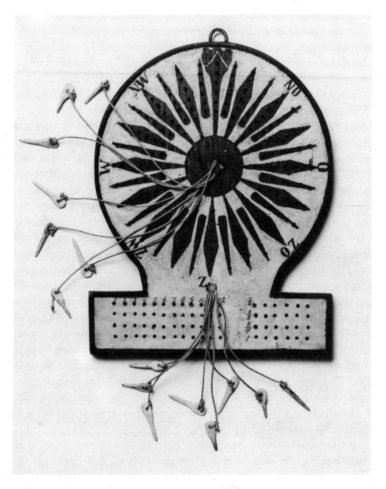

Figure XI. Traverse Board, used for dead reckoning, nineteenth century. *Courtesy Nederlands Scheepvaartmuseum, Amsterdam.*

With the invention of tables the level of accuracy of calculating the position increased, although the lack of knowledge of tides and ocean currents could not be overcome. In the late sixteenth and early seventeenth century, English, French and Dutch authors were independently publishing navigational manuals, often including new and original knowledge. For example, an important table for navigation was the *streektafel* with which an observer knowing his course and sailed miles, could calculate his position. The table was of great use when steering courses other than north-south or east-west. It was based on tables developed by a Portuguese scholar in Spanish service, published in 1535. Based on these was the *krom-streektafel;* this version, published by Cornelis Jansz. Lastman in 1621, was calculated for charts on Mercator's projection. Some years later logarithms, invented by the Englishman John Napier in 1614, were introduced into navigation. Although tables were available, seamen often preferred to use logarithms through instruments. Popular examples of these were the gunter's scale, developed by the Englishman Edmund Gunter in 1620 and the plane scale by his countryman John Aspley, first published in 1627. At the end of the seventeenth century the sinical or nautical quadrant was being manufactured by instrument makers. With known course and distance the change in latitude could be read. Again it was an instrumental method of solving a problem which, by that time, could be solved by calculation.

Navigational techniques and methods, many of which were developed as early as the fifteenth century, were perfected during the seventeenth century. At the beginning of the eighteenth century a high standard of accuracy had been achieved. The basis for modern navigation was established and navigational science was on the eve of important inventions such as the octant, the timekeeper and the reflecting circle.

SUGGESTIONS FOR FURTHER READING

J. A. Bennett, *The Divided Circle. A History of Instruments for Astronomy, Navigation and Surveying.* (Oxford, 1987).

C. H. Cotter, *A History of Nautical Astronomy.* (London, 1968), pp. 57–83.

C. A. Davids, *Zeewezen en wetenschap. De wetenschap en de ontwikkeling van de navigatietechniek in Nederland tussen 1585 en 1815.* (Amsterdam/Dieren, 1986).

J. B. Hewson, *A History of the Practice of Navigation.* (Glasgow, 1951).

Derek Howse, *Greenwich Time and the Discovery of Longitude.* (Oxford, 1980), Chapters 1 and 2.

G. Schilder and W. F. J. Mörzer Bruyns, "Navigatie," in *Maritieme Geschiedenis der Nederlanden.* (Bussum, 1977), volume II, pp. 159–199.

G. Schilder and W. F. J. Mörzer Bruyns, "Navigatie," in *Maritieme Geschiedenis der Nederlanden.* (Bussum, 1977), volume III, pp. 191–225.

Alan Stimson, *The Mariner's Astrolabe.* (Utrecht, 1988).

E. G. R. Taylor, *The Haven Finding Art.* (New York, 1957).

David W. Waters, *The Art of Navigation in England in Elizabethan and Early Stuart Times.* (London, 1958), pp. 127–250.

Supplementary Reading

E. Crone, *Pieter Holm and his Tobacco-box.* Translated by Dirk Brouwer with an introduction by Edwin Pugsley, (Mystic, 1953).

E. Crone, *How did the Navigator determine the Speed of his Ship and the Distance Run?.* (Coimbra, 1969).

C. A. Davids, "The Use of Globes on Ships of the Dutch East-India Company', in *Der Globusfreund,* (1987), pp. 69–80.

G. Forty, "The Backstaff and The Determination of Latitude at Sea in the 17th Century," *The Journal of Navigation,* 39 (1986), pp. 259–268.

C. Koeman, "Flemish and Dutch contributions to the Art of Navigations in the XVIth Century" in *Instituto de Investigacao Cientifica Tropical.* (Lisbon, 1988).

C. Koeman, "The Astrolabium Catholicum," *Publicacoes do Centro de estudos de cartografia antiga,* 134 (1980), pp. 65–76.

M. S. Mahoney, "Christiaan Huygens: The Measurement of Time and Longitude," in H. J. M. Bos, ed., *Studies of Christiaan Huygens.* (Lisse, 1980), pp. 234–270.

W. F. J. Mörzer Bruyns, "Prime Meridians Used by Dutch Navigators," *Vistas in Astronomy,* 28 (1985), pp. 33–39.

W. F. J. Mörzer Bruyns, "A History of the Use and Supply of the *Pleynschael* by Instrument Makers to the VOC," *International Journal of Nautical Archaeology,* 11 (1982), pp. 293–296.

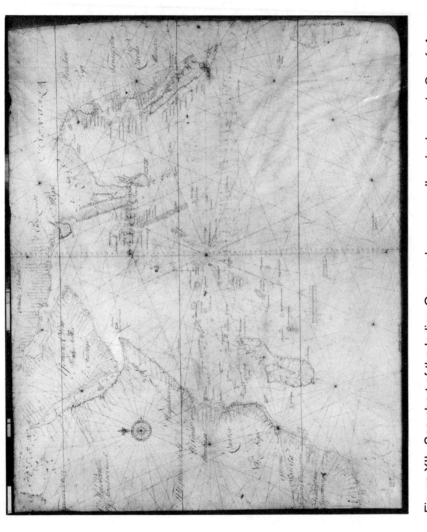

Figure XII. Sea-chart of the Indian Ocean, drawn on vellum by Isaac de Graaf, Amsterdam, in 1731. De Graaf was the official chart-maker of the Dutch East India Company. *Courtesy Nederlands Scheepvaartmuseum, Amsterdam.*

7

SOURCES OF KNOWLEDGE: CHARTS AND RUTTERS

Willem F. J. Mörzer Bruyns

Charts and rutters are as essential for safe navigation as are instruments. A chart depicts part of a coastline with islands and surrounding waters. It contains information such as latitude and sometimes longitude of the depicted area, compass directions, the water depths and underwater dangers to navigation, mountains and hills visible from sea, ports, conspicuous trees and towers and magnetic variation. Later charts also contain tidal information, the scale and information on the cartographic projection used.

A rutter, from the French *routier,* is a book containing written information on part of a coastline and its surrounding waters. A rutter almost always also contains coastal views. It provides advice as to safe navigation in the particular area, such as on courses to steer, areas to avoid and safe anchorages. Since Abraham Ortelius published the first modern atlas, his *Theatrum Orbis Terrarum,* in Antwerp in 1570, the knowledge of cartography moved north from the Mediterranean to be concentrated in the Low Countries. Ortelius's contemporary and countryman Gerard Mercator devised a projection, later to be named after him, which would prove to be revolutionary in maritime cartography. This method depends on the principle that the convergence of meridians is in proportion to the cosine of the latitude. A proportional misplacement is introduced into the spacing between parallels of latitude on the chart increasing toward the poles. The consequence of the method is that the spiral rhumb lines on the earth's surface become straight lines in the chart. At the time the significance of Mercator's invention was not fully realized. However, in 1599, the English scholar Edward Wright explained it and made it available in his *Certain Errors in Navigation.* It still took considerable time before sea-charts were generally drawn according to Mercator's method.

Sea-atlases and Rutters. A sea-atlas was in fact a combination of a sea chart and a rutter, nevertheless rutters were also published separately. A sea-atlas always contained charts and often accompanying texts. Rutters contained texts and sometimes charts and views. In some cases a rutter consisted of reprinted texts from sea-atlases.

In 1584, the Dutch pilot Lucas Jansz. Waghenaer from Enkhuizen was the first to compile and publish a sea-atlas. This was the first book to contain large-scale charts of European coastal waters, between the White Sea and Strait of Gibraltar, in combination with sailing directions. The charts in a sea-atlas were far smaller than the traditional sea-charts but as the scale was larger they contained more information. Coastal views were also incorporated in the charts. The *Spieghel der zeevaerdt* by Waghenaer became an extremely popular navigational aid and was published in English as *The Mariners Mirrour* (1588), in German (1589) and French (1600). The popularity of Dutch sea-atlases did not end here and in the years after Waghenaer also included the Mediterranean. In the early seventeenth century, Willem Jansz. Blaeu published a number of similar sea-atlases. His *Licht der zeevaert* appeared in English in 1612 as *The Light of Navigation* and, in 1619, in French as *Le Flambeau de la navigation*. His 1623 rutter *Zeespieghel* appeared in the same year as *Sea Mirror*. Contemporaries of Blaeu, such as Hendrik Doncker and Jacob Colom, published similar sea-atlases and rutters which were also translated into English, French and sometimes Spanish. The Blaeu family was, between 1633 and 1704, official chart maker to the Dutch East India Company. In this capacity they had direct access to hydrographical information returned by ships' captains and mates returning from Asia. The activities of the Company necessitated the founding of a separate hydrographical office in Batavia, the headquarters of the Company in Asia. Besides producing increasingly accurate sea-charts, it was possible for the Blaeu's to compile and publish beautiful general cartographical works, such as atlases and globes, as a spin-off of their official function.

In 1671, the English cartographer John Seller, trying to break the Dutch monopoly in maritime cartography, published *The English Pilot*. It was, however, based on Dutch charts and he had even bought old Dutch copper plates reengraving them for his pilot. In 1680, the Amsterdam cartographer Johannes van Keulen produced his first sea-atlas the *Zee-Atlas* and, in 1689, the first edition of the very popular *Zee-Fakkel*. This was also published by Van Keulen in English as *The Lightning Columne,* and also in French, Spanish and, one volume in Italian. By that time, however, the English and

French had started to break the Dutch monopoly in maritime cartography, although the quality of the Dutch charts remained far superior for many years. At the death of Isaac de Graaf, in 1743, Johannes II van Keulen was appointed cartographer of the Dutch East India Company and that position remained in his family until the Company was dissolved in 1799.

In 1681, the Admiralty in London appointed a naval captain, Greenvile Collins, to survey the British coast and its harbors. The *Great Britain's Coasting Pilot* appeared in 1693. In the same year, *Le Neptune François,* ordered by Louis XIV and containing charts of the French coast on Mercator's projection, appeared. It was immediately translated and published in Dutch. *Le Neptune* was the result of a process started in 1667 with the establishment of the l'Observatoire in Paris. The longitude of the meridian of the French capital, established through the observing the eclipse of Jupiter's moons, triggered off the triangulation of the entire country. Although Dutch maritime cartography retained its international popularity throughout the first half of the eighteenth century, the French eventually took the lead. In 1720, the Depôt des Cartes et Plans de la Marine, the French hydrographic service, was established through which the further publication of sea-atlases was to be directed. Although France was the first country in which chartmaking was recognized as a responsibility of the state, it took some years before the work of the Depôt actually got underway.

By the middle of the eighteenth century, the British had also introduced triangulation in order to chart their isles. The Admiralty, in 1751, appointed the civilian surveyor, Murdoch Mackenzie, to chart the British west coast in this manner. In 1752, the Scot, Alexander Dalrymple, was sent out to Asia by the East India Company. In the years to follow, he traveled a great deal, collecting hydrographical information, eventually to be published in 1770 as *An historical Collection of the Several Voyages and Discoveries in the South Pacific.* In 1771, Dalrymple published the first specialized work on marine surveying, titled *Essay on Nautical Surveying* and, in 1774, Mackenzie published his *Treatise on Marine Surveying.* Both were to become the eighteenth-century standard works in this subject. In 1779, the East India Company appointed Dalrymple as the first hydrographer to the Company. In his *Essay,* he had recommended the use of the sextant for surveying. This had been developed in 1759, providing a means of accurate angle measurement for navigation and hydrography. In 1795, the Admiralty followed the example of the East India Company and appointed Dalrymple as

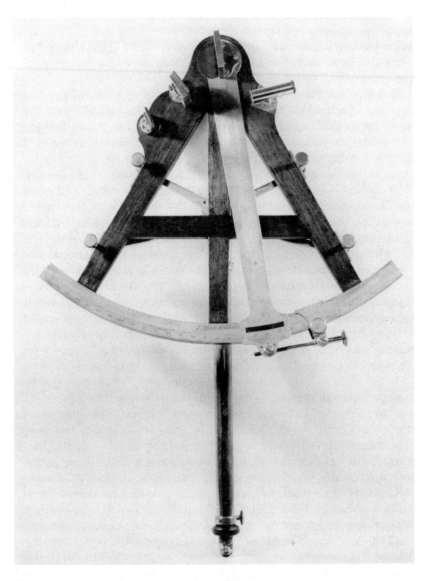

Figure XIII. Sextant made by John Bird, London, c. 1770. Bird was the first to make sextants; they were used by James Cook on his voyage to the Pacific Ocean. *Courtesy Nederlands Scheepvaartmuseum, Amsterdam*

first hydrographer, thus establishing the Hydrographic Department. He remained at this post until forced to retire in 1808. Dalrymple could, by then, not meet the Admiralty's demand for charts necessary to fight the Napoleonic wars. Before this, however, in 1784 another important sea-atlas appeared. It was the *Atlantic Neptune* a compilation by the Swiss born British officer serving in North America, J. F. W. Des Barres, and containing charts of the east coast of North America. In 1796, an American, Captain Lawrence Furlong, compiled *The American Coast Pilot,* a rutter, which was subsequently published at Newburyport, Massachusetts, by Blunt & March. It was based on old English and American rutters and saw several editions. Oddly enough, it was translated into French in 1821. Meanwhile in the Netherlands in 1788, a longitude committee was established by the Amsterdam Admiralty in order to revise the sea-charts and rutters. It was, in fact, the first time that the Dutch state took the responsibility for maritime cartography.

Lastly, the name of the French hydrographer, C. F. Beautemps-Beaupré, should be mentioned. Beautemps-Beaupré, popularly known as the "father of hydrography," published in 1808 his *Methodes pour la levée et la construction des cartes et plans hydrographique* in which, for marine surveying, he proposed the use of the reflecting circle rather than the sextant. He was commissioned with surveying the coast of the French empire, an effort that was completed in the early nineteenth century.

Projections. Meridians are imaginary lines on the earth connecting the poles. They are great circles, which means that their center coincides with the center of the earth. Latitude is measured along the meridians, from the equator north and south toward the poles. The equator is a also an imaginary great circle, however at 90° angle with the meridians. Imaginary circles are drawn parallel to the equator circles toward the north and the south. The meridians converge toward the poles, so that the distance between them decreases. At 90° latitude, that is at the poles, the distance between meridians has become zero and the observer has no longitude.

In the traditional sixteenth-century sea-chart, the meridians were not drawn as converging, but as parallel north-south lines. This meant that, although the latitude could be correct, an error of longitude was introduced, increasing toward the poles on charts depicting a large area. In such charts, the image becomes increasingly deformed toward the poles, with subsequent risk for navigators attempting to use the charts. As mentioned before, the Flemish cartographer, Gerard Mercator, developed a cartographic projection, named after him, in which this deformation was avoided. Like charts on Mercator's projection, globes present a correct image of the earth. However, in order to be of practical use for navigation, a globe would have to have an enormous diameter. Such a diameter, however, would be impractical on a ship. Nevertheless, globes, too, were used at sea until the early eighteenth century, especially for navigational purposes as an accurate projection of the earth's surface. The Dutch East India Company provided globes to its ships between the early seventeenth century and 1760 (with an interruption of 30 years). Between 1746 and 1760, celestial globes were also provided. These were used in conjunction with the newly invented octant for observing stars in the twilight.

Standard or Prime Meridians. If graduation for longitude was drawn on a chart at all, the prime or zero meridian, where longitude was measured from, would generally be the one over the most westerly parts of the Old World, like Cape Verde, the Cape Verdes, the Azores or the Canaries. The French used the meridian over Paris, after the Observatory was established there in 1667. The Dutch, at first, used the meridian over the island of Tenerife in the Canaries, although the meridian over Amsterdam was also used for navigation, especially in Dutch waters. In 1788, the Amsterdam Admiralty formally recognized the meridian over Tenerife. During the French occupation, however, the Dutch also used the meridians of Paris and Cadiz. In 1826, the Dutch ruled that thereafter the meridian of Greenwich would be standard. The founding of Greenwich Observatory in 1675 stimulated the use of its meridian as prime meridian. It was internationally recognized as such in 1884 by all seafaring countries.

With the successful introduction of lunar distances and the chronometer at sea in the second half of the eighteenth century, it became possible to establish with great accuracy the longitude of various places on earth. Soon the positions of halfway ports like St. Helena and Capetown and destinations like Bombay and Batavia were accurately calculated and published. Ships' chronometers could be checked by being taken ashore to an observatory or by observing signals from the land. In order to accommodate for a large number of ships at one time and to avoid the transportation of vulnerable chronometers, time-balls were erected around the world. (A time-ball is a large ball dropped as a visual signal from a staff at a prearranged time, generally noon, and often accompanied by firing a cannon, so that ships in a harbor would know the precise local time.) Although proposed as early as 1824, the first time-ball was placed in 1833. It was on the roof of the Royal Observatory in Greenwich, visible for all ships anchored on the River Thames. A year later, the British East India Company installed such a ball on the island of St. Helena and the Dutch authorities did so at Batavia in 1839.

Routes. When choosing a course, a sailing ship depends on the direction of the wind. Moreover, seventeenth- and eighteenth-century square rigged ships could not sail as close to the wind as nineteenth-century schooner-rigged ships. Also, sea and ocean currents strongly influenced the direction in which the relatively slow ships sailed. Consequently, sailing routes were almost never the shortest distance between two ports. For the Dutch, and to a lesser extent also for the English, departure from home ports into the Atlantic Ocean during southwesterly storms was difficult and sometimes impossible. Weeks of delay could be avoided by sailing north and around the British isles into the Atlantic. The next hindrance was crossing the area of the Doldrums, near the equator, where there is virtually no wind at all. It had been discovered that the area covered by the Doldrums was not the same in the whole Atlantic. Depending on the time of year, the narrowest parts were either near the coast of Brazil or half way across the ocean toward Africa. However, sailing close to the Brazilian coast meant the risk of running on the Abrolhos Islands, so named by the Portuguese discoverers. Sailing too far west could bring a ship into the South Equatorial Current and Caribbean Current, forcing it into the Caribbean. However, navigating too far east was equally risky as this could take a ship into the Guinea Current and into the Guinea Gulf, with hardly any wind at all. Once the Doldrums were passed, the South East Trade Wind and the Brazil Current were picked up and ships sailed to the Cape.

Beyond the Cape of Good Hope, after 1611, ships sailed due south to about 40° latitude. Here, the prevailing westerly wind and the South Australian Current assured a fast crossing towards the Australian west coast. Thanks to this route, discovered by the Dutchman Brouwer, the total duration of voyages between Europe and Asia was reduced from about 328 days (about 11 months) to about 240 (about 8 months). Moreover, due to the moderate climate in the higher latitude, both the health of the seamen and their food could be better preserved. Navigators, not capable of determining their longitude accurately, knew that the Indian Ocean islands of Amsterdam and St. Paul should be sighted about halfway. Nevertheless, it happened that ships ran onto the low and badly visible coral reefs off the West Australian coast. Most ships, however, managed to pick up the South East Trade Wind and sailed to Sunda Strait for Batavia.

Figure XIV. Sea-chart of the Atlantic Ocean, drawn on vellum by Isaac de Graaf, Amsterdam, in 1738. The lines drawn near the equator represent the area through which the ship should safely pass. Midday positions and course lines of a ship are visible. *Courtesy Nederlands Scheepvaartmuseum, Amsterdam.*

SUGGESTIONS FOR FURTHER READING

J. R. Bruijn, F. S. Gaastra, I. Schöffer, eds., *Dutch-Asiatic Shipping in the 17th and 18th Centuries.* (The Hague, 1987), volume 1, pp. 56–106.

M. Destombes, *Cartes Hollandaises.* (Saigon, 1941).

C. Koeman, *The History of Lucas Jansz. Waghenaer and His "Spieghel der Zeevaerdt."* (Lausanne, 1964).

C. Koeman, *Atlases Neerlandici.* volume IV, *Maritime Atlases,* (Amsterdam, 1970).

C. Koeman, "The Chart Trade in Europe from the Middle Ages to the 20th Century", in Derek Howse, ed., *Five Hundred Years of Nautical Science 1400–1900.* (Greenwich, 1981), pp. 131–141.

G. Schilder, "Organization and Development of the Hydrographic Office of the Dutch East-India Company in the 17th Century," *Imago Mundi,* 28 (1976), pp. 61–78.

David W. Waters, "The English Pilot: English Sailing Directions and Charts and The Rise of English Shipping, 16th-18th Centuries," *The Journal of Navigation,* 42 (1989), pp. 317–354.

David W. Waters, *The Art of Navigation in England in Elizabethan and Early Stuart Times.* (London, 1958), pp. 457–494.

Supplementary Reading

D. Gernez, "La libraire néerlandais Joannes Loots et sa maison d'editions maritimes," *Communications Academie de Marine de Belgique,* VII (1954), pp. 23–69.

De VOC in de kaart gekeken. Cartografie en navigatie van de Verenigde Oostindische Compagnie 1602–1795. (Den Haag, 1988).

In de Gekroonde Lootsman. Het kaarten-boekuitgevers en instrumentenmakershuis Van Keulen te Amsterdam 1680–1885. (Utrecht, 1989).

C. Koeman, *The sea on paper. The story of the Van Keulens and their 'Sea Torch'.* (Amsterdam, 1972).

P. C. J. van der Krogt, *Globi Neerlandici. De globeproduktie in de Nederlanden.* (Utrecht, 1989).

G. Schilder, P. C. J. van der Krogt and S. de Clercq, eds., *M. Destombes (1905–1983). Contributions selectionnés sur l'histoire de la cartographie et des instruments; Selected contributions to the history of cartography.* (Utrecht and Paris, 1987).

Lawrence Wroth, *The Way of a Ship; An Essay on the Literature of Navigation Science.* (Portland, Maine, 1937).

8

SOURCES OF KNOWLEDGE: JOURNALS, LOGS, AND TRAVEL ACCOUNTS

Karel Davids

The entry of Captain Cook's journal of the *Endeavour* on the 19th December 1768 reads:

Winds Northerly. Course SW. Dist in miles 116. Latd in 34° 4'. Longd. in West from Greenwich 45° 6' Steady fresh breeze and fair weather. At 1/2 past 5 pm Longitude in per observation of the Sun and Moon 43° 38' West from Greenwich. Variation 11° 3'. The observed Latd exceeds that given by the Log 7 Miles.[1]

This short fragment contains several hints about the way in which data on navigation were recorded in the late eighteenth century. First of all, Cook made a distinction between a journal and a log. Witness the reference in the last sentence; data registered in the log could differ from those entered into the journal. Second, navigators were evidently in the habit of keeping a journal. Third, there was more than one journal, each of which had a different history of use and ownership. The ship's journal from which this particular fragment was taken, was after all only one of a larger set. The copy of the journal of the *Endeavour* edited by J. C. Beaglehole was the transcript of Cook's journal handed over to the Admiralty after the ship's return and now kept in the Public Record Office, London. But there was also a holograph journal and several other transcripts, which are preserved in private collections. Moreover, the journals formed the base of a travel account written by John Hawkesworth, *An account of a voyage round the world . . . by Lieutenant James Cook,* published in London in 1773. This section deals with each of these three aspects in turn: the contents of journals and logs, the practice of keeping journals and logs and the issue of their use and ownership, including their adaptation as travel accounts and their usefulness as source of knowledge for historians.

Contents of Journals and Logs. The main difference between the contents of logs and journals was that logs contained rough data recorded per watch, the basic division of time used aboard ship, whereas journals did not. The logs contained courses steered, distances sailed, soundings, estimated position and various sorts of computations—including sometimes calculations of longitude. The nature of these aids for navigation probably explains why logs have much more rarely been preserved than journals. For the 35 ships fitted out by the Swedish East India Company between c.1730 and 1770, for example, Christian Koninckx could retrieve fifteen journals of twelve voyages, but merely two logs. Of the 130 ships sent out by the Asiatic Company of Denmark between 1732 and 1833, 117 journals have been preserved, but no logs.[2] Neither has any log been found of a ship of the Dutch East India Company (VOC), although the number of voyages made under the aegis of this Company between Asia and the Dutch Republic alone amounted to almost 8,000 in the period 1602–1795. The number of journals preserved, by contrast, runs to over 270.

What sort of data were recorded in ship's journals? Captain Cook's journal of the *Endeavour* was ordered according to a two-page system; each of the pages was divided into a number of columns. On the left-hand page, Cook used to enter each day the direction of the wind, the course steered, the distance traversed in miles, the estimated latitude in degrees and minutes and the estimated longitude in degrees and minutes. On the right-hand pages he noted down the variation of the compass, the weather, the difference between observed and estimated latitude, the observed longitude, if any, and various other bits of information subsumed under the heading: "remarkable occurrences on board His Majestys bark Endeavour." The range of data recorded by Cook and the way in which they were ordered, were hardly different from those used aboard a Dutch East Indiaman from the middle of the seventeenth century onward. The chief distinctions were, that masters and mates of the VOC before the 1780s normally only recorded observed longitudes when they had the opportunity to take bearings of landmarks, and that on voyages between Asia and Europe they entered the data, arranged in columns, into printed, standardized forms, which were issued to all Dutch ships sailing to the Indies from 1655 onward.

But the journals of Cook and the masters and mates of the VOC must be regarded as specimens of "best practice"—methods rather than as typical examples of procedures followed by seafarers of early modern Europe. They were records of long-distance ocean voyages carried out under the aegis of highly developed maritime organizations. They contained a maximum range of information, ordered in the clearest and most precise manner known in their day. The level reached by these navigators was never attained in other branches of seafaring, except in journals of ocean voyages made by warships or East Indiamen of various maritime powers in the eighteenth century. Ships' journals were normally far less extensive and not as neatly arranged. Data like the variation of the compass, estimated longitude or even observed latitude were seldom recorded or completely lacking. An arrangement in columns was rarely applied. And what is more, keeping journals had by the end of the eighteenth century in all probability still not become a generally adopted practice.

The Practice of Keeping Journals. One of the reasons why the voyage of the *Endeavour* can be extremely well studied is simply that so many members of the crew kept a journal. It was not only Cook himself who made a daily record of events, but also his lieutenants, the master, the master's mates, the midshipman, the surgeon, the gunner and the two scientists, Joseph Banks and Charles Green. On VOC ships, journals were kept by masters and first, second and third mates as well as (though of a different kind) by merchants and surgeons.

But the habit of keeping journals was in fact very unevenly spread in different branches of shipping. While the practice was adopted early on in ships sailing to the East or West Indies, and later on board many naval vessels as well, before the end of the eighteenth century it was much less used in such branches of European seafaring as whaling or merchant shipping. There are almost no journals extant of voyages in European waters during the early modern period made by ships in the merchant navy of the Dutch Republic, one of the largest in Europe. The most plausible explanation is that there may never have been many journals made in the first place. Outside navies and trading companies, it was probably not yet common practice to keep journals in the seventeenth and eighteenth centuries. Probate inventories of deceased seamen in the Dutch Republic rarely contained any reference to ships' journals; neither did inventories of managers or shipowners, for that matter. For a long time, authors of navigation manuals found it necessary to exhort their readers to keep journals. Moreover, the extant journals from the merchant navy are of a rather simple nature compared to those from the VOC.

This scarcity of journals from other branches of shipping can, at least from the late seventeenth century onward, not simply be explained by an inability of navigators to read or write. The literacy rate among pilots of the Dutch mercantile marine around 1700 was, in fact, quite high: 98%.[3] The explanation must rather be sought in the uses of journals and the arrangements concerning their ownership.

Uses and ownership. Journals could in general serve three main functions: as an aid for seamen themselves in finding their way overseas, as a piece of evidence for interested parties ashore (trading companies, private shipowners, charterers, insurers, navy authorities or other government bodies) and as a source of data for cartographers. As a fourth, derivative function, ships' journals could also be used as a source for published travel accounts.

As an aid for navigation, journals were not absolutely necessary. It was by no means impossible for seamen to find their way overseas without keeping a journal. Instead, they could plot their course on a chart, or they could rely on their experience and memory. Evidence from the eighteenth century shows that seamen sailing in European waters in that period were no less adept in using their experience and memory as the native mariners whom Captain Cook met during his voyages in the Pacific or indeed, the Polynesian seafarers studied in recent times by scholars like David Lewis, Thomas Gladwin, or E. Dodd.[4] This was probably also true for ocean navigators in Europe during the Early Middle Ages. The Vikings were able to make long voyages across open seas without, for all we know, ever keeping a journal.

The fact that ship's journals were kept (and sometimes preserved) has therefore not only to do with their possible use for seamen themselves, but also with demands made by other interested parties. Seamen were often obliged to keep journals. In trading companies like the VOC and the English East India Company, keeping a journal was almost right from the start a formal part of the duties of the navigating personnel. This obligation to keep journals was later extended to other branches of shipping. In France, for instance, all navigators were instructed to do so under a royal regulation of 1681. In the Dutch Republic, an order to this effect was issued in 1702 by the States General for vessels engaged in privateering and by the city government of Amsterdam in 1752 for merchant ships registered in Amsterdam.

The principal reason why authorities in various branches of shipping chose to make keeping journals compulsory rather than leave the decision to the discretion of navigators themselves was, in all probability, the consideration that the very practice of putting actions and observations in the course of a voyage on record made it easier to exercise control over seamen. Supervision could be improved. Journals could, if necessary, be used as evidence in court, for example, in the case of damage, shipwreck, mutiny or neglect of duty.

In addition, navigators in some branches of shipping also received instructions concerning the procedures to be followed in keeping journals at sea and handling these records after the ship's return to port. After c. 1650, the VOC ordered its masters and mates to enter all information into printed, standardized forms, which they received from the Company's storehouse at the time of departure. It was, moreover, not unusual that navigators employed in navies or trading companies were also instructed to hand in their journals after return. At the start of the voyage of the *Endeavour,* the Commissioners of the Admiralty ordered Captain Cook, that before he left the vessel after its return to Britain, he was "to demand from the officers and petty officers, the log books and journals they may have kept, and to seal them up for our inspection, and enjoyning them, and the whole crew, not to divulge where they have been until they shall have the permission so to do."[5] This very obligation had also been imposed on masters and mates who sailed with the Dutch expeditions to the East Indies almost 200 years before. In these cases, ownership of journals no longer rested completely with the navigators themselves. They could not freely dispose of their own records.

The reason for the introduction of such instructions was, of course, first of all the wish to prevent data on geographical discoveries and trade routes or information of political and military value being divulged to possible competitors. A second reason was the need to use data collected by seafarers for improvement of rutters and charts. In 1617, the VOC ordered that all journals had to be delivered to the Company's hydrographer on a ship's return. The introduction of printed, standardized forms for ship's journals in the 1650s may well have been occasioned by the sheer increase in the amount of data which had to be processed by the hydrographic office of the VOC.

But, in reality, information was often not entirely secret. Part of it *was* divulged, and some of it was indeed divulged on purpose. Journals of the voyages of Captain Cook were, after all, published under the auspices of the Admiralty itself, albeit in a heavily edited version. Ships' journals could also be copied and diffused in spite of the strict prohibitions issued by naval authorities or the boards of trading companies. Ownership rights were surely not always safe. Journals from Cook's voyages appeared in nonauthorized editions, too. But the practice of piracy was much older than that. Publishers in the Dutch Republic were already, from the 1590s onward, busily engaged in producing travel accounts based on ships' journals acquired by "unofficial channels," or by stealth. An account of the first successful voyage from Holland to the Indies, 1596–1597, was published in the very year those ships returned. In the summer of 1601, it took Jan van Waesberghe in Rotterdam barely a month to rush through the press an abstract travel account of the first Dutch voyage around the world under the leadership of Olivier van Noort. A full account appeared a few months later.

In the Dutch Republic, interest in travel accounts of seafarers was, from the late sixteenth century onward, as lively as it was in England. Publishers also found it lucrative to market compilations. While England boasted the great collections of Richard Hakluyt, Samuel Purchas, the Churchills and John Harris, Holland saw the appearance of compilations by Isaac Commelin, *Begin ende voortganck van de Vereenigde Nederlantsche Geoctroyeerde Oost-Indische Compagnie* (1645), Joost Hartgers (1648) and Gillis Saeghman (1660).

From the historian's point of view, travel accounts are less valuable as sources for the reconstruction of navigational practice than ships' journals. A key difference between travel accounts and ships' journals is precisely that, in the former records, most of the technicalities of navigation have been suppressed. They do not represent a faithful testimony of the technology that had actually been applied. On the other hand, the value of travel accounts resides in their usefulness as sources for the study of culture, both of the observers, i.e., the seamen, and the observed, the foreign peoples. A ship's journal, by contrast, is one of the best sources for the knowledge of navigational practice a historian could wish for. Nevertheless, even journals do not offer a complete picture. They are records of data collected by seafarers rather than of the methods by which these data have been obtained. Historians would, therefore, do wisely to consult other sources as well: notably, archaeological evidence, museum collections, navigational manuals, probate inventories from seamen, instrument makers and booksellers as well as lists of charts and instruments issued by naval authorities or trading companies.

NOTES

1. J. C. Beaglehole, ed., *The Journals of Captain James Cook.* volume I, *The Voyage of the Endeavour 1768–1771*. Hakluyt Society, Extra Series, no. XXXIV, (Cambridge, 1955), p. 35.

2. Christian Koninckx, *The First and Second Charters of the Swedish East-India Company (1733–1761).* (Courtrai, 1980), pp. 112–114; Eric Gøbel, "The Danish Asiatic Company's Voyages to China, 1732–1833," *Scandinavian Economic History Review,* 27 (1979), pp. 23–45, esp. pp. 24–26.

3. P. C. van Royen, *Zeevarenden op de koopvaardijvloot omstreeks 1700.* (Amsterdam, 1987), p. 128.

4. David Lewis, *We, the Navigators. The Ancient Art of Landfinding in the Pacific.* (Canberra, 1972); Thomas Gladwin, *East is a Big Bird. Navigation and Logic on Puluwat Atoll.* (Cambridge, Mass., 1970), E. Dodd, *Polynesian Seafaring. A Disquisition on Prehistoric Celestial Navigation and the Nature of Seagoing Double Canoes.* (London, 1972).

5. Beaglehole, ed., *The Journals,* vol. 2, p. cclxxxiv.

SUGGESTIONS FOR FURTHER READING

J. R.Bruijn, F. S.Gaastra, I. Schöffer, eds., *Dutch-Asiatic Shipping in the 17th and 18th Centuries.* (The Hague, 1987), volume 1, pp. 56–106.

C. A. Davids, *Zeewezen en wetenschap. De wetenschap en de ontwikkeling van de navigatietechniek in Nederland tussen 1585 en 1815.* (Amsterdam/Dieren, 1986).

Eric Gøbel, "The Danish Asiatic Company's Voyages to China, 1732–1833," *Scandinavian Economic History Review,* 27 (1979), pp. 23–45.

Christian Koninckx, *The First and Second Charters of the Swedish East-India Company (1733–1761).* (Courtrai, 1980).

David W. Waters, *The Art of Navigation in England in Elizabethan and Early Stuart Times.* (London, 1958).

9

THE DEVELOPMENT OF NAVIGATIONAL TECHNIQUES, 1740–1815: GENERAL BACKGROUND

Karel Davids

The principles of the methods of finding longitude that were brought into practice in the last decades of the eighteenth century had already been known more than 200 years before. What conditions had to be fulfilled before this advance could finally be achieved? This is the first issue that will be discussed in this chapter. I will restrict myself to the astronomical method: finding longitude by lunar distances. Second, the chapter will deal with other, "softer" methods for checking longitude which were sometimes used before the more accurate methods were adopted at the end of the eighteenth century. Third, this chapter will explore the reasons why England and France were ultimately more successful in developing effective solutions for the problem of finding longitude than the leading seafaring nation in the seventeenth century, the Dutch Republic.

Finding Longitude by Lunar Distances. The principle of the method of finding longitude by lunar distances consisted in comparing the time at which a given distance between the moon and the sun, a planet or a star is observed on board and the time at which this same phenomenon is observed at a prime meridian, be it the meridian of Greenwich, Paris, Tenerife or another place. The difference in time yields the longitude east or west of the chosen prime meridian; one hour difference in time is 15 degrees in longitude.

The operation of the method can be explained with the help of Figure XV:

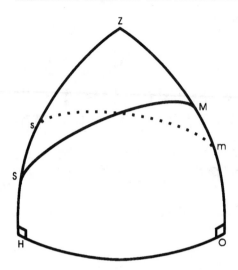

Figure XV. Principles and practice of the lunar method for finding longitude at sea.

arc HO	observer's horizon
arc MO	true altitude of moon's center
arc ZM	true zenith distance of moon's center
arc SH	true altitude of star
arc ZS	true zenith distance of star
arc MS	great circle arc through true positions of moon's center and star: true lunar distance
arc mO	apparent altitude of moon's center
arc Zm	apparent zenith distance of moon's center
arc Zs	apparent zenith distance of star
arc ms	great-circle arc through the apparent positions of moon and star: apparent lunar distance

The apparent distance between sun and moon measured by an observer (= the angular distance between sun and moon) is here denoted as "ms." It is called "apparent," because the observed distance due to the combined effects of atmospheric refraction and parallax-in-altitude differs from the distance in reality. Atmospheric refraction is the bending of a ray of light as it passes from a medium of one density into one of a different density. Parallax-in-altitude is the angle at the center of a celestial body between lines terminating at the observer's position and the earth's center. The first phenomenon has an elevating effect: the apparent altitude of a celestial body is higher than its true altitude. The second one has a depressing effect: the apparent altitude is lower than the true one. In the case of the moon the depressing effect of the parallax-in altitude is always greater than the elevating effect of atmospheric refraction, so that the altitude of the moon (mO) appears to be lower than it actually is (MO); in the case of the sun, a planet or a star the reverse holds true. In order to find a true lunar distance on board the seaman therefore has to take four steps: (1) observe the apparent altitude of the moon, (2) observe the apparent altitude of the sun (or a planet or a star), (3) observe the apparent distance between the moon and the other celestial body and (4) reduce the apparent distance (ms) to the true distance (MS), that is: "clear the distance" from the effects of refraction and parallax-in-altitude. Clearing the distance is the most laborious part of the application of the lunar distances method. True lunar distances measured on board can then be compared with true lunar distances observed at a given prime meridian.

The time on board can be measured with the help of astronomical observations plus a watch to serve as a timekeeper between observations. In order to know the time at which a given true distance is observed at the prime meridian, the seaman consults an almanac in which angular distances between the moon and the sun (or a planet or a star) which can be observed from this prime meridian at particular points in time are predicted for a certain period in advance, normally a year.

In order to put the method of lunar distances into practice navigators thus needed the following methods and equipment: (1) a method for calculating local time by astronomical observations plus a watch, to serve as a timekeeper between observations; (2) instruments to measure accurately both altitudes and lunar distances, even if these were larger than 90 degrees; (3) a method for clearing the distance; (4) a nautical almanac, listing predicted lunar distances for a given meridian.

Methods for calculating local time were known long before the middle of the eighteenth century. The development of accurate instruments in the course of the eighteenth century will be described in the next chapter. As far as methods for clearing the distance were concerned, navigators enjoyed an *embarras du choix*. By 1797, the total number devised by astronomers, mathematicians and other nautical experts already amounted to 40. The making of nautical almanacs containing predicted lunar distances, however, was an extremely complicated business. To predict lunar distances one needs to know (aside from the motions of the sun and the planets and the positions of the stars) the regularities of the moon against the background of the heavens. This required long series of regular observations as well as high mathematical and astronomical skills and imaginative power to detect the hidden key in the large amount of collected data. When Johann Werner in 1514 first propounded the idea of finding longitude by lunar distances, the accumulation of data had barely begun. It did not start on a large scale until the foundation of the Royal Observatory of Paris in 1667 and of the Greenwich Observatory in 1675.

Other Methods. Seamen, meanwhile, were before the end of the eighteenth century not completely at a loss when it came to checking the longitude of the position of a ship. Apart from taking bearings of landmarks of known longitude at different points en route (for example, the Cape of Good Hope), they sometimes used observations of the variation of the compass needle as a rough indication for longitude. True, evidence on navigation practice on ships of the VOC shows that the use of this method was largely discontinued after c. 1635, probably due to the discovery of the phenomenon of "secular variation"—the change of magnetic declination at the same place in the course of time. But the idea of a relation between variation and longitude did not pass into total oblivion. The method was in fact reintroduced on Dutch East Indiamen after 1740, not as an infallible clue for finding longitude but as an aid for locating the position of a ship in specific areas at sea on the route between Europe and Asia.

This revival was probably due to two factors. First of all, the pattern of magnetic declination across the globe was by the middle of the eighteenth century much better known than a century before. This advance in knowledge was to some extent due to the work of Edmond Halley. Halley had in the 1690s not only vastly expanded the body of data on variation, but had also devised a new type of chart in which points of equal variation at a given moment in time were connected by lines called "isogonic lines." His "isogonic chart" of the world, published in 1701, was in the eighteenth century expanded and updated several times. The second factor was the increase in the amount of data on magnetic declination in various parts of the globe thanks to regular observations by navigators on ships of the Dutch East India Company. These observations were recorded in ships' journals, which were made available for analysis by examiners of pilots of the VOC. Inferences drawn from the analysis of ships' journals by examiners of pilots in turn formed the basis for revisions of sailing directions issued to navigators on the order of the Company's Directors.

After ca. 1740, sailing directions of the VOC devoted increased attention to the use of observations of the variation of the compass as indicators for the ship's position. The sailing directions of 1768 concerning the crossing of the equator, for example, read as follows: "for one or two degrees to the north as well as below the Equator, between 356 and 359 degrees longitude magnetic declination is now found to amount to 5 to 7 degrees westerly; East of 359 degrees, the westerly variation increases, West of 356 degrees it diminishes."[1] In other words, given that you knew you were near the Equator, knowledge of the magnitude and tendency of variation could provide you with a rough indication about the longitude of your ship's position. Similar directions were given, among other places, for the area near the Cape of Good Hope and the islands of St. Paul and Amsterdam in the middle of the Indian Ocean. As ships' journals attest, the method remained in use for a long time on board Dutch East Indiamen. It was still being employed in the 1780s, when the method of lunar distances finally became part of navigational practice in ocean shipping.

A Comparative Perspective. Why were England and France ultimately more successful in developing effective solutions for the problem of finding longitude than the leading seafaring nation in the seventeenth century, the Dutch Republic? The need for such solutions was in the Dutch shipping in principle not less than in England or France, considering the dozens of ships sailing to and from Asia, Africa and the West Indies each year. The reward offered by the States General in 1600, which in the course of the seventeenth century was raised to the amount of 25,000 guilders,[2] shows that the need was by the Dutch government indeed keenly perceived. But demand was clearly not enough. Adequate supply of knowledge was required as well, before the problem could finally be solved.

A crucial difference between on the one hand England and France and on the other hand the Dutch Republic was precisely that governments in the former countries were more active in providing the means to seek "perfect" solutions for the problem of finding longitude at sea than the States General or provincial and local authorities in the Dutch Republic. England and France had state-sponsored observatories from the third quarter of the seventeenth century onward, where permanent staff could collect astronomical data on a regular basis. State funds were supplied for trials with new methods for finding longitude in the 1760s and 1770s. Successful inventors were supported with state pensions and rewards. The persistent rivalry between England and France played in this active encouragement of innovations no small part. Innovative activity in the field of longitude-finding was in the eighteenth century further stimulated by the large "consumer demand" for almanacs, chronometers and altitude-measuring instruments on the part of the navies and trading companies.

In Holland, by contrast, state sponsorship for the search for solutions to the problem of longitude was until the end of the eighteenth century not very extensive. There were observatories at the universities of Leiden and Utrecht sponsored by provincial governments since about 1640, to be sure, but these were not concerned with making regular observations relevant for the advance of the science of navigation. There was no permanent staff of observers and hardly any money at all for the purchase or repair of instruments. The substantial reward offered for successful inventors by the States General in 1600 was in the end never paid. It was only from the 1780s onward that state sponsorship somewhat increased in the form of funds for the adaptation of foreign nautical almanacs for the use of Dutch seafarers and the supply of sextants and chronometers.

But why was support from the very organization that must have had overriding interest in the matter, the VOC, lacking as well? The VOC *did* indeed spend some money on examinations and even on trials of new proposals for the finding of longitude at sea. A notable example was the sponsorship of trials with the marine chronometer developed by Christiaan Huygens in the 1680s and 1690s. But the East India Company never provided funds for research on a regular basis. It did not pay for the upkeep of observatories or for the design of new timekeepers. The most probable explanation for this policy is, that this was precisely the rational behavior to be expected from a highly developed trading company like the VOC. Why should the VOC have made large investments in research with an uncertain outcome, which moreover, if successful, would have benefitted its competitors as well, while it could easily wait and see what efforts by private inventors or public authorities would produce? The Company rather acted as a free rider. When the method of lunar distances finally became available for use by seafarers, the directors were not slow in introducing this innovation into its own organization. Up to that time, they had backed the most useful alternative at hand: using observations of the variation of the compass as an indicator of the ship's position at sea.

NOTES

1. *Verbeeterde instructie van de eygenschap der winden en de courssen te houden in het vaarwater tusschen Nederland en Java.* (Amsterdam, 1768), pp. 8–9.

2. To put the size of the reward in proper perspective, the daily wage of a laborer in the Dutch Republic during most of the seventeenth and eighteenth centuries was one guilder.

SUGGESTIONS FOR FURTHER READING

Charles H. Cotter, *A History of Nautical Astronomy*. (London, 1968).

C. A.Davids, *Zeewezen en wetenschap. De wetenschap en de ontwikkeling van de navigatietechniek in Nederland tussen 1585 en 1815*. (Amsterdam/Dieren, 1986).

Karel Davids, "Finding longitude at sea by magnetic declination on Dutch East-Indiamen 1596–1795," *The American Neptune,* 50 (1990), pp. 281–290.

R. T. Gould, *The Marine Chronometer. Its History and Development.* (London, 1960–62).

E. G. Forbes, *The Birth of Scientific Navigation: The Solving in the 18th Century of the Problem of Longitude.* (London, 1974).

E. G. Forbes, *Greenwich Observatory.* volume 1, *Origins and Early History.* (London, 1975).

Derek Howse, *Greenwich Time and the Discovery of Longitude.* (Oxford, 1980).

David S. Landes, *Revolution in Time. Clocks and The Making of the Modern World.* (Cambridge, Mass., 1983), chapters 9–11.

M. S. Mahoney, "Christiaan Huygens: The Measurement of Time and Longitude," in H. J. M. Bos, ed., *Studies of Christiaan Huygens.* (Lisse, 1980), pp. 234–270.

F. Marguet, *Histoire générale de la navigation du XVe au XXe siècle.* (Paris, 1931).

W. E. May, "How the Chronometer went to Sea," *Antiquarian Horology* (1976), pp. 646–664.

W. F. J. Mörzer Bruyns, "Navigation on Dutch East India Company Ships Around the 1740s," *The Mariner's Mirror,* 78 (1992), pp. 143–154.

S. Moskowitz, "Three Studies in the History of Celestial Navigation," *Navigation. Journal of the American Institute of Navigation,* 12 (1965), pp. 192–200; 17(1970), pp. 101–121; 20(1976), pp. 1–16.

10

THE DEVELOPMENT OF NAVIGATIONAL METHODS AND TECHNIQUES, 1740–1815

Willem F. J. Mörzer Bruyns

During the eighteenth century, navigational methods and techniques were greatly perfected. At the beginning of the century navigators could establish their latitude, but longitude was still an inaccurate factor. The noon position, found every 24 hours providing the sky was not clouded at the moment of culmination, consisted of the latitude from the sun's altitude and the sum of the hourly speeds. Altitude observations of stars, taken during the twilight, could give additional daily latitude checks. Since the charts containing Halley's data on variation had been published, it was possible to establish the ship's position more accurately.

The Octant and the Sextant. The process of further perfection of navigational techniques and methods commenced in 1731 when John Hadley presented his quadrant, better known as octant, to the Royal Society of London. There is evidence that Thomas Godfrey from Philadelphia invented the same instrument at the same time. However, due to the distance from London his invention did not arrive there until after Hadley had been acknowledged as the inventor. With the octant seamen could find their latitude with great accuracy. Observations up to 2′ of arc could be made, the same as on few cross-staffs only. As important as the improved accuracy was the ease of using the compact octant. It was provided with two mirrors and worked on the principle of double reflection of light. As, through reflection, the observed angle was halved, the arc of the instrument being 45° (octant = 1/8 of a circle = 45°) altitudes could be measured up to 90°. Toward the end of the century the instrument was equipped with two horizon mirrors so that it could also be used with the back toward the sun. This was especially useful when the

horizon directly beneath the sun was obscured through weather conditions or land.

An early application of the octant, in addition to the traditional
noon observation of the sun, was the double observation with known
time lapse in between. The advantage of this method was that, even
if the sky were overcast at culmination, the observer could still find
his latitude. The altitude of the sun before and after culmination
was observed and the time between observations accurately measured. Obviously, in the case of clouds, several observations would
be made in the forenoon. The time between the observations was
measured with an accurate watch which, for a period of a few hours
at the most, would not be influenced by the ship's movement. This
method was developed by the Dutch teacher of navigation and examiner of mates and lieutenants in Amsterdam, Cornelis Douwes,
and made available in 1747. Douwes's method became popular in his
own country and was also used by English, German, Spanish, Italian, Danish, Swedish and American seamen. It was supposedly published in England by officers in 1759 and a year later in the *Transactions* of the Philosophical Society. Later, under the direction of the
Astronomer Royal, Nevil Maskelyne, tables for Douwes's method
were published. In America the method was definitely established
through the 1799 Newburyport edition of J. Hamilton Moore's *The
Practical Navigator,* edited by Nathaniel Bowditch.

Soon the octant was also used for finding longitude through the
method of lunar distances. The principle of this method is based on
the fact that the moon moves across the sky more rapidly than the
stars. Because earth and moon are far apart, the constantly changing distance between the moon and the fixed stars is, at any one moment, the same for every observer on earth. When computed for a
period in the future for a standard meridian and arranged in tables,
an observer at sea measuring the distance and calculating his local
time will, against his measured distance in the table find the standard meridian time. The difference with his local time, found from
a sun's altitude in fore- or afternoon and known latitude, gave the
difference in longitude between his and the standard meridian. This
laborious method, as mentioned before developed in theory in the
sixteenth century, became available for practical use as the necessary tables were calculated and published. These were compiled in
1752 by the German astronomer Tobias Mayer. His contribution to
the solving of the longitude problem was recognized by the British
Board of Longitude which, in 1765, awarded £3,000 to his widow.
For use at sea the tables appeared in the first edition of the *Nauti-*

cal Almanac published in 1766 for the years 1767–69. One of the first to use this almanac was James Cook who, in 1769, established the longitude of several places in New Zealand.

The range of the octant soon proved too limited for use with lunar distances, as the angle between moon and fixed star often exceeds 90°. By 1757, the British naval officer John Campbell instructed the London instrument-maker John Bird to construct an octant with an arc extended to 120°, thus creating a sextant (1/6 of a circle = 60°). Initially, like octants, Bird made his sextant frames of wood. However, soon brass was used. The advantage of this was that a brass frame was far more rigid, increasing the reliability of the instruments. After Bird, English instrument-makers like Jesse Ramsden, George Adams, Benjamin Martin and Edward Throughton and in France Etienne Lenoir made high quality sextants. Outside these countries the Amsterdam firm of Van Keulen manufactured sextants, using a dividing machine acquired from Ramsden.

The next step in perfecting this instrument was made when, in 1770, Jesse Ramsden invented a circular dividing engine. This was a machine with which the scale of circular instruments could be divided with great accuracy. Prior to Ramsden's invention scale division had been done by construction, necessitating instruments with a large as possible radius. Although Bird's dividing work was of a high quality, the invention of Ramsden made far more compact instruments available. As the range of sextant, and even quintant (1/5 of a circle = 75°) with which angles up to 150° could be measured, proved too limited, the reflecting circle or circle of Borda came into use. It was developed in 1770 by the French naval officer Chevalier De Borda and based on an earlier sketch by Mayer. It was in fact a full-circle sextant with which angles up to 180° could be measured. It was Throughton in England and Lenoir in France who manufactured reflecting circles. The reading accuracy of both sextants and circles could be as fine as 10″, ten times that of an average eighteenth century octant. Both reflecting circle and sextant were used for hydrographical purposes.

The Ships' Chronometer. The method of finding longitude from the time difference between two meridians became available as timekeepers were developed. Encouraged by an Act of Parliament of 1714 offering a reward of £20.000 for an invention by which the problem of finding the longitude at sea was solved, scholars, scientists and instrument makers worked on inventions for the rest of the century. The full sum was, eventually, in 1774 awarded to the English carpenter John Harrison (1693–1776) for his fourth timekeeper. Although

Harrison had received several installments and advance payments over the years, it was not until after the king's intervention that the full sum was paid out to him shortly before his death. By order of the Board of Longitude an exact copy of the winning number four had been made by a well-known London watchmaker Lacum Kendall. After a trial at the Royal Observatory in Greenwich it was, with great success, tried out at sea by James Cook during his second voyage in 1772–1775. While Harrison was perfecting his timekeeper in England, in France Pierre le Roy and Ferdinand Berthoud were doing the same. Making his own timekeepers, Le Roy, *"horloger du Roi,"* improved on Harrison's chronometer number four. Berthoud started making timekeepers, named by him *"horologie à longitude,"* in 1763. Eventually he made seventy, perfecting them over the years. They were used by the French navy on expeditions of discovery, such as by Cook's contemporary, La Pérouse, to the Pacific.

By the end of the century, the chronometer, as the perfected timekeeper for use at sea was now called, was commercially being made. This was mainly thanks to the English chronometer-makers John Arnold and, especially, Thomas Earnshaw. His compact instruments were used on naval ships, both English and Dutch, toward the end of the eighteenth century for establishing the longitude of geographically important places. By 1815, the introduction of these time pieces at sea was well under way on board ships which were not specifically commissioned for hydrographical or scientific work. Those who could not afford the relatively expensive chronometer could still find their longitude through the method of lunar distances. Next to chronometer-longitude, this method of finding longitude remained in use throughout the ninteenth century and it was also used in order to establish the daily error and rate of chronometers at sea.

Other Instruments. Despite the development of sophisticated instruments like the sextant, older instruments like cross-staffs and back-staffs remained in use at sea all during the nineteenth century. An important reason for this was the difference in price. A Dutch octant in 1750 cost around 75 guilders while a cross-staff could then be purchased for about 5 guilders. For back-staffs, the difference was very similar. They were made and used on both sides of the Atlantic Ocean. In Amsterdam, van Keulen, the chart-makers, instrument-makers and publishers, made, among other instruments, cross-staffs and back-staffs. In New York, the mathematical instrument-maker, Anthony Lamb, made these instruments, of which several are kept in American museum collections.

Like the instruments for measuring altitude, the compass, too, underwent developments in the eighteenth century. The most noticeable change was with the needle. A London medical practitioner, Dr. Gown Knight, experimented in order to improve the magnetic strength of compass magnets. In 1745, he demonstrated his method before the Royal Society. Using large compound needles, he was able to magnetize compass needles much more effectively than had been possible by using a lodestone. To accomplish this, the magnetized needles had to be heavier and larger than before, when they had been hardly more than a symmetrical piece of iron thread. The heavier type of compass needle came into general use in the second half of the century.

Already in the seventeenth century, seamen had been aware of the fact that a compass would be influenced when iron was placed near it. In 1658, an examiner of the mates for the Amsterdam chamber of the VOC, Abraham de Graaf, warned ships' officers taking compass bearings that metal objects in their clothing, such as buttons and buckles, could seriously deflect the compass. For the same reason, VOC ships after 1671 were armed with bronze rather than iron cannons, near the compass. It is, therefore, surprising that Captain James Cook kept iron keys in the binnacle and William Bligh, even a pair of pistols in the same place. It was not until the nineteenth century that there came a general awareness of deviation, the influence of ships' metal on a compass. This recognition was the result of investigations by the British Captain, Matthew Flinders, when surveying the coasts of Australia in 1810.

As early as 1779, a Dutchman suggested the use of a liquid compass. In such a compass, the card and needle were submerged in a closed bowl containing water. Due to the upward pressure of the water, a heavier, thus stronger, needle could be used. Also, the water acted as a buffer, absorbing sudden movement, in heavy weather conditions. Although several experiments were made, the liquid compass was not developed until well in the ninteenth century.

Conclusion. During the eighteenth century, the navigational techniques and methods greatly increased and, by 1815, had reached a high standard. After 1747, through the method of double altitude, latitude could be found not only at the moment of culmination, but several times a day. For finding longitude, two methods became practically available. After 1769, the *Nautical Almanac,* including lunar distance tables, and the development of sextant and reflecting circle had made the method of distances available for practical use. Lastly, the commercial production of timekeepers toward the end of the century, gave seamen a method of finding their longitude by chronometer.

SUGGESTIONS FOR FURTHER READING

C. H. Cotter, *A History of Nautical Astronomy.* (London, 1968) pp. 180–208.

E. G. Forbes, *The Birth of Scientific Navigation: The Solving in the 18th Century of the Problem of Longitude.* (London, 1974).

H. L. Hitchins and W. E. May, *From Lodestone to Gyro-Compass.* (London, 1955), Chapters 1 and 2.

David S. Landes, *Revolution in Time. Clocks and the Making of the Modern World.* (Cambridge, MA.,1983), Chapters 9–11.

W. F. J. Mörzer Bruyns, "Navigation on Dutch East India Company Ships Around the 1740s," *The Mariner's Mirror,* 78 (1992), pp. 143–154.

Supplementary Reading

C. H. Cotter, "Matthew Flinders and Ship Navigation," *Journal of the Royal Institute of Navigation,* 29 (1976), pp. 123–134.

C. H. Cotter, *A History of the Navigator's Sextant.* (Glasgow, 1983).

Karel Davids, "Finding longitude at sea by magnetic declination on Dutch East-Indiamen, 1596–1795," *The American Neptune,* 50 (1990), pp. 281–290.

R. T. Gould, *John Harrison and his Timekeepers.* (Greenwich,1958).

R. T. Gould, *The Marine Chronometer. Its History and Development.* (London, 1960).

Derek Howse, "Captain Cook's Pendulum Clocks," *Antiquarian Horology,* (1969), pp. 1–15.

F. Marguet, *Histoire générale de la navigation du XVe au XXe siècle.* (Paris, 1931).

W. E. May, "How the Chronometer went to Sea," *Antiquarian Horology* (1976), pp. 646–664.

S. Moskowitz, "Three Studies in the History of Celestial Navigation," *Navigation. Journal of the American Institute of Navigation,* 12 (1965), pp. 192–200; 17 (1970), pp. 101–121; 20 (1976), pp. 1–16.

11

THE DIFFUSION OF NAVIGATIONAL KNOWLEDGE: COMPARATIVE APPROACHES

Karel Davids

The previous chapters dealt with the important changes in navigation technology after the initial advance achieved by Portugal and Spain in the fifteenth and sixteenth centuries. These changes, pioneered by England, Holland and France, mainly took place between 1590 and 1630 and in the last two thirds of the eighteenth century. The voyages of Cook and French expeditions like those of Bougainville and La Pérouse show the application of this technology at its best. But significantly, the overall level of sophistication of navigation technology in the seventeenth and eighteenth centuries was rising as well, as ships' journals attest. How was this technical knowledge diffused? This chapter will look at the institutional arrangements that underpinned the spread of nautical knowledge. It will look, more specifically, into the development of nautical training and examination in a comparative perspective, viz. by making a comparison between the Dutch Republic, France and England.

The Starting Point: Portugal and Spain. State-sponsored institutions for the diffusion of nautical knowledge emerged in Portugal and Spain already in an early stage of overseas expansion. The *Armazém da Guiné e Indias,* a central agency for the production and distribution of nautical charts in Portugal was presumably established as early as the last quarter of the fifteenth century. In 1547, a position of *cosmógrafo-mor* was created. Its first incumbent was the well-known author of books and tracts on navigation, Pedro Nunez. The duties of the *cosmógrafo-mor* included (according to an instruction of 1592, but probably already from 1559 onward) the inspection of nautical charts, globes and instruments, the teaching of classes on navigation to mariners, the examination of pilots and the registration of naval officers. These institutional arrangements persisted throughout the seventeenth and most of the eighteenth centuries.

The organizational build-up in Spain started only a few years later. It was marked by a greater division of labor. In 1508, an office of pilot-major was created at the *Casa de Contratación* in Seville (the body responsible for organizing trade with the Indies), in 1523 a position of cosmographer-major and in 1552 a chair of the art of navigation and cosmography. The task of the first official consisted of the examination and licensing of pilots and masters, of the second one in the supervision of the manufacture of charts and nautical instruments, and of the third one in the training of pilots and masters. Both the pilot-major and the cosmographer-major were in the execution of their duties assisted by a number of cosmographers, masters and pilots.

This institutional structure for the diffusion of nautical knowledge established in Portugal and Habsburg Spain in the late fifteenth and sixteenth centuries left its impact upon developments in northwest Europe in various ways. Examiners, teachers or cosmographers in the service of the *Casa* or the *Armazém,* like Pedro Nunez, Pedro de Medina and Rodrigo Zamorano, produced some of the most important tracts and textbooks which found their way to the North. Institutional structures established in northwest Europe were moreover perhaps to some extent modeled on the examples provided by Portugal and Spain. There was also a significant difference, though. In northwest Europe, institutional arrangements concerning nautical education and examination were a mixture of public interference and private initiative rather than purely a matter of state sponsorship as in Portugal or Spain.

The Dutch Republic. This mixture of public interference and private initiative differed by country. At one extreme was the Dutch Republic. In the Dutch case, the diffusion of nautical knowledge was mostly effected through the private sector. The majority of the seafarers in Holland learnt the art of navigation by serving apprenticeship on board ship or by attending courses given by private teachers. These "mathematical practitioners," who often combined teaching on navigation with courses on surveying, gunnery, gauging or book-keeping, the writing of textbooks and sometimes the making of nautical instruments, could be found in many port cities and even places in rural areas in the maritime provinces of the Dutch Republic from the end of the sixteenth century onward. Nautical education was, thus, largely left to the market.

The role of public authorities on the other hand was much more subdued than in Portugal or Spain. The States General and the

States of Holland from 1600 onward encouraged the search for effective methods for finding longitude at sea by offering substantial rewards to successful inventors, but refrained from interfering in nautical education or in quality control of masters and mates in the mercantile marine. In so far as public authorities *did* play a role in the field of navigation technology, it was local governments and admiralties which showed the most active interest. Local governments made a modest contribution to the growth of nautical education by subsidizing private teachers, supporting teaching on navigation by common schoolmasters or sponsoring special public lectureships. The first method was practiced in several port towns during the early stage of Dutch overseas expansion, notably in Rotterdam and Flushing around 1610. The second one was widely adopted in the countryside of the maritime provinces of the Dutch Republic from the late seventeenth century onward. The third one was introduced in a number of port cities in the course of the eighteenth century. The city of Amsterdam between 1711 and 1838, for example, subsidized a public lectureship in astronomy, mathematics and navigation at the municipal institute for higher learning, the *Athenaeum Illustre*. The lectures were all given in Dutch. Both the governments of Amsterdam and Rotterdam from ca. 1750 onward, together with the Admiralties of Amsterdam and the Maze and, in Amsterdam, the local Chamber of the VOC, contributed to the upkeep of training colleges for masters, mates, gunners and naval officers, the *zeemanscolleges*. But even local governments never went so far as to introduce compulsory examinations for navigating personnel in the merchant navy, the fisheries or the whaling industry. The assessment of technical competence of masters and mates in these branches of shipping was entirely left to the discretion of shipowners. Statutory examinations for naval officers and masters and mates in the navy, which were first introduced by a number of admiralties at the end of the seventeenth century, did not become general until after ca. 1750. Separate training institutes for navigating personnel on naval vessels did only come into being after the five admiralties had finally been merged into a single organization under the Batavian Republic (1795–1806).

The closest parallel to the institutional structure developed in Portugal and Spain was offered by the organizations which coordinated a large share of Dutch ocean shipping, the trading companies, and especially the Company which monopolized Dutch trade with Asia, the VOC. Not that the VOC, like the *Armazém da Guiné* or the *Casa de Contratación*, normally provided its own facilities for nautical education. Its support for the *zeemanscollege* in Amsterdam was the exception rather than the rule. The Company commonly preferred to tap the supply of masters and mates educated by private teachers or public lecturers instead of spending money on "in-house" training. Nevertheless it took measures to control the quality of its navigating personnel from a very early date, and the institutional arrangements which were created show a remarkable resemblance to those that had been established in Portugal and Spain. The Chamber of Amsterdam introduced a compulsory examination for mates and created a separate position of examiner in 1619. The other five chambers followed Amsterdam's example before 1730. By the middle of the eighteenth century, the Company employed ten examiners in all. The statutory obligation to pass exams was gradually extended to all masters and mates who sought employment with the VOC; by 1750, it was impossible to attain a higher rank in the hierarchy of navigating personnel without first giving proof of competence in the presence of one or more examiners of pilots. To become a captain of a Dutch East Indiaman, one had to pass no less than four exams: as third mate, second mate, first mate and master. Like the examiners, teachers and cosmographers in the service of the *Armazén* or the *Casa,* the examiners of pilots of the VOC were the leading authorities in the field of navigation technology. It was the examiners of the Chambers of the East India Company who composed many of the tracts, tables and textbooks discussed in another chapter in this volume.

France. At the other extreme was France. As in Holland, nautical education in France was partly left to market forces. Private teachers of navigation proliferated in Dieppe, Rouen, Honfleur, Le Havre and other major or minor ports during the sixteenth, seventeenth and eighteenth centuries. But the institutional structure in France also showed striking differences with arrangements in the Dutch Republic. The principal trading company in France, the East India Company, had by the middle of the eighteenth century not only developed a fully fledged system of promotion via compulsory examinations, but had also established its own training college in Lorient and created a separate corps of officers modeled on that of the Royal Navy.

In contrast with Holland, France, moreover, saw from an early date a far greater measure of government interference in the field of navigation technology. After a first attempt to set up state schools of navigation in the 1620s had ended in failure, a large-scale organization was created in the time of Colbert. This expansion of state-sponsored nautical education was directly related with Colbert's effort in the 1660s and 1670s to endow France with a powerful navy.

The institutional structure was built in three phases. First of all, royal chairs in the art of navigation were created in port cities like Le Hâvre (1660) and Nantes (1672). Some of these posts were held by Jesuits, or even established in Jesuit colleges, although the courses could also be attended by pupils from outside. Jesuits were most active in the spread of nautical knowledge in France. The *Societas Jesu* included in fact two of the best-known authors of textbooks on the art of navigation in France, Paul Hoste and Georges Fournier. Second, a state regulation was enacted in 1681, which both contained detailed rules concerning public schools of navigation in the main ports of France, and introduced compulsory examinations for masters and mates in ocean shipping and coastal navigation; this examination system thus covered the entire mercantile marine. Third, training colleges for naval officers were in 1682 created in Brest, Rochefort and Toulon. A large part of the teaching was again done by Jesuits. The introduction of these educational arrangements was further accompanied by the development of a system of examinations. The ambitions of the French state in the field of navigation technology were not fully realized in practice. Creation of facilities did not automatically imply that they would serve their purpose. Some schools did in fact hardly function at all. The quality of naval cadets did not become as high as the "planners" had expected. Yet, the remarkable thing about France was precisely that public authorities had such a grand conception of the proper role of the state in the diffusion of nautical knowledge.

England. England stood midway between Holland and France. On the one hand, developments in England showed clear similarities with those in the Dutch Republic. The role of private teachers in the supply of nautical education was in the case of England during the seventeenth and eighteenth centuries no less prominent than in Holland. London bristled with mathematical practitioners as much as Amsterdam. A difference resided in the context in which many of these practitioners worked. Patronage in England was more important than in Holland. Experts in the art of navigation like Edward Wright, Thomas Hariot or Thomas Hood enjoyed lavish support from noblemen or rich merchants. In contrast with Holland, patronage even crystallized in the creation of a separate, permanent, privately funded institution intended for the diffusion of knowledge among "commoners." This was the college founded in London in 1597 as implementation of the will of a rich merchant, the founder and builder of the Royal Exchange, Sir Thomas Gresham. Gresham College was endowed with seven chairs: law, rhetoric, divinity, music, physics, geometry and astronomy. The geometry professor was expected to teach one term on arithmetic, another term on theoretical geometry and a third one on practical geometry. The professor of astronomy was instructed to teach on "principles of the sphere and theoriques of the planets," explain the use of "common instruments for the capacity of mariners" and "apply these things to use by reading geography and the art of navigation." Courses were given both in Latin and in the vernacular. They could be attended free of charge by whomever wished to listen.[1]

The ideals of the founder were never fully realized. Recent research has cast doubt on claims put forward by scholars like E. G. R. Taylor and Christopher Hill about the eminent importance of Gresham College as a teaching institution. Mordechai Feingold and Ian Adamson have contested the view that Gresham professors really did everything they were expected to do and truly reached a public of "commoners." On the contrary, Sir William Boswell in 1639 observed that the professors of Gresham College "excepting few [had] beene very idle . . . Only Brigs, Gelebrand and some other few have beene doing any thing there."[2] But the role of this institution as a center for the production of knowledge is undisputed. In the first half of the seventeenth century, Gresham College was a prominent meeting place for people committed to the advancement of science. Whatever the failings of its staff in the field of teaching, its professors of geometry and astronomy were, at least, very active in designing new instruments and composing tracts, tables and textbooks relating to the art of navigation. Just as the luminaries in the art of navigation in Portugal and Spain were attached to the *Armazém* or the *Casa,* and in Holland, distinguished experts were connected to the VOC, so leading authorities in this field in England during the first half of the seventeenth century held, for a time, positions at Gresham College: Henry Briggs, Edmund Gunter and Henry Gellibrand.

Trading companies in England no more concerned themselves with nautical education than chartered companies in Holland. The East India Company only briefly, in 1614–1615, sponsored a lectureship in the art of navigation held by Edward Wright. When the Directors of the East India Company at the end of the eighteenth century considered knowledge of the method of finding longitude by lunar distances a requirement for mates serving on the ships hired for the trade to Asia, it obliged those who were not familiar with this technique to follow courses with a private teacher, Lawrence Gwynne in Hackney. By then, the East India Company, like its Dutch counterpart, had also introduced compulsory examinations for navigators. Statutory examinations for masters and mates in other branches of shipping were not introduced until the middle of the nineteenth century.

The role of public authorities in the diffusion of nautical knowledge in England, by contrast, resembled more the pattern prevalent in France than that in the Dutch Republic. The drive to create educational facilities for seafarers and introduce regulations on examinations started earlier in England than in Holland and originated first and foremost from the central government. Statutory examinations for lieutenants in the Royal Navy were, thanks to Samuel Pepys, introduced during the 1670s. In 1673, a mathematical school "for young scholars" was founded by Charles II at Christ's Hospital, London. In 1730, a Royal Naval Academy was established at Portsmouth for the education of "young gentlemen for your majesty's service at sea." The curriculum of the Naval Academy, which provided an alternative channel for the training of future naval officers next to the time-honored way of serving as "volunteer per order" aboard ship, included, among other subjects, mathematics and navigation. But in fact, this institute remained of minor importance until the nineteenth century. In addition, the naval authorities from 1702 onward created opportunities for nautical education on board by the appointment of "naval schoolmasters." Naval schoolmasters, whose qualifications were tested by the corporation of Trinity House, were instructed to teach volunteers aboard ship in the theory and practice of navigation. The total number active in the eighteenth and early nineteenth centuries has been estimated at 500 to 600.[3]

In all five countries discussed in this chapter, institutional arrangements for the spread of navigational knowledge in the early modern period were considerably enlarged. This expansion was essentially the result of two forces: the rise of ocean shipping and the growth of the centralized state. The relative strength of these forces differed by country. While in the Dutch Republic the former was stronger than the latter, the reverse was true for France. In all countries, the spread of educational facilities was sooner or later followed by the introduction of compulsory examinations for navigators. The pattern in which this occurred again varied by country. A trading company took the lead in Holland. In the other countries, it was the state itself which led the way. But neither England nor Portugal or

Spain matched the extent of state interference in France. France was in the early modern period the only country to have the statutory examinations for seafarers extended to all branches of shipping.

NOTES

1. David W. Waters, *The Art of Navigation in England in Elizabethan and Early Stuart Times.* (London, 1958), p. 245.

2. E. G. R. Taylor, *The Mathematical Practitioners of Tudor and Stuart England.* (Cambridge, 1968): Christopher Hill, *Intellectual Origins of the English Revolution.* (Oxford, 1965): Ian Adamson, "The Administration of Gresham College and its Fluctuating Fortunes as a Scientific Institution in the Seventeenth Century", *History of Education,* IX (1980), pp. 13–25; Mordechai Feingold, *The Mathematician's Apprenticeship. Science, Universities and Society in England, 1560–1640.* (Cambridge, 1984), chapter 5; the quotation of Boswell is on p. 176.

3. F. B. Sullivan, "The Naval Schoolmaster during the Eighteenth Century and the Early Nineteenth Century," *The Mariner's Mirror,* 62 (1976), pp. 311–326.

SUGGESTIONS FOR FURTHER READING

A. Anthiaume, *Évolution et enseignement de la science nautique en France et principalement chez les Normands.* (Paris, 1920). Two volumes.

C. A. Davids, *Zeewezen en wetenschap. De wetenschap en de ontwikkeling van de navigatietechniek in Nederland tussen 1585 en 1815.* (Amsterdam/Dieren, 1986).

A. E. Fanning, *Steady as she goes. A History of the Compass Department of the Admiralty.* (London, 1986).

David C. Goodman, *Power and Penury. Government, Technology and Science in Philip II's Spain.* (Cambridge, 1988).

G. Schilder, P. C. J. van der Krogt, and S. de Clercq, eds., *Marcel Destombes, Contributions sélectionnées à l'Histoire de la Cartographie et des Instruments Scientifiques; Selected Contributions to the History of Cartography and Scientific Instruments.* (Utrecht, 1987).

E. G. R. Taylor, *The Mathematical Practitioners of Tudor and Stuart England.* (Cambridge, 1968). Third impression.

E. G. R. Taylor, *The Mathematical Practitioners of Hanoverian England 1714–1840.* (Cambridge, 1966).

A. Teixeira de Mota, "Some Notes on the Organization of Hydrographical Services in Portugal before the Beginning of the Nineteenth Century," *Imago Mundi,* 28 (1976), pp. 51–60.

David W. Waters, *The Art of Navigation in England in Elizabethan and Early Stuart Times.* (London, 1958).

Figure XVI. Chronometer for finding longitude at sea, No 40, made in 1788 by Ferdinand Berthoud and sold to the Amsterdam Admiralty. It was used on Dutch ships in 1793. *Courtesy Nederlands Scheepvaart-museum, Amsterdam.*

12

THE APPLICATION OF NAVIGATIONAL AND HYDROGRAPHICAL KNOWLEDGE, 1740–1815

Willem F. J. Mörzer Bruyns

The application of navigational and hydrographical knowledge has very much been a matter of exchange of knowledge between seaman and with scientists, technicians and scholars ashore. The seamen collected practical knowledge during voyages which was subsequently handed over to the specialists ashore. There, the practical knowledge was developed and transformed into new methods and techniques, after which the process started over again.

During the sixteenth century, when the English and Dutch maritime expansion commenced, it was necessary to acquire navigational knowledge and experience which had not been needed for local seafaring. For this knowledge, the north European countries initially had to depend on Iberian seamen and scholars. In 1548, the English bribed the Spanish pilot-major, Sebastian Cabot, into disclosing to them Spanish navigational secrets, enabling the English to sail beyond European waters. Petrus Plancius, the Protestant minister who fled Antwerp in 1585 for Amsterdam, was also a scholarly geographer. Through contacts of his publisher, Cornelis Claes, he obtained secret cartographical information on the route to Asia from the Spanish pilot-major, Bartholomeo de Lasso. This, in combination with practical information acquired and published in 1596 by the Dutchman, Jan Huygen van Linschoten, who worked for the Portuguese in Goa, the Dutch acquired the knowledge to sail halfway around the world to Asia.

The Organization. When the Dutch East India Company was founded in 1602, Plancius was appointed as its official cartographer.

The Company maintained this function until it was liquidated in 1799. From 1633–1704, three generations of the Blaeu family of cartographers were appointed to this position. In 1704, Isaac de Graaf was appointed and remained in that office until his death in 1743. Between 1743 and 1799, members of the Van Keulen family of cartographers, instrument-makers and publishers filled that official position. This firm, in addition to charts, also provided a large portion of the ships' navigating instruments. The main task of the cartographer was to supply updated charts to the Company's ships before sailing. It was also his task to collect hydrographical and cartographical information in order to improve and update the charts. This was done in workshops in Amsterdam. Both the Blaeu and the Van Keulen families generated a fruitful relationship between their official functions and their commercial activities. The main source that Plancius and his successors tapped to improve their charts were the masters and mates of the Company ships and the logs they were compelled to keep during their voyages. To facilitate this, ships were supplied with blank logbooks and with blank sheets of "compass lines paper," in which they had to plot new discoveries and return them to Amsterdam. By 1620, the distribution of charts of Asian waters was concentrated in Batavia and, before 1688, the Company was operating a large cartographical bureau there. Local hydrographical information was collected by cartographers and processed into charts and sent to Amsterdam. The Batavia office operated well into the second half of eighteenth century.

On the basis of the information returned by masters and mates, Plancius prepared instructions for making a safe voyage from the Netherlands to Asia. Over the years, as meteorological and magnetic data was returned, Plancius's successors modified these instructions. In 1654, the cartographer and the examiner compiled a list of mates' equipment to be handed to every ship. In 1655, the list was printed and became a Company standard. Over the years, it was amended according to new developments in cartography, instrument-making techniques and the increase of knowledge of the art of navigation.

Charts. It can be said that, in 1602, the Dutch East India Company was instrumental in establishing a structure for the improvement and distribution of sea charts, as Spain and Portugal had done in the two centuries before. The Company's initiative preceded any similar organization among north European countries. Besides the navigational aspect, the Company, through strict rules and regulations, also hoped to keep the information secret from its commercial rivals, such as the English. A way of doing this was to forbid the printing of charts of the area to the east of Africa and the west of America. In these areas, basically the Indian and Pacific Oceans, Company ships were provided with manuscript charts drawn in the workshops of the chart-makers. By the second half of the eighteenth century, however, the French and especially the English had, by their own means, obtained sufficient information to produce charts of a quality superior to the Dutch. Because of the repeated reproduction of the East India Company's charts by hand, their accuracy diminished and mistakes had unwittingly been introduced. For this reason, and as foreign rivals began to produce better charts than the Dutch, the examiner of the mates advised that Dutch charts should be printed. In 1753, a sea-atlas of Asian waters was published by the Van Keulen firm, with permission of the Company. Although the element of secrecy was no longer necessary, the organization of chart supply on a private basis continued until the liquidation of the Company in 1799.

In 1720, the Depot des Cartes was founded in order to organize French cartography and, later in the century, a similar organization for the same purpose was founded in England. Both the English and the French organizations were state funded, a situation which in the Netherlands would not occur until well into the nineteenth century. The accuracy and the quality of maritime charts increased dramatically in the second half of the eighteenth century. This was mainly due to voyages of discovery such as undertaken by Cook, Bougainville, La Pérouse, D'Entrecasteaux, Vancouver and Flinders, during which modern methods for astronomical navigation, such as lunar distances and longitude by chronometer, were applied. In the Netherlands in 1788, the Amsterdam Admiralty established a longitude committee. Besides centralizing knowledge on the subject of longitude at sea, the committee's task was to improve the sea charts and navigational instruments.

Instruments. The provision of instruments to the ships of the Company was organized in a way very similar to that of the charts. The main difference was that the instruments were, with the exception of the Van Keulen period, usually obtained from commercial instrument-makers rather than from an official functionary. The popular mariner's astrolabe had been used by the Spanish, Portuguese, Dutch, English and French since the end of sixteenth century. Besides making these instruments themselves, both the English and the Dutch obtained them from the Iberian Peninsula. By

1675, the mariner's astrolabe was less popular and by 1700 it had become obsolete. Joan Blaeu, examiner of the Amsterdam mates of the East India Company, successfully advised the directors to remove the astrolabe from the ships' lists. It was heavy, cumbersome in use and gave readings to an accuracy of no more than half a degree. Moreover, it was expensive in comparison to the cross-staff, which remained popular. Improvements and additions to this instrument, such as sights for the use with the back to the sun, made it far more accurate than the astrolabe. The back-staff or Davis quadrant, too, underwent improvement. In the second half of the seventeenth century, the English Astronomer Royal, Flamsteed, added a lens making it also possible to observe the sun even when the sky was slightly overcast. However, the most important improvement in altitude measuring instruments was John Hadley's invention of the octant in 1731.

In the Netherlands around that same time, naval officers were strongly critical of the current state of knowledge about navigation and navigational instruments. This lead to the appointment of Cornelis Douwes as official teacher of navigation in Amsterdam. It also lead to the appointment, in 1748, of the Amsterdam instrument-maker, Benjamin Ayres, as a teacher of this skill. Ayres was also commissioned to provide both the Amsterdam Admiralty and the East India Company with accurate instruments, such as octants. The criticism moreover lead to the development of an azimuth compass which could be used to take accurate bearings of the sun. In combination with the variation charts compiled by Halley, it became possible to roughly calculate longitude. A further improvement of the octant and the sextant, which was developed in 1757, was the dividing machine invented by Jese Ramsden. With this, it became possible to divide circular instruments accurately. Ramsden was compelled to share his invention with others for the improvement of navigation. The Dutch firm of Van Keulen, chart-makers to the Dutch East India Company, obtained such a machine around 1780. In the eighteenth century, the Van Keulens were the only manufacturers of sextants in the Netherlands, which, after 1788, they sold to the VOC for use with lunar distances. Through the efforts of the French instrument-maker, Lenoir, and his English colleague, Throughton, the reflecting circle was perfected for use with the lunar distance method. Lastly, at the end of the century, the marine chronometer became generally available. Nevertheless, it was not until the early nineteenth century that this sophisticated instrument was widely used on ships which were not solely equipped for scientific research and discovery.

Books. In 1580, De Medina's book, *Arte de Navegar* (Valadolid, 1545), a Spanish manual on the art of navigation, was translated into Dutch and published in Antwerp together with an appendix written by the Antwerp scholar, Michiel Coignet, updating the book. De Medina's book was extremely popular and had been translated into French in 1553 (the first of 14 editions), into Italian (1554) and into English (1581). It was by no means the only Iberian book on the art of navigation to be translated for the north European market. The English navigator, William Bourne, had published *A Regiment for the Sea* (London, 1574) which was mainly based on Marten Cortes's, *Breve Compendio de la sphera y de la arte de navegar* (Sevilla, 1551). Around 1600, books on other navigation-related subjects were published. Among these were books on the use of globes for navigation such as *Tractatus de globis coelesti et terrestri* (London, 1593) by the Englishman Robert Hues. His countryman, Thomas Hood, wrote *The Mariner's Guide* (London, 1596) on the use of the sea chart and Edmund Gunter published *The description and use of the sector, cross-staffe and other instruments* in 1623. The first seventeenth-century Dutch navigational manual to become a standard work was written in 1621 by the examiner of mate's at the Amsterdam chamber of the VOC, Cornelis Jansz. Lastman. It enjoyed great popularity and had a great many reprints. After 1660, it was superseded by the books of Gietermaker and Klaas de Vries. These books dealt with the art of navigation in a general way and could well be used for self-study. In an eighteenth century navigation book, the first chapters dealt with basic mathematics and astronomy. The seaman was taught to calculate the date, the time of full and new moon, and the date of Easter. Besides "rules" to follow, several exercise examples were given for each problem. Data on the moon's phase was of great importance to calculate tidal information, and additional tables with tidal information were included. The manual contained tables with "rules" of explanation and exercises to calculate the position of the sun and moon in the heavenly sphere. The reader was also taught how, during night time, to find the number of hours before or after midnight. A list of astronomical definitions was provided, such as the ecliptic, declination, right ascension, amplitude and refraction. The next chapter dealt with navigational instruments, such as the mariners's astrolabe, the cross-staff and also, after 1731, the octant. Their use was explained and, in the case of the cross-staff, an explanation of its construction was often included. The manual would also contain information on refraction and a table with the daily declination of the sun.

Similar books appeared in other countries. Andrew Wakely's *The Mariners-compasse rectified* was first published in the early seventeenth century and, after many reprints, was still in use in the eighteenth century. Other books crossed the Atlantic Ocean. In 1754, John Robertson first published in London *The Elements of Navigation,* a manual on the theory and practice of navigation. In 1772, his countryman, John Hamilton Moore, revised the book and published it in London under the title, *Practical Navigator and Seaman's New Daily Assistant* later shortened to *The New Practical Navigator.* In 1799, the American publisher, E. M. Blunt, pirated this book and published it in Newburyport, Massachusetts, after he had it thoroughly revised by the Salem navigator and mathematician, Nathaniel Bowditch. Bowditch's book, in fact, was the first American navigational manual. In 1802, now with Bowditch's name on the title page, it was published as *The New American Practical Navigator* and, with this title, was reprinted many times.

SUGGESTIONS FOR FURTHER READING

Silvio A. Bedini, *At the Sign of the Compass and Quadrant. The Life and Times of Anthony Lamb.* Transactions of the American Philosophical Society, vol. 74, part 1. (Philadelphia, 1984).

A. E. Fanning, *Steady as she goes. A History of the Compass Department of the Admiralty.* (London, 1986).

E. G. Forbes, *Greenwich Observatory.* Volume 1, *Origins and Early History.* (London, 1975).

D. Gavine, "Navigation and Astronomy Teachers in Scotland outside the Universities," *The Mariner's Mirror,* 76 (1990), pp. 5–12.

Derek Howse, *Greenwich Time and the Discovery of Longitude.* (Oxford, 1980), Chapter 3.

G. S. Ritchie, *The Admiralty Chart: British Naval Hydrography in the Nineteenth Century.* (London, 1968; revised 1994), pp. 1–106.

G. Schilder, "Organisation and Development of the Hydrographic Office of the Dutch East India Company in the 17th Century." *Imago Mundi,* 28 (1976), pp. 61–78.

N. J. W. Thrower, ed., *The Three Voyages of Edmond Halley in the Paramore, 1698–1701.* Publications of the Hakluyt Society, Second, Series, volumes 156–157. (London, 1980), volume I, pp. 15–82.

Part III
The Struggle for Empire

The seventeenth century witnessed a progressive enlargement of the role of European governments in the global struggle for maritime advantage. What had once been mainly carried on by chartered companies, settlers, merchants, privateersmen, and freebooters was now carried on by navies and armies of the state. Thus, the state became predominant in overseas as well as European warfare. By the early eighteenth century, only the most distant theaters of rivalry, such as the Pacific and Indian Oceans, remained the responsibility of chartered companies. By 1750, state navies operated even in these waters. A small British naval squadron under Commodore George Anson, for instance, crossed the Pacific on a voyage of destruction and plunder in the years 1740–44. More important, from the later 1740s onward, British and French naval squadrons were to be regularly found in the Indian Ocean, supporting the land forces of their respective East India companies.

It is well known that Great Britain and France were the primary adversaries in the eighteenth-century struggle. Dutch claims after 1714 were largely confined to what is now Indonesia; in Europe, the Atlantic, and the Caribbean, the Dutch sought to avoid expensive involvement. Thus, Spain became the more important third party. French governments never gave up hope of using their influence at Madrid to monopolize the trade of Spanish America. Moreover, as the Spanish navy grew in numbers and tonnage (from the later 1720s onward), it became an axiom of French maritime strategy to try to unite the House of Bourbon's naval forces against Great Britain's. The Spanish navy, though its difficulties in finding skilled seamen and gunners were congenital and serious, was certainly not a factor to be ignored. At times, Spain was indeed actively allied with France, resentment of British high-handedness and hopes of recovering Gibraltar being the most prominent Spanish motives. But, just as often, Spanish commercial and strategic concerns pointed toward a policy of watchful neutrality.

The outcome of the eighteenth-century global struggle for empire rested ultimately upon seapower. As will become evident in the chapters that follow, seapower must be understood not just in terms of superiority in battle but of strategic comprehensiveness and staying power. Britain achieved all this. The achievement came to fruition within a specific historical period, between about 1650 and 1760. The accomplishment is often taken for granted, as if it were a natural consequence of Great Britain's insular situation. To be sure, fundamental factors of geography and of international and commercial rivalry were present, but the accomplishment should also be traced to political choice: the English nation's inclination to support a strong navy.

Part of our task in this section will be to show the ways in which the European states' expansion of empire and their capacity to develop seapower were fundamentally intertwined. In doing so, we shall explore not only the reasons for Britain's achievement, but also the disadvantages and difficulties that France encountered when attempting to rival it. A century ago, Captain Alfred Thayer Mahan, in the introduction to his famous work, *The Influence of Sea Power upon History, 1660–1783* (1890), listed "six points" which underpinned a nation's capacity to develop seapower. Readers will notice some significant differences between the conceptual basis of Mahan's six points and what is set forth here.

13

ELEMENTS OF NAVAL POWER IN THE EIGHTEENTH CENTURY

Daniel A. Baugh

It is useful to make a distinction between *elements of naval power* and *foundations of seapower*. Elements of naval power include, first off, all matters relating to warships: their design and construction, guns, timber and naval stores, home dockyards and facilities for upkeep and repair, and distant naval bases for meeting far-flung strategic needs. Second, the preservation of a ship's company from deficiency of food and drink was as important as the preservation of the ship itself. Keeping the men fed and healthy, wherever they might be deployed, was an extremely challenging task in the sailing-ship era. This was of course a vital matter because of its bearing on the strategic reach and staying power of naval forces. These topics will be taken up in this chapter.

In the next chapter, two other elements of naval power will be discussed. One was the ability to obtain or to train sufficient numbers of skilled seamen for wartime needs. It will be seen that this problem posed very serious difficulties for all navies of the eighteenth century. The other was the shaping of a competent corps of sea officers, something that could not be accomplished without a concurrent development of administrative means to coordinate their activities and mold them into a distinct profession. Both elements were vital to the formation of efficient ships' companies and well managed squadrons—difficult attainments in the sailing-ship era.

The *elements of naval power* were created and sustained by the *foundations of seapower*. The latter extend broadly and deeply. They encompass such factors as geographical situation, concern for trade (in which overseas colonies often played a role), financial capacity, and political will. These foundations will be explored in Chapter 15.

Warships. In the eighteenth century, unlike the twentieth, warships were the sole fighting instruments of naval power. There were three basic categories:

1. ships of the line (or line of battle ships) of 60 guns or more;
2. frigates (50 to 20 guns) and sloops of war;
3. armed vessels (brigs, schooners, etc.).

Ships of the line represented a huge capital investment. There were four "rates," according to size. The first rate (100-gun) *Victory,* launched in 1765, cost £63,000 (whereas the largest cotton factory built in the 1790s cost £5,000). Even a third rate 74-gun ship of the line cost almost four times as much to build and fit out as a fairly large frigate of 32 guns.

In 1920, a distinguished naval historian, Admiral Sir Herbert Richmond, compared the battleship of the eighteenth century to its coal-fired, modern counterpart:

> She was then offensively superior and could not be approached by anything afloat except her own kind. She had no enemies to interfere with her at sea and the menace of the fire-ship was dead. She had perfect freedom of movement, limited only by the weather; a radius of action in time limited only by her three months' supply of fresh water and provisions . . . . [1]

Certainly her freedom of movement was, by modern measures, severely restricted by unfavorable winds, but that applied equally to her opponents, and Admiral Richmond's observation serves to remind us that, although the introduction of steam power in the nineteenth century eliminated this restriction, it sharply reduced a battleship's radius of action and degree of self-sufficiency. By the end of the nineteenth century, the advent of torpedoes and mines rendered battleships vulnerable to attacks by smaller vessels. It is worth emphasizing that in the eighteenth century the ship of the line was, indeed, invulnerable to anything but her own kind and her oceanic reach was enormous.

John Keegan has made a comparison which enables us to grasp the order of magnitude of the battle-fleet's firepower in those days. He compares the artillery that Napoleon took into battle at Waterloo in 1815 with the cannonry aboard Lord Nelson's fleet when it engaged at Trafalgar in 1805. Napoleon took 366 six to twelve pounders to the battlefield. These required 9,000 artillerymen plus 5,000 horses for ammunition wagons; more horses were needed to bring up fodder (50 tons a day). Nelson's fleet (27 ships of the line) carried 2,232 guns; the *lightest* was a twelve pounder, the heaviest fired a 68-pound shot. To handle these guns 14,000 men were needed. In land warfare it would have required 50,000 gunners plus 30,000 horses for the train to furnish the equivalent firepower. The horses and wagons would have had to bring up 300 tons a day of fodder and 75 tons a day of human food. Of course, in Nelson's fleet, the powder, shot, and food were carried aboard. Keegan concludes: A fleet could transport to the place of battle six times as many guns of much heavier calibre at one-fifth the logistical burden, and, given an average sailing wind, five times the speed.[2]

The superior weight-carrying efficiency afforded by water transport in respect to trade was the central technological-economic factor of the Early Modern era. Clearly, this same factor served to escalate massively the firepower of navies, whose function, ultimately, was to guarantee or deny the use of sea transport in wartime. It was with ships of the line that navies contended for naval mastery, but the endless chore of guaranteeing or denying the use of sea transport was carried out by cruisers.

Shipbuilding, Design, and Technology. Most French warships were built on building slips in royal dockyards and, in peacetime, British ships of the line were built in royal dockyards, too. In wartime, however, Britain's dockyards were so heavily occupied by the tasks of fitting out and repairing that new ships of the line were built by contract in private yards; these were constructed according to Admiralty plans, under inspection of a dockyard supervisor. Practically all of the British navy's smaller warships were similarly contracted for in private yards.

Naval arithmetic in this era must begin by counting ships. Did Great Britain enjoy an advantage in respect to shipbuilding capacity? The answer is yes, mainly because of the availability of private shipyards. For instance, all but four of the two dozen 74s and 64s ordered during the American Revolutionary War were set up in private yards; it was an impressive, indeed rather desperate, effort that involved mobilizing the total shipbuilding resources of the realm.

Yet, even with this mighty effort, the British navy did not by the end of the American war manage to surpass the warship tonnage possessed by France and Spain combined. The Bourbon powers had increased the total tonnage of their navies during the preceding period of peace from about 300,000 in 1765 to 400,000 in 1775, on the eve of war. Total British naval tonnage during those ten years fell, from 377,000 to 337,000. Although the degree of imbalance that developed by 1775 was unusual for that century, it was not unusual after 1750 for the Bourbon navies combined to outbuild the British navy in peacetime. During the eight years of peace from 1748 to

1755, the combined Bourbon navies caught up with Britain in the tonnage race, but in 1755 Britain nevertheless met a "two-power standard" (about 275,000 tons on each side).

Clearly, then, British naval tonnage expanded chiefly during time of war. In fact, there was a net gain of 80,000 tons during the 1740s, a gain of 100,000 between 1755 and 1765, and one of 110,000 between 1775 and 1785.[3] This points to a conclusion that capacity to build ships in wartime was the decisive factor behind British naval success, but we shall see in a moment that there were other factors of greater importance.

Ship design was not one of them. Most of what has been written on this subject takes the position that French ships were better designed than British. Some historians have recently questioned whether French superiority in this sphere was of much significance, and there is literally more to the question than meets the eye of an expert looking at hull drawings. The proportioning of masts, rigging, and ballast—best guided by sea experience—mattered greatly. Besides, there were other factors to consider: the ratio of firepower to cost, toughness, and sea-keeping; also the capacity to sail and fight under a variety of sea conditions. Like any engineering problem, ship design involved "trade-offs," and we should not forget the clear evidence that both navies valued the enemy ships they captured. There are reasons to think that British hulls were inferior in some respects prior to mid-century, but after that time the balance of considerations does not indicate an overall inferiority.

In practical operation at sea, British squadrons and cruisers enjoyed some important advantages. First, a clean hull produced a speed advantage, and British facilities for cleaning and maintaining hulls, both at home and overseas, were more numerous and better equipped. The British advantage was amplified after 1780 by a technological innovation, namely the rapid introduction of copper sheathing in the British navy. A coppered hull stayed clean longer. The metal sheathing also gave superior protection against the marine boring worm and thus enabled distantly deployed ships to remain on station longer.

Another material British advantage lay in the superiority of British ordnance. It was superior in both quality and quantity. The French and British were not technological equals in casting and drilling cannon, and the French had chronic difficulties in manufacturing heavy naval guns in sufficient numbers, because the French civilian market for heavy iron products, unlike the British, was not large. There was, thus, a greater contraction of iron production in France in time of peace, and a resulting shortage of capacity in time of war.[4] As for quality, evidence is anecdotal, but it seems that French crews had more reason to fear disaster when their guns became hot. In 1759, *Le Souverain* experienced five burst guns in two separate engagements, with resulting death and mayhem on the gun deck in each instance. This sort of thing had a certain effect on morale.

Naval Materials. Wooden ships of war were built chiefly of oak; their masts were of fir. A half-century ago, historians commonly supposed that the primary administrative problem of the British navy in the eighteenth century was a growing scarcity of these items. Whatever the merits of R. G. Albion's *Forests and Sea Power,* published in 1926, and there are many, the book promoted the profoundly incorrect notion that a growing scarcity of timber and masts not only seriously troubled the British navy, but was also more keenly felt by the British navy than the French.[5]

To be sure, administrators often expressed anxiety about timber and masts and were sometimes caught short. The largest oak timbers, especially those with curvature, had always been scarce, and so had very large fir trees for lower masts. In general, however, timber shortages were remediable by reaching farther afield for those of more difficult access, where the huge logs had to be dragged to streams and rivers, and floated to tidewater. The problems were mainly those of transportation and cost.

The French navy was particularly worse off in respect to masts. For one thing, its access to Baltic sources could in time of war be seriously hampered by British seapower. Also, the French treasury's recurring foreign-exchange weaknesses put naval purchasers in an inferior position. To be sure, there were occasions, particularly during the American Revolutionary War, when the British navy was hard-put to find the large fir trees for lower masts. It had to resort to "made masts," fabricated from a number of trees. Thus, as is often the case when vital raw materials are in short supply, labor was substituted to solve the problem.

Masts, spars, rope, and sailcloth make up the "engine" of a sailing ship—what enables it to go—as well as the "brakes." Anchors served as emergency brakes. These items routinely deteriorated, became worn out, or were lost in rough weather, and, in time of war, they might be destroyed in maneuvering and combat, most often, it appears, by extreme press of sail in a chase.

Spars, being generally smaller than masts and subjected to less stress, seldom posed supply difficulties. Sailcloth posed a problem for Britain in 1700, because English manufacturers did not know how to make a tough, high quality fabric and, therefore, bought canvas from the Dutch. However, they soon learned. Rope was made from hemp and tar. For all European naval powers, the leading source of hemp and tar was the Baltic.

Perhaps the worst materials shortage that the British navy confronted occurred in the first decade of the eighteenth century, when the warring of the Northern powers rendered supplies of hemp, tar, and pitch from the Baltic precarious. This shortage provoked measures to encourage the production of these commodities in the American colonies. But, only the pitch from America attained a quality that the British navy cared to use. For the French, aside from money, the main problem may have been the wartime impact of British seapower. During the Seven Years War, for instance, the British navy stopped and searched all shipping from the Baltic—it was mostly Dutch—and detained all naval materials; the presumption (almost always correct) was that these were destined for French dockyards. The stores were landed in England and sold, recompense being made to the shippers. The Dutch authorities protested but could do little. During the American Revolutionary War, the British adopted the same policy. This time, the Dutch were not only neutral but less fearful of British power and they resisted more strenuously. They also used interior waterways to convey the materials to France. The British government's response was firm. Although Britain hardly needed an additional naval enemy in 1780, it pertinaciously adhered to a policy that provoked war with the Dutch—a sign of how seriously London viewed the issue.

Regarding naval materials, one conclusion is that access to the Baltic was a crucial consideration for Britain and for the French Atlantic bases. In this respect, an advantage attached to Toulon, for France, and Havana, for Spain, was that those shipyards drew timber and many other naval materials from sources not easily interdicted by the British navy.

Upkeep of Ships. Hull cleaning and repair could be accomplished either by dry-docking or heaving the ship down on a careen. Dry-docking put less stress on the vessel's frame. There were other advantages, and they all added up to a longer life for the ship and a more rapid turnaround during cleaning and refitting. Dry docks represented a huge capital investment. Their justification was twofold. Financially, they helped preserve ships from decay during the time they were laid up in peacetime (drydocking greatly facilitated hull inspection as well as repair). Operationally, in wartime, they speeded cleaning and repairs.

The royal yards in England had had dry docks for a long time. Five royal dockyards were in existence in 1688. Of these, only Portsmouth lay outside the Thames basin. After the Revolution of 1688, when France became the leading naval adversary, the English government decided immediately (1690) to establish a dockyard to the westward; a glance at a map is sufficient to reveal why. In the course of the eighteenth century this new yard in Plymouth Sound was responsible for three-quarters of the growth of British naval dockyard employees.

France, like the Dutch Republic, lagged behind in constructing dry docks. The brand new naval arsenal at Rochefort, built in the 1660s by direction of Louis XIV and Colbert, was given dry docks, but it was not until the 1740s that dry docks were constructed for the forward base at Brest. Toulon did not get a dry dock until about 1775, after the Spanish navy built one at Cartagena in 1772. Toulon was an important naval arsenal, and there can be no doubt that the delay in providing a dry dock was owing to the meager range of tides in the Mediterranean. At Cartagena the Spanish assigned 390 prisoners to manning the pumps. The prisoners were divided into three watches working round the clock, and, according to reports, any press of activity pushed them beyond human limits. Horses were substituted but they died too; the solution was a steam pump, which antedated the use of steam in British yards by a quarter century.

There were no dry docks in the naval bases established across the Atlantic during the eighteenth century, even at Havana, which was otherwise a large, well equipped arsenal. After 1750, however, the British navy could use the East India Company's dry dock at Bombay. Otherwise, warships had to be careened. A pair of ships of similar size could careen each other if one of them possessed the large blocks and tackles needed for the purpose, but a careening wharf, with large, purpose-built capstans and storehouses close by, afforded far greater efficiency. Ships could careen at the stone wharves of Port Mahon, and with difficulty at Gibraltar's mole. In the West Indies permanent naval bases with careening wharves were established by the British navy at Antigua and Jamaica in the 1730s—an indication of the expanded view of seapower that developed in Britain during the first half of the eighteenth century. The main French base in the West Indies was at Fort Royal, Martinique. On the North American coast, the British cruisers relied upon private facilities in Boston, New York, and Charleston; the development of Halifax did not begin until 1749. The French used Louisbourg, though its situation was not favorable for ship repair. By the time the great struggle for empire

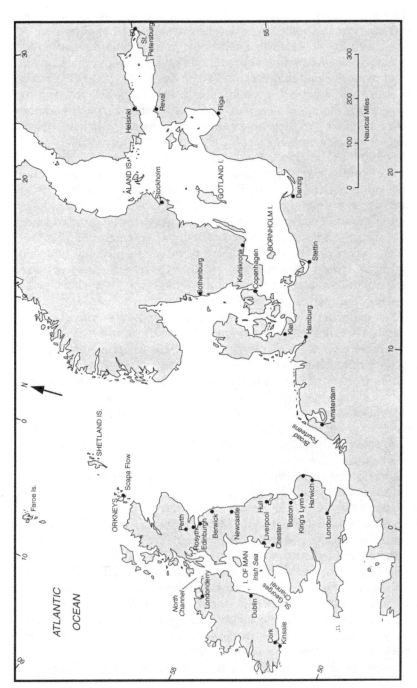

Figure XVII. Map of the North Sea and the Baltic Sea.

reached its height in mid-century, the British navy was considerably better equipped than the French navy to maintain ships overseas.

Preservation of Crews. Strategic coverage involved, of course, the ability to keep ships at sea and on distant stations. Since the most visible features of a naval base are the facilities erected for hull cleaning, maintenance, and refitting, it is easy to forget that the requirements that most affected the operational endurance of sailing warships were food and drink. Another requirement—needed all too often in those days—was a hospital of some sort to receive and minister to the sick.

Popular writers of the eighteenth century continued, as Nicholas Rodger has noted, to draw upon the scandalous lore of the preceding century about rotten navy victuals, and the influence of such writings on many modern accounts has served to hide one the greatest achievements of British naval administration of the eighteenth century. In 1700, the victualling department's administration was completely overhauled and placed on a sound footing, the old system of employing great contractors having been abandoned in the 1690s. The reforms initiated in 1700 had lasting effect. The result was a quality of service unique among navies of the time.

The biggest administrative task, namely the victualling of ships in home waters and prior to their departure on distant assignment, was handled directly by the Victualling Office. Ships overseas were usually replenished by contractors, but the Victualling Board confined its contracting arrangements to merchants of known capacity who had connections and experience in the particular far-flung region. The contractors were fully aware that ship captains would unhesitatingly complain to the Admiralty and Victualling boards about bad service or provisions.

In the West Indies, the superiority of British over French naval victualling has been historically established. French arrangements for sending provisions to the Caribbean often miscarried, and when that happened even a small French squadron based at Martinique, for instance, would quickly generate famine prices in the island if it resorted to emergency local purchase. Among the British navy's many wartime victualling advantages in West Indies was its contractors' ready access to British North American supplies. By the time of the Seven Years War, the advantages enjoyed by the British navy in the Caribbean theater were huge.[6] The larger history of French naval victualling remains uninvestigated; that is why the discussion here is so heavily concentrated on the British experience.

Although the spread of sickness through a ship's company was one of the foreseeable hazards of naval life, a well fed crew was less

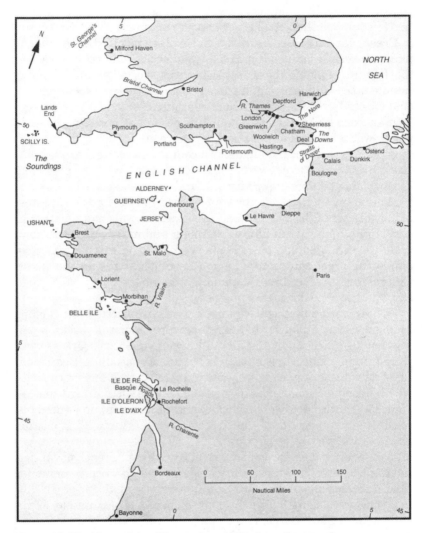

Figure XVIII. Map of the Channel and Western Approaches

likely to get sick. The standard seamen's diet in the British navy was plentiful. It afforded 4,000 calories a day, enough to sustain long hours of hard work. It was not very palatable: the main items were salt beef and pork, cheese, and unleavened bread (sea biscuit). The allowance of beer was a gallon a day per man. As is well known, the diet was deficient in vitamin C, and, on long cruises, the seamen fell victim to scurvy.

It was not until the mid-1790s that the problem of scurvy was solved by the issue of bottled lemon juice to the sick, and this medicinal remedy was soon followed up by the preventive measure of incorporating fresh lemons in the regular dietary issue. (Limes were substituted later—an unfortunate change because their vitamin C content was lower.) It is thus easy to see why the most often asked question about British naval victualling in the eighteenth century has been: Why did it take so long to hit upon the solution?

Was it not well known that lemons and oranges kept the disease in check? Mediterranean squadrons usually purchased them, and so did East India Company ships. And had not Dr. James Lind—perhaps the most famous name in naval medicine—conducted an experiment involving a "control group" that demonstrated the distinctive efficacy of oranges and lemons in 1747, the results of which he published in *A Treatise of the Scurvy* in 1753? The recent Navy Records Society centenary volume (*British Naval Documents, 1204–1960*) contains Lind's report of this experiment. It also contains some documents illustrating the difficulties of taking out fresh beef to the "Western Squadron" (that watched Brest) under the command of Admiral Hawke in 1759: live bullocks had to be hoisted aboard in slings in open ocean. Compared to supplying fresh beef, the carrying out of fresh vegetables was easy. The Victualling Office could have coped with the difficulty and expense of routinely supplying fresh vegetables or lemons in nearby seas if it had been ordered to do so. A regular supply of "fresh greens" to the Western Squadron was strongly urged by an enlightened purser in 1747 and, after some deliberation, the proposal was approved by the Admiralty. The practice was revived for Hawke's squadron in 1759. But it did not become permanent; in fact, nothing like the impressive effort of 1759 was repeated for more than 30 years. The Admiralty's failure in this matter did not arise from unconquerable administrative obstacles. Nor did it arise from complacency. It arose from scientific confusion.

The symptoms of scurvy in its advanced form were well marked out, but the circumstances under which the onset of the disease occurred were mystifying in their variation and gave prodigious scope for false theorizing. One puzzle was why some men came down with scurvy sooner than five weeks at sea and others later. This puzzle may be connected with another: why, considering that in wartime most seamen were confined aboard, was scurvy not rampant in the ships moored at Spithead? Perhaps, the answer is that men bought fruits and vegetables from the bumboats, or else their visiting friends and wives—some of the women were wives—brought such items aboard. The first cases to show up at sea were quite possibly those of men who did not eat enough fruit and vegetables while in port.

Not least among the obstacles to a solution was existing medicinal theory. The most eminent London physicians focused their attention elsewhere than on dietary deficiency. Observers at sea were inclined to dwell on the notion of salt, and that is one reason why fresh beef was so highly valued. Early in the century, the Admiralty began to direct the Victualling Office to provide, wherever possible, "fresh provisions" on a regular basis to ships in port, commonly twice a week. (The phrase "fresh provisions" really meant, "fresh meat," which was substituted for the salt ration.) This was an expensive undertaking. Also worth noting is the fact that naval vessels heading out on long voyages commonly left port with live animals on deck. When I first inquired into the eighteenth-century navy's responses to scurvy 30 years ago I thought that fresh beef was a total irrelevancy. That is evidently not the case: fresh-killed grass-fed beef retains some vitamin C. Still, the difficulty and expense of resupply at sea was very great. Vegetables would have been more feasible in home waters. As for the adoption of lemons, even Dr. Lind himself did not push single-mindedly for this remedy. There were too many competing conceptions, and the solution was ultimately reached within the naval organization, chiefly as a result of the disciplined empiricism and determined advocacy of a former naval surgeon who served in the 1790s as physician to Lord Howe's fleet, Dr. Thomas Trotter.

It is not easy to convince the modern reader that eighteenth-century British naval authorities really did care about and give serious thought to the health of seamen—that the delayed triumph over scurvy should be attributed to scientific confusion rather than indifference and complacency. An illustrative example, therefore, seems in order.

At the beginning of 1782, on a long return voyage from the Cape of Good Hope, Captain Thomas Pasley of HMS *Jupiter* recorded in a diary his apprehension and horror as he watched the progress of scurvy in his ship.[7] He had on board some large boxes of earth for, he wrote, "my Garden (which it has been my Practice to raise daily Sallad in)." Having taken sick men aboard from another ship, and seeing his own men falling ill, he decided to put his garden to use for the benefit of the crew. This is what he did:

> I have given [it] up, and Buried as many Men in it as possible, greatly to their Satisfaction. They are happy and seem to have faith in it. So have

I, not for an absolute cure on board, but as putting an undoubted check to the Scurvey's progress—God grant it!

The next day he recorded:

Yesterday the Garden did wonders; the Men who were carried and lifted in and out of it, incapable of moving a Limb, walked of themselves to day—wonderful effect. I have dismantled my third Tray of Earth likewise . . . ,

Each day 36 men were thereafter immersed in the soil, each for an hour's duration. But it was a race with death to the island of Fernando de Noronha, the only salvation. "The island will be a most joyfull sight, and the men landed a burthen off my heart and mind; for I am in hopes that all that is [sic] landed alive will recover—God Grant it!"

When he reached the island, his great anxiety was that all the bullocks might have been already slaughtered to serve a ship that preceded him, but he soon learned from a message carried through the surf by a Portuguese swimmer to his boat that there were plenty of bullocks available. The trouble was that the unusually high surf prevented his boats from taking the sick ashore. After three days, the Portuguese governor "sent off one Bullock and two Sheep with a quantity of Greens" as a present. Pasley planned to slaughter them the next day to provide the crew with fresh meat and a "Broth stuffed with the Greens," but he was convinced that the lives of the sick men depended upon getting them landed. On the fifth day, he risked a boat with 15 men aboard, but it "overset and Turned Bottom up" in the surf; all 15 were saved, thanks to the exertions of people on shore. By this point, he had 196 men sick with scurvy, and "an addition of 5 and 6 every day." Finally, six days after arriving, he was able to get the seriously ill men ashore: "In all I landed of the *Jupiter* 146, of the *Mercury* 36. I have now on board complaints of the number of 40; but Beef and Broth every day will soon set them on their legs." The Portuguese governor ashore, "civil and attentive" beyond expectation, visited the sick and "distributed among them fruits." At the end of 18 days, Pasley recorded: "four only of 150 I sent on shore required assistance to return." He sailed the next day, mindful of how grateful he was to the island's governor.

Captain Pasley's belief in the efficacy of beef broth and contact with earth—Will scientific study someday verify the therapeutic value of the latter or was he merely witnessing a placebo effect?—and the secondary attention he gave to greens and fruits are repre-

sentative of the era. His humane concern for the health of his ship's
company was equally representative. It was strongly bolstered by a
distinctly unsentimental consideration: in the event of combat, he
observed, "My Character depends on being well man'd."

At a more general level, the success of the navy depended on "being
well man'd," and, accordingly, eighteenth-century naval authorities
gave high priority to seamen's health. After the massive typhus epi-
demic of 1740, which seriously impeded the fleet mobilization, the Admiralty petitioned the Privy Council to have naval hospitals built in
order to avoid the ill-consequences of hired sick quarters, which were
erratic nursing care, convalescence wrecked by drunkenness, and the
impossibility of preventing desertion. The result was the founding of
Haslar Hospital near Portsmouth and, subsequently, a naval hospital near Plymouth as well. By the 1780s, the principle of the "receiving ship" where new recruits could be scrubbed and given clean
clothes was adopted, and the spread of typhus at times of mobilization was much reduced. In the meantime, Admiralty instructions
placed strong emphasis on fumigating, airing, and scrubbing with
vinegar the lower decks. Thus, the second great scourge, infectious typhus, was brought under control. A third was the virulent form of
malaria known as "yellow fever," which caused service in the West Indies and other tropical areas to be dreaded by officers as well as seamen. Only by keeping ships out of port in certain seasons of the year
was it possible to reduce the risks of deadly mosquito-borne fevers.
The British navy learned to favor such a procedure, but cleaning, refitting, and replenishment in those seasons was often unavoidable.

Requisites for Command of the Seas. My reason for dwelling
at length on preservation of crews is that these matters were of far
greater importance to the establishment of naval supremacy in the
eighteenth century than is commonly recognized.

Consider, for instance, the most desired naval objective—destroying the enemy's main force—the objective that used to be regarded
as the beginning and end of naval strategy. Undeniably, the task of
exercising command of the sea is made easier and safer if the enemy's main force has been eliminated. Certainly in the old days, the
idea of positioning a battle-fleet off the enemy's main base in hopes
of bringing about a decisive sea battle early in the war was a sensi-
ble strategy. The trouble is that a fleet that knows its inferiority will
not come out and risk annihilation; it will stay in port and wait. Unless there is a dire strategic or administrative reason why it must
accept the risk of battle, it will delay its sortie until, either by acci-
dent or exhaustion, the superior fleet departs. All this is incontro-

vertible and was well argued 80 years ago by Sir Julian Corbett.[8] An obvious implication is that it was not enough for the power that wished to hold command of the sea simply to have a stronger battle-fleet. That fleet had to be continued on station—whether off Brest or somewhere in the Caribbean—for a long time. The conditions of sea warfare in the eighteenth century (chancy weather, limitations on sailing capabilities, scurvy) made this task especially difficult. These same conditions added a further dimension to the problem, because under favoring circumstances a French fleet commander could reasonably gamble that his forces would be able to escape interception. The watching British fleet, therefore, had to be able to chase, perhaps to chase across an ocean. To sum up, in order to reap the advantages of naval superiority, Britain not only had to keep its squadrons on station to the extremities of their endurance, but also had to anticipate that those squadrons might need to depart on a long voyage, perhaps across the Atlantic.

Regardless of whether the hoped-for early destruction of the enemy battle-fleet occurred, it would be necessary for the superior naval power to have a multiplicity of cruisers on various stations to protect trade from enemy predators that could not easily be prevented from getting to sea. In short, ensuring safe use of the sea for one's own military and economic purposes while denying the benefits of sea transportation to the enemy required a vast array of smaller ships, as well as facilities to sustain them on distant deployments. Battleships contended for command of the sea, but cruisers exercised it—a point that Admiral Mahan's writings too readily obscured. And it should not be forgotten that the assiduous exercise of sea power provided significant advantages to naval administration itself. It was earlier noted that the British government worked to deny naval stores and materials to the French. Similarly, especially in the Seven Years War, the British navy disrupted the marshalling of French victualling convoys in Biscayan roadsteads.

As a nation pursuing dominance, Great Britain was bound to keep more vessels at sea for longer periods of time. The British navy had to deploy not only more fighting ships with more capable crews, but also more and better means of sustaining and preserving those crews. Its facilities for ship cleaning and repair had to be more comprehensive, and its access to naval materials more assured, not just because of greater numbers, but because of the wear and tear incurred by greater time at sea. It is possible to go much further—to assert that the requirements of true command of the sea in the eighteenth century were of a character that involved not just more of everything, but a unique degree of comprehensiveness and preparation.

To underline this point, the importance of which has only gradually impressed itself on my mind, I shall end on a personal note. When I got to Cambridge many years ago to begin the study of naval administration for my Ph.D. degree, Professor E. E. Rich, the Professor of Imperial and Naval History, who also happened to be Master of my college, tested my resolve to do naval administration. I remember one of his arguments as if I had just heard it yesterday. The gist of it was: "But what is the point? All the navies of the time had to deal with the same problems, and their administrative efforts failed or succeeded in coping with them to about the same degree." I went ahead anyway (under the direction of Mr. John Ehrman), but ruled out in advance any attempt to gauge the impact of administration on operations, knowing that nothing could be concluded without a comparative study of Britain's naval opponents. One consequence, unfortunately, was that I further contributed thereby to the separation of administrative and operational naval history—a separation which has caused a good deal of traditional naval history to be fundamentally unsound. Now, many years later, I know far better than I did at the time of my thesis examination (wherein Professor Rich showed himself to be a generous and helpful examiner) that he was only partly right in imagining that both sides experienced "the same problems," and profoundly wrong in supposing that all eighteenth-century navies solved their naval administrative problems with about the same degree of success. In fact, it seems that the spheres in which British naval administration came to differ most markedly during the eighteenth century from French or Spanish were those relating to the preservation of crews. This conclusion runs counter to popular notions. I believe it to be correct, but it must be regarded as tentative, awaiting more extensive studies of French and Spanish naval administration.

NOTES

1. H. W. Richmond, "The Future of the Battleship," *The Naval Review*, 8 (1920), pp. 368–9.

2. John Keegan, *The Price of Admiralty: The Evolution of Naval Warfare.* (New York, 1989), p. 47.

3. These figures are based on the work of Jan Glete, *Navies and Nations.* (Stockholm, 1993). They include all ships above 20 guns that were deemed suitable for fitting out.

4. See Chapter 9 of James Pritchard, *Louis XV's Navy.* (Toronto and Montreal, 1987).

5. Paul W. Bamford, *Forests and French Sea Power, 1660–1789.* (Toron-

to, 1956) showed how much more serious France's problems in this sphere were than Britain's.

6. All this has been recently set forth in Christian Buchet's remarkable comparative study, *La Lutte pour l'Espace Caraibe*. (Paris, 1993).

7. The following account is drawn from Captain Thomas Pasley, *Private Sea Journals, 1778–1782,* edited by Rodney M. S. Pasley. (London, 1931), p. 217ff.

8. Julian S. Corbett, *Some Principles of Maritime Strategy*. (London, 1911; annotated edition, Annapolis, 1988).

SUGGESTIONS FOR FURTHER READING

Daniel A. Baugh, *British Naval Administration in the Age of Walpole*. (Princeton, 1965).

Christian Buchet, *La Lutte pour l'Espace Caraibe et la Facade Atlantique de l'Amerique Centrale et du Sud (1672–1763)*. (Paris, 1991).

Robert Gardiner and Brian Lavery, eds., *The Line of Battle: The Sailing Warship, 1650–1840*. (London, 1992).

Jan Glete, *Navies and Nations: Warships, Navies and State Building in Europe and America, 1500–1860*. (Stockholm, 1993).

Brian Lavery, *The Ship of the Line*. Volume I, *The Development of the Battlefleet, 1650–1850*. (London, 1983).

Christopher Lloyd, ed., *The Health of Seamen: Selections from the Works of Dr. James Lind, Sir Gilbert Blane and Dr. Thomas Trotter*. Publications of the Navy Records Society, vol. 107. (London, 1965).

James Pritchard, *Louis XV's Navy, 1748–1762: A Study of Organization and Administration*. (Kingston and Montreal, 1987).

N. A. M. Rodger, "Le Scorbut dans la Royal Navy pendant la Guerre de Sept Ans," *Revue du Nord,* Extra Number (1986), pp. 455–462.

N. A. M. Rodger, *The Wooden World: An Anatomy of the Georgian Navy*. (London, 1986).

14

OFFICERS AND MEN
N. A. M. Rodger

It is a commonplace of military history and a staple theme of officer training everywhere that the best men will always beat the best weapons. This tends to absurdity if it is understood, as it sometimes has been, to mean that national character makes both numbers and equipment irrelevant, but it is certainly true in the sense that the best trained force is likely win against the best-armed, assuming no gross inequality of numbers or firepower. Naval warfare was in the eighteenth century, as it has always been, quintessentially the warfare of capital and technology, and the key components of success were the abilities to handle the complex and sophisticated technology of the sailing man-of-war, and to manage the no less complex naval administration ashore. Moreover the business of handling ships and fleets involved not one but many skills, and perhaps the hardest of all was the skill of integrating them effectively. Victory at sea sprang from the harmonious cooperation of many different abilities; defeat might spring from failure in any one of them. The skill of the admiral is often thought of as consisting primarily in tactics (in reality the weak point of all squadrons in those days); it is more realistic to see his essential skill as being that combination of leadership and management which brought a squadron to its highest collective efficiency.

The officers and men who worked these hugely complicated and delicately balanced sailing machines, belonged themselves to shipboard societies which were of corresponding complexity. Popular misconceptions tend to arise from a military model, in which a small number of officers control a large number of subordinates by means of mechanical drills enforced by rigid discipline. This may be useful as a crude picture of an eighteenth-century infantry regiment, but it bears no relation to the reality of a ship's company. On board ship, professional skill was the most important index of status, and many professions were represented. Seamen were the most numerous, and among them the warrant officers and petty officers took the lead by authority and experience, while the smart young topmen enjoyed the status earned by their skill and daring. Carpenters, caulkers, sailmakers, soldiers, coopers and clerks enjoyed similar hierarchies of skill and experience. Commissioned officers were required to learn seamanship, as the sailors did, aloft; they added the skills of navigation and, it was hoped, command.

In each group there were boys learning the trade, and in wartime there were also adults with few or no skills. Though able seamen were indispensable as topmen, petty officers and captains of guns, much of the work of the ship was a matter of pulling and hauling on falls and tackles which led down on deck. This demanded strength and organized teamwork rather than individual skill, and could be done by men with little experience who need never go aloft. The same was true of the heavy work of serving the guns. There was therefore scope for a considerable degree of "dilution" of skills by replacing seamen with landsmen in wartime. This was also one purpose of the marines or naval infantry which formed part of the establishment of most eighteenth-century navies. They were valuable as soldiers in action, laying down small-arms fire and leading boarding parties, but in working the ship they served as unskilled decklabor. It was the marines and landsmen, rather than the seamen who knew their business, who tended to be "encouraged" about their work by petty officers with rope's ends. It was a feature of shipboard life acceptable to the seamen, who had a clear idea of the status and dignity of skilled men like themselves, and the contemptible position of the landlubber.

This brings us to the question of naval discipline in the eighteenth century, a subject about which probably more, and more inaccurate, myths are in circulation than any other. To a large extent, naval discipline was a functional response to the necessities of seafaring, resting on mutual consent and enforced by public opinion. All seamen had been bred from boyhood in a world in which survival depended utterly on skilled teamwork, not simply on every man pulling his weight on the falls of tackle or halliard, but on the intelligent and timely application of individual skill and initiative. In many maneuvers the safety of the ship depended as much on the individual topman aloft as on the captain or master on the quarterdeck. This bred a close, almost intimate world of shared dangers, in which the skilled seamen (and indeed the skilled men of every trade), enjoyed and expected to enjoy the respect due to key men on whom the whole company depended. This had nothing to do with any democratic ideas of leveling the social or naval hierarchy, which seem to have been virtually unknown before 1789; nor did it involve any challenge to the essentially autocratic nature of shipboard society, for all seamen knew that orders had to be given and obeyed at sea for the safety of all. What it did mean was that there was a natural alliance between the prudent officer and the responsible, skilled and experienced part of the ship's company, against all slackers, drunkards, incompetents and troublemakers who threw more work onto their shipmates and made life in the crowded world of a ship more difficult or dangerous than it needed to be. Successful seafaring demanded a high degree of self-discipline, and those who did not or would not acquire it were a burden on their fellows. In the hands of any reasonably capable and sensitive captain, naval discipline at sea was employed with the support of majority opinion to keep life as safe and comfortable as possible. The offenses that were typically punished seem to have been idling and shirking, failing to keep oneself and one's berth clean, drunkenness on duty and the like, and it is easy to see that responsible and hard-working men were positively keen to see the punishment of those guilty of such antisocial behavior. Flogging was the usual punishment in British ships, and it enjoyed the tacit, sometimes the vocal support of majority opinion at sea, so long as it was done fairly and consistently. A weak man who punished too little, who did not live up to his threats, was liable to be less popular than a severe but consistent captain. Most unpopular of all was the capricious commander, alternating cruelty and indulgence, whose men never knew where they stood with him.

There is, however, a clear trend for discipline in British ships to become harsher as the century proceeded. In the mid-eighteenth century, the captain of a British warship was largely responsible for recruiting his own ship's company, and in practice had the major voice in the choice of his officers. This bred a sort of free market in talent, in which officers of good reputation looked out for skilled followers (both junior officers and ratings) to man their ships, while young men of ability and ambition took care to attach themselves to captains most likely to bring them safe home and provide them with prize money and promotion. In this way the navy was divided into many followings, large and small, bound together by vertical ties of patronage and service which owed very little to central authority or formal discipline.

There are indications, however, that these ties were weakening by the time of the 1780s and were to weaken faster during the war years of the 1790s. The reasons for this are still obscure, but it has something to do with the rise of Admiralty authority, progressively taking more and more powers of promotion into its own hands, undermining the influence of admirals and captains and centralizing power within the navy. The effect was to make naval discipline harsher, as a remote and impersonal authority substituted its unyielding power for the more flexible and personal bonds which had formerly held the navy together. One clue to the trend is the growing tendency of officers to think of the marines as an arm of authority, distinct from the rest of the crew. The sharp rise in class and political consciousness generated by the French Revolution speeded up changes which were already in progress, and injected a strong element of mutual antagonism and fear in the division between quarterdeck and lower deck. We should beware of exaggerating these changes; a recent study concludes that captains in the navy administered their ships in much the same spirit that justices of the peace ashore dispensed justice in their districts, but there is no doubt that in both cases change was taking place, and that it was tending to drive officers and their men slowly apart.

At the same time there was a fundamental change (which has hardly been studied) in the naval recruitment system, which became largely centralized, so that during the Revolutionary and Napoleonic Wars captains were entirely beholden to the Admiralty for providing their men. Seldom did captains have prior social contact with their men any more. Even the officers were less and less likely to be chosen by their captain. Moreover, during these wars the 'dilution' of the skilled seamen by landsmen was carried so far that, on one calculation, the unskilled or semiskilled part of the average British ship's company in 1805 was two-thirds of the total. It was possible to turn those men into an efficient ship's company only because they were in commission and at sea for such long periods. But it was impossible to maintain the old navy's casual accommodations when so few of the men were regular seafarers, when they were unlikely to be personal connections of their officers, and when the acute manpower shortage made leave a rarity.

It is still a matter of some uncertainty what proportion of British seamen in any period were recruited by the press gang, and in any case what the press-gang meant in practice is a subject so encrusted with myth and emotion that some effort is required to address it rationally. The British were in a sense trapped by a political tradition in which the liberty of the individual was preserved by the weakness of central government. No scheme in the French style which de-

pended on the imposition of a national scheme backed by autocratic
power was politically acceptable. But some coercion was unavoidable if the navy was to be manned. The press-gang was the result.
It was universally admitted to be an evil, and an inefficient evil, but
it was that very inefficiency, the haphazard operation which testi-
fied to the weakness of the state and gave the seamen so many opportunities for evasion, which made it acceptable as a lesser evil.
Better that the liberties of seamen should be placed in jeopardy than
the liberties of Englishmen everywhere should be sacrificed.

From the navy's point of view, the press-gang was a method of
getting the seamen, above all the young topmen, which were in critically short supply. The press-gangs operated largely at sea, taking
men out of inward-bound British merchantmen on soundings, and
replacing them with others who could be trusted to return. Some
pressing was done ashore, for example by raiding dockside pubs,
but shore-based press-gangs were as much or more concerned with
recruiting volunteers (always an important part of their work) and
with controlling the movement of men on leave. Essentially the
press-gang was a method of increasing the effective supply of seamen by forcing them to work twelve months of the year instead of
the seven or eight which were usual in deep-sea trades with their
long intervals in port unloading and waiting for cargo. The navy's
target was seamen, above all topmen; it was neither legally possible nor practically useful to the navy to "sweep the streets" for anyone who could be found. There is anecdotal evidence that by the end
of the century, with the manpower shortage becoming ever more
acute, press-gangs may have been less discriminating in their recruitment, but even then the navy was not essentially short of unskilled men. Seamen, above all topmen, were always the prime requirement.

The French navy also suffered from a severe manning problem,
but it differed in two ways from the British situation. In the late seventeenth century, France instituted a system by which the seafaring population of most (though not all) the coastal districts of France
was listed and obliged to perform naval service by rotation. In principle the men had to serve in the king's ships one year in three or
four, and in return received small pensions and other privileges.
This system was reasonably fair and efficient, and was envied by
British naval administrators, who several times tried without success to persuade Parliament to adopt something similar. It also gave
the French navy a significant advantage in the early stages of mobilization. But the machine, though ingenious, was fragile. Under

eighteenth-century conditions, with larger squadrons at sea for longer periods, it rapidly broke down. All the annual *classes* together were inadequate to man the ships which France wished to commission, and the naval budget ceased to pay the promised pensions. In these circumstances the French system came to rely on compulsion and violence as much or more than the British did, applied to a seafaring population which was much smaller to begin with. According to the figures of T. J. A. Le Goff, the numbers of men available from the Atlantic seaboard in 1757 were distributed as follows:

King's service	19,000
East India Company	2,700
Commerce & privateering	8,300
Prisoners of war	10,000
Not yet called up	6,500

In France, as in Britain, the king's ships took about half the overall seafaring population, but much of the other half were in British prisons rather than in merchant shipping. In 1758 the British government deliberately exploited this advantage by altering its policy of exchanging prisoners of war, offering only unskilled or unfit men. With many fewer prisoners in their own hands, the French had no choice but to continue the exchanges on this unfavorable basis, or abandon them altogether and suffer still worse.

In general, the longer a war went on, the less well-manned the French navy became, and the better the British. The French were drawing upon, and rapidly exhausting, a manpower pool which had been too small to begin with. The collapse of deep-sea trade in wartime, and its replacement by privateering—both of which were vulnerable to heavy losses of men made prisoner—tended to drain the pool further. In all the wars of the eighteenth century, even those like the American War in which France was relatively successful at sea, the manpower crisis grew steadily worse. In Britain, by contrast, it was usual for trade in wartime to remain broadly unaffected, even to grow. The result as the navy mobilized was a forced expansion of the manpower pool as existing seamen were made to work harder (by being taken up by the press-gang), older men were drawn back by bounties into the navy or higher wages into merchantmen, and British seamen were diluted by landsmen and foreigners. The result was always worst in the opening years of the war as the navy mobilized, and the crisis eased as the supply grew to meet the new demand. Spain was in the worst position of all, for its deep-sea merchant fleet was so weak that most of the men who were registered in the *matrícula del mar,* the equivalent of the French *système des classes,* were not real seamen at all.

In all navies the recruitment of officers presented no difficulty. The honor of serving as an officer of the crown easily outweighed arduous service and indifferent pay, especially if, as in British service, prize money offered the chance of a fortune. In all navies it was expected that commissioned officers would be of the rank of armigerous gentleman, and in the French system proofs of nobility were formally required of candidates in most circumstances. In practice, however, not all these claims were authentic, while in the British navy the patronage system sometimes helped able men of very humble backgrounds to the quarterdeck. British officers, like their men, usually went to sea in boyhood, but it was common, especially toward the end of the century, for young gentlemen to spend some time borne on the books of guardships in port while they attended schools which specialized in mathematics and other subjects essential for the future navigator. French officers received a much more thorough education, taught almost entirely in the classroom ashore, but the curriculum was overly theoretical, and it seems to have been neither well taught nor well attended. In practice there was a strong tendency for British officers to be better trained as seamen, and not necessarily worse educated than their French opposite numbers.

In all navies the great problem with officers was how to maintain their professional skills during peacetime, and no navy developed an effective answer to it. Training cruises were tried on a small scale, but money was lacking to provide more than brief experience for a small proportion of officers. For the British the situation was eventually transformed by 20 years of almost continuous warfare against Revolutionary and Napoleonic France, allowing professional skills to rise to levels hitherto unknown. At the same time the French lost most of their experienced officers in the turmoil of the Revolution.

The period from 1793 to 1815 for most people sums up naval warfare under sail, and it is fair to see it as representing the culmination of many eighteenth-century trends. For France, however, and later for Spain as well, it marks the return of a nightmare from the seventeenth century; rebellion and civil disorder wrecking the structure of the state and overthrowing naval strength. Manpower and training, like every aspect of the management of a navy, were acutely demanding, and searched out every weakness of state and society; only the fittest survived, and only continuity of support over a long period could build up the necessary structure of skills and resources.

SUGGESTIONS FOR FURTHER READING

Timothy J. A. LeGoff, "Problemes de recrutement de la marine française pendant la guerre sept ans," *Revue Historique,* 564 (1987), pp. 355–361.

N. A. M. Rodger, "The Victualling of the British Navy During the Seven Years' War," *Bulletin du Centre d'"Histoire des Éspaces Atlantiques,* 2 (1985), pp. 37–53.

N. A. M. Rodger, *The Wooden World: An Anatomy of the Georgian Navy.* (London, 1986).

15

TRADE AND COLONIES: FINANCIAL AND MARITIME STRENGTH, CA. 1714–1790

Daniel A. Baugh

It was remarked at the outset of Chapter 13 that maritime trade and financial capacity were *foundations* of seapower in the eighteenth century. It was also noted that during the century the global contest for supremacy was carried on almost entirely by navies and armies of the state. Whatever disagreements may persist as to the character of the Early Modern "military revolution," no one disputes the state's central role in the process or the importance of state revenues to its continuance. It had always been impossible to mobilize an effective navy without large-scale financing. Now the mobilizing of armies also depended heavily on the state's treasury. The great practical problem of Early Modern regimes became that of meeting the growing costs of their armies and navies.

This chapter is about money and maritime commerce, their interconnection and their relation to state and naval power. The interest in fostering maritime commerce exhibited by the governing regimes of Early Modern Western Europe cannot be properly understood unless the money problems of those governments are kept in mind—a point that textbook accounts of "the mercantilist era" too often neglect. As Jean-Baptiste Colbert remarked in 1664, "Le commerce est la source de la finance, et la finance est le nerf de la guerre."

At the base lay the problem of state revenue. It might be presumed that a large, populous country such as France for instance, increasingly productive by eighteenth-century standards in both agriculture and manufacturing (and therefore a wealthy country in terms of what modern economists regard as real wealth) would have been capable of procuring a revenue adequate for its military and naval needs. In pure economic theory that may appear so. Yet in fact, wealth of that character was difficult to tax. Direct taxes on domestic property were expensive to administer and their collection was eroded by political or social resistance. This was the case in nearly all countries of the time. Moreover, tax payments in cash, which was what western European governments needed, could drain a region of its currency and thus depress the local economy to the point where further taxation was useless. On top of this, in time of war cash flowed out of the country as a whole—to pay for naval stores, wages to soldiers encamped in foreign lands, food and drink for soldiers and sailors serving abroad, and so on.[1] Economists from Adam Smith forward have scolded the mercantilist writers of the seventeenth and eighteenth centuries for their seemingly doctrinaire "bullionism," that is, their fixation on the need to import a balance of precious metals. Some writers were indeed foolish enough to confuse precious metals and wealth, but most eighteenth-century mercantilists did not do so. They well knew that countries at war or preparing for war could not avoid outflows of precious metals, and also knew what the consequence of unreplenished outflows were for the domestic economy and for being able to continue a war. It was not only easy but fairly logical to suppose that there could never be too much gold and silver in a country that lacked indigenous mines.

For countries without mines, trade was the only means of replenishment. But foreign trade offered many additional advantages of equal, perhaps greater, importance. Duties on imports were politically more convenient than domestic levies. The domestic economy was enlivened by foreign commerce, and excise and other internal tax yields were enhanced. No tax is without its problems, political and economic, but in those days indirect taxes such as customs and excise duties, if properly administered, were capable of generating ever larger yields at reduced political cost. During the sixteenth century direct taxes (levies upon property) had accounted for 60% of English royal revenue. During the period from 1689 to 1714, the average was about 40%. After 1714, only 20% of peacetime revenues, and 28% of wartime, came from direct taxes; indirect taxation produced about 75% of British revenue in the eighteenth century. The French monarchy had also moved toward greater reliance on indirect taxes, but not to the same degree; indirect taxes accounted for only 47% of France's total revenue during the century.[2]

The advantages of trade were not just fiscal; they were also financial. Taxation alone could not meet wartime costs. As wars dragged on, the states of Europe, in all cases, spent money they did not have—they borrowed. When eighteenth-century observers made remarks such as "the longest purse must win," as they commonly did, it was understood that the outcome depended not merely on revenues but crucially on the state's credit. A healthy public credit depended partly on the availability of accumulated money capital. This capital was first mobilized by merchant bankers, many of whom were raised up to great wealth by their connections with foreign commerce. The rise of the Amsterdam money market—that newly emergent, magical ingredient of seventeenth-century Dutch success—was correctly ascribed to such connections. The lesson was not lost on eighteenth-century statesmen: no country of Western Europe that wished to remain a great power could afford to pass up the phenomenal range of advantages spawned by commerce.

Yet before focusing on maritime commerce and its relation to power, we must give some attention to financial administration, for in fact the state's financial capacity in time of war was as dependent upon this factor as much as it was upon wealth and commerce.

The Financial Revolution. The subject of financial administration is all the more important because an immense change occurred during the half-century before 1714, a change that transformed the English state. This change was identified and traced by P. G. M. Dickson in a book entitled *The Financial Revolution in England,* published in 1967. No similar "financial revolution" occurred in France, and, as contemporaries came to recognize, Britain thus enjoyed a decisive war-winning advantage in the eighteenth century.

One must go back to the mid-seventeenth century when there was nothing remarkable about English treasury administration except that it was quite centralized and could draw upon the traditions of a well-established customs service. Otherwise, early Stuart finance suffered from serious diseases. When the English Civil War erupted the costs were met by improvisation and confiscation, and the Cromwellian regime's inability to raise enough revenue for both an army and navy contributed to its demise in 1660.

After 1660, strange as it may seem, the Restoration monarchy under the famously nonchalant Charles II laid down some key underpinnings of the financial revolution. Prompted by parliamentary complaints as well as his own desire to maximize yields on the taxes granted to him, Charles allowed men familiar with business and finance (and Dutch practices) to design and implement certain treasury reforms. Customs collection was taken out of "farm" in 1671; excise, in 1683. Revenues, thereafter, responded fully and immediately to a growth in trade, whereas hitherto the farmers (syndicates of financiers), having contracted for a fixed payment to the crown, kept surplus collections as profit. These reforms could not have stuck if the royal regime had been unwilling to restrain its habit of borrowing from the farmers. The change had a broad impact as well, being the key to a trend toward ridding English public finance of "undertakings," that is to say—and this is important—of those renewed great contracts that had hitherto kept collections, disbursements, and loans in the hands of private financiers.

Important steps of another sort were taken in the later 1660s. In a wartime act authorizing an extra vote of supply in 1665 it was specified that the records of receipt and disbursement of the monies thus raised should be available for public inspection. Furthermore, the act provided for the issuance of Treasury Orders, each of which was to be numbered sequentially by date of issue and paid "in course"; they were assignable. Thus, though the number of months that might elapse before payment remained uncertain, the receiver or buyer could count on straight dealing: neither favoritism at court, nor bribery, nor assiduous solicitation could cause the queue to be jumped. The practice was soon extended to other Treasury Orders. The upshot was a money market in which ordinary investors could participate. The designers had intended this, knowing that it would lessen government dependence on wealthy financiers. It is to be noted that the motive force behind these reforms was ultimately parliament. The aim and tendency was to separate Treasury administration from court influence—in other words to make "royal" finance more "public."

The beginnings of English financial reform were thus in place before 1688, but the central achievement of the financial revolution, namely the massive enlargement of the British government's capacity to borrow through long-term instruments of debt, occurred after the Revolution of 1688. The partnership of crown and parliament which thereupon developed was based on a common agenda: defending the Revolution Settlement and England's future position in the world against Louis XIV's formidable challenge. The Land Tax of 1690 signified parliamentary commitment to the task. The Bank of England, established in 1694, facilitated all manner of short-term borrowing. Liquidity was enhanced by paying navy, victualling, and transport bills in course, thus making them more readily transferable.

To raise new revenue parliament added prodigiously to the list of new customs and excise levies. Since the war's costs vastly exceeded revenue capabilities, the practice of pledging particular taxes and duties to service long-term annuities accelerated. This was the process of "funding" and the result was the creation of the national debt. In the quarter century after 1688 it rose from almost nothing to £40 million. Although during the period of peace after 1714 interest payments accounted for 44% of public expenditure, and there was much doubt as to whether a nation so laden with public debt could withstand another great war, the answer was fairly clear in 1749. The year after the war of 1739–48 ended, although the National Debt stood at £75 million, the government's credit standing enabled it to refinance 6% bonds at just above 3%. As an instrument for supporting the prosecution of wars the financial revolution was by mid-century an obvious success.

By contrast, the history of French royal finance under the Old Regime is a story, dismal yet fascinating, of administrative drift and stifled reform. There is neither space nor need to trace that story here. Instead, we shall examine the structural shortcomings under three categories: the position of the *financiers,* especially their role in lending; treasury administration and accounting; and taxation.

French royal finance remained substantially in the hands of great *financiers,* men who could mobilize wealth and employ it to secure royal favor, gain control over large portions of the state's revenues and profit thereby, and profit further from lending money to the state. The French monarchy never really broke away from direct dependence upon the credit and conduct of private entrepreneurs. The *financiers,* whether foreign bankers or powerful French merchants who managed to acquire court favor, were known to be profiting exorbitantly and were reviled by one and all. It was the habit of the monarchy from time to time to satisfy its resentment, and the public's, by subjecting the accounts of individual *financiers* to audit by a *chambre de justice,* the common result being that they were broken and imprisoned for peculation. Naturally, mindful of this form of risk if for no other reason, the *financiers* while they lasted provided their services at high cost. The Bourbon kings borrowed from tax farmers, from collectors of the revenues contributed by the provincial estates and the clergy, and through the agency of municipalities. For reasons to be discussed in a moment, the monarchy could not borrow by the efficient method of direct treasury issues attached to a specific revenue stream. It was not until after 1750 that royal debt of that type began slowly to emerge, but it never dominated Bourbon finance.

Administratively, there was no dominating central treasury to keep track of the crown's financial position, nor were the sums that were received and disbursed by various entities brought under current and comprehensive accounting. Royal accounting was either fragmentary or clogged by medieval irrelevancies. Some monies traveled ancient paths, and some traveled no traceable path, or at least none that could be trusted, because so much of financial administration was expediential and dominated by private agency. As John Bosher has observed in his book *French Finances*,

> For all practical purposes the accountants were private businessmen, and the Crown could control them only by occasional legal process, not by continuous administrative direction. It follows that the financial administration was not a bureaucracy even in the loosest sense of that abused term.

Finally, there is the matter of taxation. Whether the people of France in the eighteenth century were overtaxed or undertaxed, and whether the burden of taxation fell more heavily on the poorer classes in France than in Britain, are matters of dispute. Two things seem clear, however: one is that the French people as a whole, notwithstanding their copious expressions of grievance and outrage, paid less per capita than the British; the other is that the French government had less to show for its fiscal efforts. Practically all French royal taxes, direct or indirect, were collected by intermediaries. Moreover, there was a corrosive drain on royal revenue from the pervasiveness of venality (the sale of offices); in most cases the original sale price actually functioned as a loan and the annual salary as an interest payment.

Why the French monarchy of the Old Regime, administratively advanced in so many ways, was worse than backward in respect to its financial arrangements is a deep and difficult question. Whether in the early years of Louis XIV's rule Colbert might have tried to reform treasury administration along English or Dutch lines is by no means certain, but the recurrent pressure of heavy royal spending and borrowing made it difficult to defy or sidestep the *financiers.* In the largest sense the answer may be that the Bourbon kings considered themselves above it all. By the laws of absolutism the king could not be compelled to pay his debts, a point that goes a long way toward explaining the necessity of borrowing through intermediaries. There was also an issue of prerogative: the king, it was held, should not be required to expose his finances to public scrutiny. (Some of Charles II's absolutist-minded courtiers raised this point when the English treasury reforms of the 1660s were instituted but he did not agree with them.) Yet one must ask why, somewhere along the line, the Bourbon kings were not persuaded by trusted advisors or councils of state that reforms had to be undertaken. Actually, reforms were from time to time proposed, but they were defeated by near-term revenue concerns and especially by the entrenched influence of the *financiers.*

These great men of finance, who were regarded as a necessary evil at best and often ended as victims when they lost monarchical favor, ultimately made the monarchy itself their victim. During the 1780s when a huge naval debt had created a dangerous financial situation, jealous contentions happened to erupt among some of the leading *financiers,* and the resulting financial crisis opened the way toward the French Revolution.

The Rise of the Atlantic Commercial Systems. Both British and French commerce grew dramatically during the eighteenth century. Both nations had established transatlantic colonies in the seventeenth century and in each case the metropolitan governments undertook during the second half of that century to integrate them in an imperial-commercial system, a "mercantile system" as Adam Smith termed it. Whatever the initial failures, the statistical record of eighteenth-century trade shows that in both cases their efforts were ultimately successful. The most astonishing increases occurred in the Atlantic basin. The nexus was the West Indies.

No attempt will be made to retrace the history of this development. What will be offered here is a comparative discussion of these two imperial-commercial systems in the eighteenth century. First I shall take up four aspects in which the goals and achievements of the British and French systems were broadly similar: production and sale of new commodities; increase of national shipping; establishment of naval bases and entrepôts; nurture of the state's financial capacity. After this, two most important differences will be identified and their impact considered.

Most discussions of eighteenth-century colonial empires and of mercantilism focus on commodities and, clearly, both Atlantic systems increased their production and seaborne trade in sugar, coffee, tobacco, indigo, rice, and cotton. Following in the footsteps of the Dutch, England doubled, by some measures tripled, its transoceanic trade between 1660 and 1700.

Although in the period after 1714 British total trade in the Atlantic basin continued to grow impressively, the fact is that in the same period French Atlantic trade grew faster. In the 1720s the total seaborne commerce of France, measured by cash value, amounted to about half the British total; in the 1780s it was nearly equal. The monopoly companies founded by Colbert, though drained of profits by their operatives, leaving the state to hold the financial bag, nevertheless had laid the groundwork for later growth. In the early 1720s, French Atlantic trade was freed from the monopoly companies and belonged thereafter to the merchants of the ports. The periods of greatest growth were 1730–1755 and the 1780s. Around 1740, the growth of Saint-Domingue (Haiti) began to dominate, and as early as 1750 five times as many slaves were imported by Saint-Domingue as by Martinique or Guadeloupe.

The dominant commodity in both the British and French islands was, of course, sugar, and its production depended utterly on slave labor. Not all slaves were field hands; some were household servants; some were skilled in sugarcane processing and other trades. But the stark fact is that these humans were treated as a commodity and their death rate in the islands (let alone the passage from Africa) was extremely high and did not come just from tropical diseases but also from overwork. From 1708 to 1735, 85,000 slaves were imported to Barbados with the effect of lifting the total slave population from 42,000 to 46,000. By 1790, the British West Indian islands as a whole had received 1,230,000 Africans to achieve a black population of 387,000. In the French islands the pattern was the same: huge importation and a high death rate.

In both cases the great growth of West Indian production was bound up not only with the commerce in slaves but also with a commerce in reexports. This was especially the case with France. Between the 1720s and 1780s, France's exportation of domestic products grew three-fold; her reexportation of colonial products grew eight-fold. Some of the reexports went to the Levant. Most went to German ports in northern Europe, where they accounted for 60% of the value of French trade to those ports. France's reexports grew from a level of 55% of Britain's reexports in the 1720s to 90% in the 1780s, and the high value of colonial products gave France a favorable balance of trade with northern Europe.

An argument can be made—I have outlined it in an article entitled "Maritime Strength and Atlantic Commerce"—that the increase of national shipping was the British system's top priority. The earliest Navigation Acts (1651, 1660) were intent on this goal, and the pattern of enforcement in the eighteenth century suggests a high degree of pertinacity. The main object was to build up a large national pool of experienced seamen for the use of the navy in time of war. One reason the transatlantic fisheries were so much valued was that they were "nurseries for seamen." But it was also useful to have a large number of ships available to answer the logistical needs of overseas campaigning. In France, however, the top priority may have been different. Colbert's decision to build up French shipping was part of a larger program to reclaim the commercial activity of France from Holland, since much of French Atlantic commerce in the seventeenth century was not only carried on in Dutch ships but managed by Dutch businessmen in French ports. Still, Colbert knew France needed a navy (sooner or later the Dutch were likely to use their navy to resist his program) and therefore France needed more seamen, but it was not his primary goal. Whatever Colbert's motives, after 1714 France's Atlantic and reexport trades were normally carried on with French ships. One interesting difference between the two nations was that French shipping was based on French ports whereas in the eighteenth century British shipping came to include a large proportion of British Empire shipping; the Navigation Acts allowed New Englanders to operate vessels and crews anywhere in the British trading system, and in the period from 1714 to 1776 about 30% of total British shipping was American.

Overseas bases served three main functions: as entrepôts; as naval refreshment and repair facilities for stationed cruisers, and sometimes large squadrons in time of war; and as privateering centers. Louisbourg was mainly an entrepôt. Port Royal, Jamaica, Cap Français (Cap Haitien), and Fort Royal (Fort-de-France), Martinique served all three functions. English Harbor, Antigua, was mainly important as a naval station. In wartime, such bases were primary targets. The capture of an enemy base served at once to reduce depredations upon one's own trade while depriving an enemy of advantages for protecting of his own. Yet, without an established colony surrounding it, an overseas base was not only difficult to sustain but extraordinarily dependent for its safety upon both seapower and an expensive garrison (Gibraltar was a clear case in point). Even stout fortifications provided no more than temporary safety. The French found this out twice at Louisbourg. Great Spanish Caribbean strongholds such as the ones at Cartagena and Havana, if they could hold out for a few weeks, were protected by mosquitoes which propagated yellow fever among the besieging soldiers. Louisbourg's mosquitoes lacked this capacity.[3]

As remarked at the outset of the chapter, Early Modern regimes were keenly intent on the financial benefits of Atlantic commerce. First, there was the quest for specie and the fear that access to specie would be blocked. Frenchmen were alarmed because it appeared that British domination of trade at Lisbon was, in effect, monopolizing

Brazilian gold. Englishmen were continually anxious lest the Bourbon connection should place the trade of Spanish America under efficient French control, and thus cut off British trading for silver that was based (mainly) on Jamaica. In addition to raising up seamen, one reason why the Newfoundland fisheries were important, to both powers, was that the dried cod were chiefly sold to Iberia, thus helping to earn specie returns. Finally, this concern for precious metals was the main reason why each nation was wary lest the other get the upper hand at Cadiz, the leading entrepôt for (legitimate) Spanish-American trade.

Finally among the similarities, there was the concern for finance. The concern was intense on both sides, but there was a difference with regard to the availability of customs revenue. The British government operated a well-established customs service which had become geared entirely to external trade. A substantial revenue was thus raised at British ports, and the particular ("enumerated") colonial products that were required by the Navigation Acts to be shipped to England were in many cases dutied. For instance, in 1675 tobacco duty accounted for 25% of English customs revenue. (Customs officers were established at British transatlantic ports too, but before 1763 their intended function was enforce regulations aimed at channeling trade rather than generating revenue.) The customs in Britain itself continued to provide a substantial revenue in the eighteenth century, even though that branch of revenue did not grow as much as the Treasury hoped.

By contrast, the French customs system was not very efficient, nor was it clearly focused on external trade. French customs were collected by the Farmers General (a monopoly company) and not just at the ports but at internal barriers and check points. Reformers sought to rid the kingdom of the internal tariffs but it was not done, and therefore the customs records that survive do not make it easy to separate revenues generated by French maritime trade from those generated internally. The French monarchy tapped the wealth of the Atlantic-oriented ports—principally Bordeaux, La Rochelle, Nantes, and Saint-Malô—mainly by means of direct taxes on the municipalities and by mobilizing their capital for loans.[4]

The usual historical emphasis on colonial commodities and monopolized colonial markets conveys the impression that the British and French governments were mainly concerned with avoiding purchase from foreign sources and maintaining protected markets. This accords with commonplace ideas about mercantilist doctrine and its influence, but results in far too narrow a view of policy, especially in the case of Great Britain, but also in the case of France. Just to cite one salient fact, the emphasis on import substitution and market monopoly ignores the palpable linkage between magnified colonial production and growing levels of reexportation to Europe (especially northern Europe), a practice which both British and French traders pursued vigorously and successfully—and with strong government approval. This fact, one of many that could be mentioned, serves as a reminder that, from the state's viewpoint, commodities were means to other ends. Chief among these ends were increased national shipping and seamen, influx of gold and silver to support the currency as well as fiscal and financial needs, and new sources of revenue and wealth which might be taxed or loaned. Both nations pursued these goals with determination.

The great differences between the British and French Atlantic maritime systems concerned colonial settlement and naval protection. After examining these we shall observe how they affected each system's degree of dependence and vulnerability.

In the Caribbean, the patterns of original settlement were similar. The Lesser Antilles were populated first, then the larger islands of Jamaica and Saint-Domingue. In the eighteenth century the proportion of white settlers sharply diminished. A 1687 census of the French islands showed a total of 19,000 whites and 27,000 slaves. Fifty years later the number of whites was about the same (20,000), but the slave population had multiplied 10 times. Most of the whites who remained were young, seeking their fortunes or trying to put their inherited plantations on a good footing before leaving, and hoping not to die first of disease. As a result, in 1715 the median age of whites of both sexes in Barbados, for instance, was 19. As one British islander remarked, "We have assistant judges sitts upon the bench that are minors." After 1740, the greatest growth occurred in Jamaica and Saint-Domingue where fresh acreage was available, especially for sugarcane and coffee. By the later 1780s, Saint-Domingue had a slave population of about 400,000, in comparison with 84,000 on Martinique and 89,000 on Guadeloupe. The ratio of slave to white population became at that point extreme: 13 to 1 in Saint-Domingue, versus 8 to 1 in Martinique and Guadeloupe. With its extensive territory and mountainous hinterlands, Saint-Domingue was at great risk of becoming ungovernable, and when French revolutionary politics hit the island in the 1790s, its slave system and plantation production disintegrated.

The truly great difference between British and French colonial settlement lay in North America. Both nations began with fishing

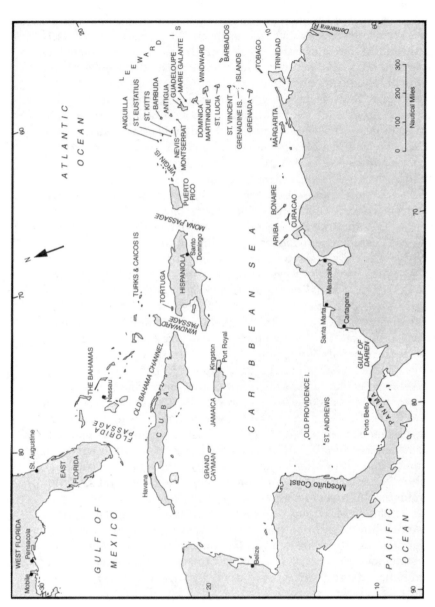

THE CARIBBEAN

on the Grand Banks and small settlements on the mainland that were dedicated to no particular economic task. After 15 years Virginia colony, then Maryland and later North Carolina, began to prosper from tobacco planting, but that was not the original plan for them. The Middle Atlantic and New England colonies remained colonies of settlement, earning their way by agriculture, fishing, and shipping and, in time of war, privateering. The settler population in British North America grew at an extraordinary pace, both from natural increase and periodic surges of immigration. In 1700, the white population was 234,000; in 1750 it stood at 964,000 (with the black population added, 1,206,000), and in 1770 at 1,816,000. (The population of England and Wales in 1750 was about 6,200,000.) With minimal direction from London and little more than the rudimentary essentials of governance, North America grew up to become a great market for British exports, a fact that became well known in British manufacturing centers. Whereas in 1700 the West Indies had received more British goods (by value) than North America, by 1750 North America received double the amount sent to the West Indies. The capacity of North American colonies to purchase British goods was limited, however, by their chronic shortage of money; for replenishment they depended heavily upon their own trade with the West Indies, chiefly selling flour and lumber. The key point is that, between 1714 and 1750, North America rose to a prominent position in the British Atlantic trading system.

Nothing like this can be said of French North America. Emigration to New France was thin; non-Catholics were screened out; Quebec and its riverine satellites were ruled by a military-bureaucratic elite. The *habitants* were brave and armed, but the colony could not survive without a costly permanent army plus the cooperation of Native Americans. The fur trade was the financial mainstay, and that too of course depended upon Native Americans. The prospects for a transatlantic shipbuilding industry that seemed so promising did not materialize, but Canadians built excellent canoes. The growing season for grain was short and chancy, and the St. Lawrence River was closed by ice half the year. Far from supplying the French West Indies with food (as authorities in Paris imagined it should), Canada could not even meet the basic provisioning needs of Louisbourg, and often its harvests were so deficient as to necessitate food importation from France. The French West Indies were fed initially by exports from France, Ireland, and Denmark, but increasingly they had recourse to the cheaper and more convenient food supplies of British North America. This trend was reinforced by metropolitan France's refusal to import molasses from its own sugar islands (the brandy interest was able to fend off rum). And so, legally or not, French molasses went to British North America—the prohibitive duty imposed at the behest of the British sugar planters in 1733 was not enforced at Boston—and food went to the French islands in return. Clearly, Canada, Louisbourg, and the French West Indies (and Louisiana for that matter) were drawn into the orbit of British North America's prodigious economic growth. The French Atlantic system became dependent upon its rival.

The second major difference stemmed from the French navy's inferior capacity to protect French trade. It must be realized that there was no chance of sea control being made absolute in the age of sail. On both sides convoys were the common practice during eighteenth-century wars, and the weaker naval power, as France generally was, could still hope to evade, and often to protect by naval escort, its major commercial and expeditionary sailings. For commerce there was the option of neutral shipping. Britain made less use of this, but France came to depend upon it in wartime as a matter of policy; upon the formal declaration of war with Britain in 1756, the French colonies were permitted by decree to carry on their trade in neutral vessels. This was especially necessary for the trade to northern Europe, which Great Britain by its naval power and geographical position could easily bring to a standstill. In the 1750s, the British government, determined to deprive France of the economic and financial benefits of seaborne trade in wartime, responded to the use of neutral shipping by instituting a policy that would remain famous in maritime history, the "Rule of War of 1756": neutrals were warned that the British navy would stop and search ships of all flags to see if they were carrying goods for a belligerent adversary. The practice was regarded by the international maritime community as outrageously high-handed, but the high hand was upheld by the British battle-fleet and when all the protests were heard and acknowledged, that was that. Deterred from sailing by offshore British cruisers, waiting interminably for convoy escorts to materialize, facing the risks of loss by capture, and suffering from the diversion cargoes to neutral vessels, many French shipowners responded by switching over to privateering.

Observing the secular growth of French shipping during the century, one must recognize the merchants' and shipowners' remarkable adaptability and resilience, yet the sharp downturns of trade that were common in wartime were devastating. In fact, the wartime disruption of external trade was one reason why the monarchy could not give up internal tariffs; a purely external system of tariffs would have meant a sharp fall off of customs revenue in wartime.

All in all, the French Atlantic system, notwithstanding its impressive growth in the eighteenth century, experienced chronic dependence as well as recurrent and serious disruptions in time of war. Were there no weaknesses of an equally serious nature in the British Atlantic system? The broad answer is that the British system's problems were temporary rather than chronic, except perhaps in one respect where the issue is controversial.

Two points are clear. First, British shipping was highly vulnerable to enemy privateering. When war broke out the French rapidly flooded the seas with privateers, before Britain could mobilize and build enough cruisers to cope. Also, there was the problem of manning the Royal Navy. Britain's surging wartime requirements for naval seamen, for privateering crews, and for deploying supply ships and troop transports were added on top of undiminished needs for commerce. Whereas the reduction of French navigation and trade in wartime allowed a release of seamen for the French navy and privateers, reduction of commerce was not tolerable to Britain: aside from the impact on the domestic economy, the ongoing returns of trade were crucial to carrying on long wars of financial attrition. The consequence was a wartime need for seamen that posed a problem of huge proportions, and the use of impressment as a means of solving the problem was corrosive to public life. On the other hand, the necessity of dealing with this problem—the concept of "challenge and response" fits here—forced the nation to enlarge its stock of the most vital resource of seapower in the age of sail.[5]

In terms of commerce, we have seen that the French Atlantic system involved certain chronic weaknesses. Can the same be said of the British system? It is an interesting question and any response must center on the eighteenth-century rise to importance of the British North American settlements. They were a substantial element in the strength of the British Atlantic shipping industry. They became the most efficient suppliers of food for the West Indies. They became a flourishing market for British manufactures, a market that no European power could seriously try to close down. And their economic and maritime growth was by no means slowing down as the century progressed. The metropolitan country was thus placed in a position where the prosperity of North America was becoming ever more significant—indeed vital to the growth and success of the system. As it became more and more evident that these colonial "children" of the American mainland were growing rapidly into a powerful commercial and maritime adulthood, it was easy to worry about signs of unruliness as well as to believe that one reason they were prospering so mightily was that they had not borne their proper share of the costs of imperial defense. After 1763, such thoughts dominated British policy toward America. The actual seriousness of the imperial problem as it was thus defined must still be regarded, however, as a matter for historical controversy, and it is too large a subject to be taken up here.

Yet it should be noted that the problem posed by the growth and conduct of British North America was generated not by failure but by extraordinary commercial and maritime success. It should be further noted that if an imperial solution was missed in the 1760s, that was not just because the British government wished to extract a substantial revenue from America. At that moment in time the government, confident in its supremacy and in some respects willfully ignorant, failed to pursue the only line of policy that could have worked, namely a continuance of the de facto modes of commercial and political reciprocity that had hitherto prevailed. For in fact the impressive growth of British North American commerce and settlement had been achieved during the century before 1760 through selective modification and relaxation—sometimes deliberate, sometimes neglectful—of the early laws of colonial trade, and under a light imperial grip on the political life of the settlers. In the 1760s imperial reformers at Whitehall sought to change the situation in both respects. The moment had come, they believed, to define rigorously who depended upon whom. They overreached, with an ultimate result that is well known.

The British government's failure to handle what it considered to be a serious North American problem in the 1760s suggests the most important point to bring out in conclusion. The reforms that backfired were motivated by Whitehall's genuine anxiety about the future of the British Atlantic fiscal and maritime system. The system's vitality, dependability, and utility to Great Britain mattered deeply—however correct or flawed the diagnosis and remedies may have been—for the nation's security was seen as resting without question upon financial and maritime capacity, to which the Atlantic system had become a major contributor. The posture of Versailles was of a different character. After Colbert, the French government displayed, with rare exceptions, a mixture of carelessness, capricious intervention, inconstancy, and often excessive exploitation. At bottom, the Bourbon monarchy's attitude toward the French Atlantic system was akin to its attitude toward its institutions of public finance. They were matters of concern, to be sure, but they were appurtenances rather than essentials, more to be used than cared for. In the final decades of the Old Regime this attitude was changing, as the policies of Choiseul and Vergennes indicate, but even then the court's attention was diverted by other concerns that were seen to be more vital.

NOTES

1. D. W. Jones's *War and Economy*. (Oxford, 1988) uses the wars of 1689–97 and 1702–14 for an extended case study of this problem.

2. Peter Mathias and Patrick K. O'Brien, "Taxation in England and France 1715–1810," *Journal of European Economic History,* 5 (1976), pp. 601–650.

3. See John Robert McNeill's *Atlantic Empires of France and Spain.* (Chapel Hill, 1985), chapter 4.

4. *E.g.,* John G. Clark, *La Rochelle and the Atlantic Economy during the Eighteenth Century.* (Baltimore, 1981), p. 18.

5. For statistics, see David J. Starkey, "War and the Market for Seafarers in Britain, 1736–1792," in L. R. Fischer and H. W. Nordvik, eds., *Shipping and Trade, 1750–1950.* (Pontefract, 1990).

SUGGESTIONS FOR FURTHER READING

Daniel A. Baugh, "Maritime Strength and Atlantic Commerce: The Uses of 'A Grand Maritime Empire,'" in Lawrence Stone, ed., *An Imperial State at War: Britain from 1689 to 1815.* (London, 1994), pp. 185–223.

John Brewer, *The Sinews of Power: War, Money and the English State, 1688–1783.* (New York, 1989).

Richard Bonney, "The State and Its Revenues in *ancien-régime* France," *Historical Research,* 65 (1992), pp. 150–176.

John Bosher, *French Finances 1770–1795: From Business to Bureaucracy.* (Cambridge, 1970).

Paul Butel, "France, the Antilles, and Europe in the Seventeenth and Eighteenth Centuries: Renewals of Foreign Trade," in James D. Tracy, ed., *The Rise of Merchant Empires.* (Cambridge, 1990).

Julian Dent, *Crisis in Finance: Crown, Financiers and Society in Seventeenth-Century France.* (London, 1973).

P. G. M. Dickson, *The Financial Revolution in England: A Study in the Development of Public Credit, 1688–1756.* (London, 1967).

William J. Eccles, *France in America.* 2nd ed. (East Lansing, Mich., 1990).

D. W. Jones, *War and Economy in the Age of William III and Marlborough.* (Oxford, 1988).

John Robert McNeill, *Atlantic Empires of France and Spain: Louisbourg and Havana, 1700–1763.* (Chapel Hill, NC, 1985).

Patrick O'Brien and P. A. Hunt, "The Rise of a Fiscal State in England, 1485–1815," *Historical Research,* 66 (1993), pp. 129–176.

Henry Roseveare, *The Treasury, 1660–1870: The Foundations of Control.* (London, 1973).

16

AMERICAN COLONIAL COMMERCE

Benjamin W. Labaree

The sea connects all parts of the world, its peoples, its resources, its cultures. The broad Atlantic hid from European view the vast continents of the Americas until, paradoxically, it provided the means by which Europeans led by Columbus, the Cabots, Vespucci, and other mariners at the turn of the sixteenth century encountered, gradually explored, and eventually colonized the Americas over the next two centuries. Then that self-same Atlantic Ocean became the highway by which the resources and produce of the New World would so greatly enrich the Old. Although the Spaniards gained the first and apparently greatest riches, their South American gold and silver mines were eventually exhausted. Having acquired a foothold along the middle latitudes of the North American coastline, Great Britain methodically eliminated its competition for empire, first by removing the Dutch from the Atlantic carrying trade by 1660 and a century later by ousting the French from virtually all of their North American possessions. Long before that, however, the British Empire had established itself as the premier colonial power of the Atlantic world.

The success of what historians used to call the "old British Empire" can be attributed to a number of factors. First, its American colonies ran through 40 degrees of latitude, from the tropical islands of Trinidad, Barbados, Jamaica and other possessions in the Caribbean to the subarctic lands around Hudson Bay. Its overseas possessions thus produced the widest possible variety of goods, few of which competed with the produce of Great Britain itself. Second, unlike the French and Spaniards, the English actively encouraged the settlement of their overseas dominions by giving colonists free land and extensive political rights. Third, although like other mercantilist powers the Britons valued their overseas possessions primarily as providers of raw materials, they realized, as their rivals

163

did not, that those colonies could also become significant markets for the mother country's manufactures. They also permitted colonial settlers to participate in trade within the empire, not only with the mother country but with other colonies as well.

Resources. A survey of British dominions in North America during the seventeenth and eighteenth centuries illustrates the remarkable variety of their natural resources. From the Hudson Bay Company trading posts Great Britain tapped the rich fur resources of the North American interior by trading with Native American tribes. At the continent's northeast corner, the island of Newfoundland gave access to the world's most abundant fishing grounds, the Grand Banks, as did Cape Breton Island, and Nova Scotia. The latter was taken from the French in 1713. Until the end of the Seven Years War in 1763, however, France controlled most of the interior of Acadia, and both British and French possessions in this area were sparsely populated, making the development or exploitation of other resources like timber difficult to achieve.

To the south and west lay the province of New England, densely populated by New World standards. Here fish, fur and forest became the basis for the region's expanding maritime trade. Here too the role of the sea as connector was most readily apparent. Settlers required vessels to reach the fishing banks offshore. Shipbuilders needed timber with which to build those vessels as well as ships to carry the fish, the furs, and forest products to markets in other colonies and overseas. The glaciation that had provided New England with many small harbors had also created numerous rivers that made land transportation difficult. Coupled with the poor soil and challenging climate these facts encouraged numerous enterprising New Englanders to turn to the sea for a living. Most of the settlers remained subsistence farmers through the colonial period, but some of the farms, especially along the eastern seaboard where grazing was good, produced surplus livestock, meat products, and vegetables for market.

The middle colonies, New York (formerly New Netherland) Pennsylvania, and Delaware, depended at first on furs for a marketable commodity. But here both climate and topography encouraged agricultural enterprise. An abundant labor force of indentured servants soon turned the broad fertile valleys of the Hudson, Delaware, and Susquehannah Rivers into productive fields of wheat, corn, and other grains. A lively coastal trade quickly developed, built around the shipment of flour and other grain produce from these so-called "bread colonies." Shell-fishing in New York and Delaware bays provided another source of food. The region's topography did not provide so many natural harbors as in New England, with the important exceptions of New York and Philadelphia, both of which had excellent access into the interior. Until the early eighteenth century much of the region's commerce was carried in vessels from the mother country or the other colonies, but then both New York and Philadelphia grew rapidly as major seaports.

Nature most favored the British colonies located along the shores of Chesapeake Bay and the Carolina coasts. Excellent soil, relatively flat terrain well drained by numerous creeks and rivers, and above all a moderate climate and lengthy growing season made them particularly well suited for plantation agriculture. Almost from their founding the southern colonies imported African slaves for labor and exported valuable market crops, especially tobacco from the Chesapeake and North Carolina, indigo and rice from South Carolina, and in the eighteenth century, Sea Island cotton from Georgia.

Trade Markets. In a world in which European rivals believed they were competing for a finite amount of world wealth, the goal of seventeenth-century mercantilism was the "self-sufficient empire." In what would be called today a "zero-sum" situation colonies provided their nation with a source of raw materials and deprived their rivals of those same resources. In time they could also become markets for the mother country's manufactured articles. Furthermore, surplus goods produced by one's colonies could be used to acquire needed materials from other countries. Finally, by restricting the carrying trade within one's empire to its own ships an imperial power could encourage a wide range of maritime activities.

Laws of trade (more commonly known as navigation acts) provided the means for carrying out the policies of mercantilism, along with a navy powerful enough to enforce their terms against interlopers from other nations. The British Empire was built on a series of laws originally enacted by Cromwell's Commonwealth in 1650 that were reaffirmed and expanded under the Restoration government of Charles II in the 1660s. Together the most important of them provided, first, that trade between ports within the empire was reserved for British or colonial vessels (i.e., built and owned in Great Britain or the American colonies). Second, certain specific ("enumerated") articles, including sugar, tobacco, cotton, indigo, rice, and dyewood (naval stores would be added later), could only be exported to the mother country. These were the commodities that England hoped to use itself, distributing the surplus throughout Europe for its own profit. And some of these materials, notably naval stores and indigo, were so important to England that it offered bounties for their production. Third, to prevent competition with producers at home Great Britain prohibited colonial artisans from sending certain products, ironware and hats were the most significant, into its other colonies. Finally, Britain alone among the imperial powers of Europe, recognized the importance of its colonies as markets for their own manufactures. Similar goods from other countries (except wine and salt) could only be imported into the colonies via Great Britain, where they faced high tariffs. The Navigation Acts were administered by the Board of Trade, a committee of the Privy Council, and were enforced through custom houses located in the major ports throughout the empire, by the vice-admiralty courts (no juries), and ultimately the Royal Navy.

Under the English mercantile system the American colonies could and did trade with the colonies of all other nations that permitted them to do so. They could not export enumerated goods like tobacco to those foreign colonies, of course, or trade with the possessions of Britain's enemies during wartime. Some goods, like molasses from foreign West Indian islands, were dutied after 1733. Colonial merchants could carry enumerated goods to Great Britain in their own ships (i.e., a Boston vessel might carry Virginia tobacco to Glasgow, or Barbados sugar to London) and after 1735 they could carry rice to ports south of Cape Finisterre. They could export nonenumerated goods to any port where a market could be found in the empire or in Europe in their own ships. One of the most important advantages of membership in the empire, particularly to New England shipwrights, was that they could sell American-built vessels to British purchasers, who could and did use them in imperial trade, an "export" worth perhaps £100,000 annually by 1770 but one which rarely showed up in official statistics.

Trade Patterns. A variety of trading patterns became well established by the turn of the eighteenth century. Among the most important were New England vessels carrying fish and lumber products, provisions, and livestock to the West Indies and returning with molasses, rum, and sugar. New Englanders also carried fish and provisions to southern plantation colonies, where they picked up cargoes of tobacco, indigo, and rice destined for England. Other vessels took masts, ship timber, pitch, and turpentine, along with rum and furs directly from New England to the old country. There these cargoes helped pay for the vast quantities of British manufactured articles in such demand back home, particularly textiles, household goods, and hardware. Vessels from the middle colonies brought wheat, flour, and other grain products to the south and West Indies, where they too picked up plantation goods to take to England. Vessels from both New England and the middle colonies carried their own produce to the Iberian Peninsula and the Atlantic islands in exchange for raisins, currants, wine, and salt. The plantation colonies of the Chesapeake and Carolinas carried relatively little of their own produce to market, but they did invest in voyages to Africa for slaves, paid for in gold, silver, firearms, and rum, among other commodities.

While in one sense "geometric," North Atlantic trading voyages were as often the "out and back" variety as the more famous triangular design. More important factors that determined how goods moved were prevailing winds, vessel sizes and rigs, and the nature and amounts of cargo. In his search for "returns," goods that he could sell in England or Europe, a Philadelphia shipowner would likely use several smaller vessels, sloop or schooner rigged, to trade with the numerous West Indies islands, and order them to bring their cargoes of sugar and molasses back home. Not until sufficient quantities had accumulated in his warehouse would he load one of his larger square-riggers, which were more suitable for the North Atlantic run to England. Because the goods carried to England were bulky raw materials, and the return cargoes finished goods, American vessels returning from the mother country almost always had extra space on board, often used for the transportation of indentured servants.

Much has been made by some authors of smuggling and other illegalities in American colonial commerce. Of course merchants in all the colonies occasionally violated the Navigation Acts if they thought the chance of detection was remote. The most common violations involved the importation of manufactured and East India goods, particularly textiles, gin, and tea from Amsterdam and other European ports. After 1733, when Parliament placed a special duty on the importation of molasses from foreign-owned West Indian islands, New Englanders smuggled in a fair amount of the illegal commodity, sometimes making a deal with the custom officer to pay a fraction of the duty (plus a generous bribe!). Another common violation involved trading with the French or Spanish West Indies during those frequent occasions when the mother country was at war with one, another, or both of her arch-rivals. Although some contraband trading went on at most ports, little evidence exists to suggest that it was extensive or that large fortunes were made through illegal activities.

As shown below the 10 principal exports of the American continental colonies on the eve of the American Revolution were the following:

PRINCIPAL EXPORTS FROM THE
CONTINENTAL AMERICAN COLONIES 1770

ARTICLE	COLONIES OF ORIGIN	VALUE £
1. tobacco	Chesapeake	906,638
2. bread & flour	Middle	504,906
3. fish	New England	397,945
4. rice	Carolinas	341,308
5. wheat, oats, corn	Middle	176,086
6. timber & products	all colonies	161,262
7. livestock & products	New England & middle	151,392
8. furs & skins	all colonies	149,236
9. indigo	Carolinas	131,552
10. whale products	New England	127,822

Total value of domestic exports: £3,356,160

Source: David Macpherson, *Annals of Commerce, Manufactures, Fisheries and Navigation.* (Edinburgh, 1805), volume III, pp. 564, 585, 596; Colonial Office Customs 16/1.

Not surprisingly, Great Britain received the largest share of American colonial exports, accounting for just over half of the total. Twenty-five percent went to the British West Indies, 20% to Southern Europe and the Atlantic islands, and the rest principally to Ireland and Africa. These figures do not include the very extensive coastal trade between continental colonies, however, or an undetermined amount of traffic with the Spanish and French West Indies. One can only estimate how much colonial trade was carried in American-owned vessels, probably less than a third at the turn of the eighteenth century but perhaps as much as half by the eve of the Revolution. On the one hand, the British shipowners dominated the valuable tobacco trade, but at the same time American merchants controlled the carriage of West Indies goods. The two peoples shared the traffic along other routes.

Economic Consequences. No historian seriously doubts what an important contribution maritime commerce made to the development of the American colonies. Its economic consequences extended through much of the continent, illustrating the principle that the sea connects all places. In New England maritime commerce provided an extended market for fish and timber, the former industry employing 4,000 fishermen and an equal number of shore-side processors. It stimulated the shipbuilding industry, over 300 vessels being built annually by the 1770s, and employed thousands of mariners. Farmers living within a day or two of the coast could export their meager surplus produce and find wintertime employment making shingles, clapboards, hoops, and staves for shipment to the West Indies. Equally important, overseas trade created the opportunity for ship-owners, merchants, and shipbuilders to begin the process of accumulating capital needed for expansion and innovation.

Further south the impact on American agriculture had greater consequences. Maritime commerce encouraged farmers of the middle colonies to grow crops like corn and wheat for market and prompted expansion into the fertile interior river valleys. It also stimulated the creation of the big flour mills around Philadelphia that became America's first factories and in the process gave hundreds of artisans the opportunity to become manufacturers. Vessels returning to the middle colonies brought thousands of immigrants, making this area the fastest growing in British America. The economies of the Chesapeake and Carolina colonies depended more heavily on overseas commerce than those of any other region of mainland America. Concentration on the culture of tobacco, rice, and indigo, in turn, led to the development of a planter class and created a perceived need for cheap slave labor. Intensive agriculture exhausted the soil of the tidewater regions by the mid-eighteenth century and encouraged migration into the interior in search of virgin lands.

Colonial Seaports. Perhaps the most important consequence of colonial American trade was the creation of seaports. By the eve of the American Revolution 19 of the 20 largest towns on the continent were seaports. Of those 19, 11 were in New England and 3 in the middle colonies, including the 2 largest (Philadelphia and New York). Though less than 10% of the population lived in these ports, they had significance far beyond mere numbers. In economic terms, their merchants, lawyers and other professionals, and shipmasters dominated their colonies by controlling exports, distributing imports, accumulating and investing capital. This group, perhaps 25% of a colonial seaport's population, provided alternative employment opportunities to the region's youth, at the least as a common laborer or mariner. These unskilled workers constituted another one-quarter of the work force. The skilled artisans, constituting almost half the population of a typical seaport, produced a remarkable variety of manufactured articles, from the smallest silver spoons to the largest full-rigged ships, newspapers, hats, wagon wheels—almost every item their customers could reasonably demand. Politically, these 19 largest seaports included nine of the colonial capitals, where contact with legislatures and royal officials opened the door to government appointments and military contracts.

Seaports were America's earliest cities, and as such were the first communities to confront urban problems like sanitation, water supply, public health, and crime, among others. The problem of the poor could not always be handled within individual families as in agricultural towns and sometimes became a major charge on the public purse. Culturally, these urban centers soon became far more sophisticated than interior towns. Schools and colleges, libraries, concerts, and theater enriched the lives of townspeople. All of the English-language newspapers in America on the eve of the Revolution were published in the seaports, for here was where printers could get the "freshest advices" from other continental colonies, the West Indies, England, and the European continent. Far more than their country cousins, the seaport dwellers had the opportunity to know what was going on in the rest of the Atlantic world.

American Revolution. Without seaports, there would probably have been no American Revolution, at least not in the closing decades of the eighteenth century. This is not, as many history textbooks have commonly suggested, because of the Navigation Acts— seaports did not protest against the mercantile system as such until the eve of Independence. Rather it is because the new British policy, introduced after the close of the Seven Years War to raise a revenue from the American colonies, struck first and foremost in seaports. The brunt of the Sugar Act (1764) and Stamp Act (1765) bore heaviest on maritime communities, as did the Townshend Act of 1767 and the Tea Act of 1773. Tangible symbols of British power abounded in the seaports. Here the governors, custom houses, admiralty courts, and troop garrisons, provided targets for the resentments, real or imagined, of the inhabitants ("the mob" if you were a loyalist; "the people" if you were a patriot). Here too could be found the means for mass communication: newspapers and broadsides, meeting places, and ready access to news from "outside," other seaports, other colonies, other lands. Urban artisans enjoyed a more flexible work schedule than their country cousins, who were often tied to the farm by the care of livestock through most of their working day. However begrudgingly, rural people except in Virginia deferred to leadership from the seaports, sending delegates to their legislatures in Boston, New York, or Charles Town, and occasionally attending protest meetings there themselves. Thousands of country people streamed into the ports of Boston, New York, Philadelphia, and Charles Town, for instance, when the East India Company's tea arrived there. America's seaports provided the grounds for confrontation between colonists and Britons long before the embattled farmers met the Redcoats at Lexington and Concord.

Atlantic maritime commerce also played a decisive role in the contest of wills that preceeded the American Revolution. British mercantile policy, succeeding in its goal of making the mother country less dependent on trade with foreign countries, ironically made it more dependent on its own continental colonies, especially as markets for the products of its rapidly expanding industries. As the Anglo-American political crisis deepened, colonists soon discovered and exploited Britain's Achilles heel. As early as the fall of 1765 merchants in several of the major colonial ports agreed not to import British goods as a protest to the Stamp Act. Six months later that tactic appeared to succeed, when British merchants fearing loss of their American business successfully lobbied the government to repeal the offensive act. Again in 1768–1770, colonial merchants boycotted British goods, this time to protest the Townshend Act. Once more the merchants of London and Bristol petitioned Parliament to accede to American demands, and the repeal of all duties save that on tea soon followed. In 1774, the British government proved that colonial commerce was a two-edged sword when it closed the port of Boston in punishment for destroying the East India Company's tea. In the ensuing months before the final Declaration of Independence both sides repeatedly "played the commerce card," the Americans reinstating their boycott of British goods, the mother country striking back by closing most other colonial seaports during the winter and spring of 1775. For a decade before the outbreak of military hostilities, the two sides struck at each other through the trading ties that had once bound them together. Interestingly enough, however, not until April 1776, twelve months after Lexington and Concord did the Continental Congress finally renounce the Navigation Acts themselves, by throwing open American ports to the vessels of all nations.

The American maritime community was reluctant to repudiate its place in the British empire because its members knew the benefits of that system to Americans had far outweighed its costs. In an era when the naval powers of the world were at war more than half the time the American colonists were protected by the world's most powerful navy, for which they paid nothing and in which they did not have to serve. They had a share in the empire's lucrative carrying trade. They enjoyed a protected market for their plantation goods, even receiving bounties for some; they could sell their vessels to

British shipowners; they were extended vast sums of money on credit, and they had access to British capital with which to expand their own enterprises. Under mercantilism the American colonies prospered beyond anyone's wildest expectations. Prosperity meant sophisticated urban centers; well-educated merchants and planters; literate artisans and farmers.

At the same time, colonial American trade had become valuable to the British as well, particularly in providing access to a rapidly expanding market (colonial America's population expanded more than eightfold in the first three-quarters of the eighteenth century). Therefore, when Americans disrupted that trade through nonimportation agreements, British leaders were alarmed. They feared, erroneously until 1776, that Americans intended political independence. The British could not afford to lose America, not only because its trade was essential to them but also because they could not risk the possibility that the colonies would fall into the hands of the French, or at least under their influence, and thereby enrich an arch-rival at Great Britain's expense. Not oppression, but prosperity, was the consequence of colonial American trade: prosperity for Great Britain that it could not risk losing; prosperity for America that led it to resent political bullying from the mother country. The result, given American conditions, was a self-fulfilling prophecy: American political independence. But, as Lord Sheffield predicted in 1782, so advantageous was the bond of commerce between the two countries that they remained each other's best trading partners for more than a century after then end of the American Revolution.

NOTE

Another version of this chapter appears in Labaree, *et al., America and the Sea.* (Mystic, 1997).

SUGGESTIONS FOR FURTHER READING

Robert G. Albion, et. al., *New England and the Sea.* The American Maritime Library, volume 5. (Middletown, 1972).

Frederick S. Allis, Jr., ed., *Seafaring in Colonial Massachusetts.* Publications of the Colonial Society of Massachusetts, volume 52. (Boston, 1980).

M. V. Brewington, *Chesapeake Bay: A Pictorial Maritime History.* (New York, 1953).

Stuart Bruchey, ed., *The Colonial Merchant: Sources and Readings.* (New York, 1966).

Converse D. Clowse, *Measuring Charleston's Overseas Commerce, 1717–1767: Statistics from the Port's Naval Lists.* (Washington, D.C., 1981).

Ralph Davis, *Rise of the Atlantic Economies.* (Ithaca, 1973).

Oliver M. Dickerson, *The Navigation Acts and the American Revolution.* (Philadelphia, 1951).

Virginia D. Harrington, *The New York Merchant on the Eve of the Revolution.* (New York, 1935).

Arthur L. Jensen, *The Maritime Commerce of Colonial Philadelphia.* (Madison, 1966).

John J. McCusker and Russell R. Menard, *The Economy of British America, 1607–1789.* Revised Edition. (Chapel Hill, 1991).

James Pope-Hennessy, *Sins of the Fathers: A Study of the Atlantic Slave Trade, 1441–1807.* (New York, 1968).

James F. Shephard and Gary M. Walton, *Shipping, Maritime Trade and the Economic Development of Colonial North America.* (Cambridge, 1974).

Ian K. Steele, *The English Atlantic, 1675–1740.* (Oxford, 1986).

17

THE EXERCISE OF SEAPOWER AND ITS CHALLENGES

N. A. M. Rodger

The older naval histories tended not to be closely interested in the practical problems involved in gaining and using naval power, with the important exception of battle tactics. The picture they presented was in essence a simple one: great fleets met and fought, and the victor was rewarded with command of the sea, from which flowed great, if not always very specific, advantages. Success was the fruit of the genius of the admiral, the talents of his officers and men, and the superiority of the national character. Failure was attributed to the corruption and sloth of politicians and civilian administrators who failed to provide the navy with the tools of victory. This was a vision which suited the Whig interpretation of history, but it was never likely to survive serious research into the archives, and as far as the Royal Navy was concerned, it was largely dispersed by Daniel Baugh's 1965 work on *British Naval Administration*.[1] With the aid of this and subsequent research we are now able to appreciate some of the many complications and difficulties of getting warships to sea and using them to effect.

Sea power was (and is) built on mastery of many advanced and difficult technologies. It was never an area in which force of character alone could surmount all obstacles. Success was the fruit of many individual skills and capacities, ashore and afloat, and of the abilities of commanders and managers to integrate them into an effective whole. Failure might be the result of failure in any one of them. Many of these essential components of sea power were, and are, obscure except to experts, but they were not the less important, and the historian of naval warfare has to be ready to understand them.

Mobilization. The nature of eighteenth-century sea power was shaped by the characteristics of navies, all of which differed in essential respects both from navies now, and from armies then. In spite of their complexity and sophistication—or rather, as a consequence of it, for complexity equaled expense—navies were not really standing forces. Officers above a certain seniority or rank in all navies, enjoyed a permanent standing conferred by their commissions or warrants, but the majority of them were not employed at sea except in wartime. Seamen and other ratings in every navy were drawn as required from the seafaring population of the country, and had no permanent connection with the fleet.

The permanent organization of eighteenth-century navies was essentially a civilian one—or, as in France, provided by a uniformed administrative corps distinct from the sea officers. This civil administration was and had to be permanent, for the great size and complexity of a navy could only be supported by an industrial and technical infrastructure which took many years to build up, and could not possibly be improvised. This was the organization which ran the dockyards, victualling yards, hospitals and gun wharfs; which designed, built and maintained ships of all sizes; which called upon, controlled or provided the resources of mines, forests, foundries and factories of all sorts; which purchased timber, masts, hemp, sailcloth, tar, pitch, iron, copper, powder, food and drink of every kind, at home and abroad. At a time when the largest private firms employed only a few hundred people, typically in a single activity such as mining or cotton spinning, the dockyards of the major naval powers employed two thousand people or more in a complex range of industrial and technical processes. In an age when the largest private enterprises were run from a single room, dockyards already required office blocks to house their managerial and clerical staff. With the significant exception of the Dutch East India Company's naval yard at Amsterdam, no private firm remotely matched the size and intricacy of even the smaller dockyards.

When navies went to war, their first and often their most critical challenge was to apply the standing administration to mobilizing the essentially part-time fighting force. The lengthy process of repairing and fitting out ships from reserve was only part of the problem, and not usually the most difficult part. More serious was the officer problem. All navies, not excepting the British, suffered acutely from the incompetence of officers, especially senior officers, on the outbreak of war. Handling a ship, still more a fleet, at sea under sail, requires a very high degree of skill, only achieved by long experience and maintained by continual practice. Officers, however talented, who had spent the past 10 or 15 years engaged in fox-hunting and county politics needed a great deal of practice to recover their former skills, and it seldom happened that squadrons, especially large squadrons, were well conducted in the opening months of a war. Decisive battles at sea, never common at any time, were almost unknown in the opening stages of a war.

The problem with ratings was quite different. These men enjoyed no half-pay and had to work more or less continually, so their professional skills did not rust ashore. The difficulty was that in every country the number of men available was governed by the number generated by the demands of commercial shipping, which never sufficed for the wartime requirements of navies, privateers and merchant shipping together. Older studies of this manning problem tended to start from the assumption that skilled men were plentiful, and invoked other explanations for the navy's shortage, but modern research (notably by David Starkey)[2] has made it clear that in the British case wartime demand for skilled seamen exceeded supply by a factor of about two to one. Moreover the British were the best provided of all the naval powers. Convinced that they ordered these things better in France, eighteenth-century British officers tended to look with envy on the French *système des classes,* which registered the coastal populations for naval service in rotation. But this system did nothing to increase the available number of seamen, and the French could not man a significant fleet by levying one-third at a time of a seafaring population which was itself only about half that available in Britain. In practice all naval powers relied heavily on compulsion to obtain the maximum possible share of the national population of seamen, and all faced acute shortages in wartime, but the British had the enormous advantage over France, and even more over Spain, of a much larger merchant fleet, and consequently manpower pool.

The navies' shortage was not of men in general; the British at least never had serious difficulty in recruiting the many technical and specialist ratings, or the marines, and unskilled landmen volunteers could usually be found in any quantity. It was able seamen who were needed, and above all topmen. To combine the skill born of long practice with the strength and agility of young manhood, seamen had to have gone to sea in boyhood. By their late teens they had mastered the difficult and arduous, but also responsible and independent business of working aloft. By their early thirties they were no longer agile enough to be topmen, though their experience was highly valuable as petty officers and forecastle men. It was the young topmen whom the press-gangs sought, not the sweepings of the streets for whom the navy had no use, and they sought them predominantly where they could always be found and with difficulty escape: at sea, on board inward-bound British merchantmen in soundings.

The significance of the French and Spanish systems of registration for naval service was not that they increased the supply of seamen, but that they provided the means to mobilize rapidly up to a certain level on the outbreak of war. Starting from the same position, France could hope to get superior squadrons to sea in the early months of the war, with the possibility of gaining a significant advantage before the slower and more haphazard British methods could fully exploit her much larger supply of manpower. This potential was well understood on both sides of the Channel, and to counteract it the British took great pains from the mid-eighteenth century onward to maintain a number of battleships (known as "guardships") in port in peacetime. Moreover in every eighteenth-century war except the American War of Independence, the British began mobilizing first and were fortunate to face either France or Spain, but not both, until the later stages of the war. Only in 1779 did the British have to reckon with a combined Franco-Spanish fleet which had mobilized early and achieved what should have been a decisive superiority in numbers.

In Command of the Sea. Such a superiority might make itself felt through a fleet action, but battle was neither the only nor even the most common means of achieving naval superiority. The doctrine of the decisive battle, promulgated to so much effect by Mahan and his disciples, has tended to obscure the fact that pitched battles were rare, and clear decisions rarer. Naval warfare, like warfare on land, was typically a war of attrition, but at sea it was a war of high technology and expense. Losses there bore on a country's financial, technical and industrial resources, and on her supply of skilled manpower, when battles on land largely involved massed infantrymen. Naval battles were important because they offered the opportunity to speed up the rate of attrition. In the two battles of Finisterre in 1747, Anson and Hawke took 12 French ships of the line, which represented a change of 24 in the balance of power, as all the prizes were in due course commissioned into British service. This was a substantial fraction of the active French fleet. The battles did not confer command of the sea in the sense of making it impossible for the French to put to sea, but they left such a disparity of forces that major naval operations and trade convoys became increasingly risky for the French. This in turn caused the decline of the rich colonial commerce, and of the many trades and industries which depended on it.

With or without battles, the process of gaining mastery at sea was invariably prolonged. In practice what it meant for the losing side was increasing difficulty and risk in mounting any major seaborne operation, and for the winning side growing freedom to exploit the sea in whatever way was desirable. No navy was ever so completely defeated that it could never get ships to sea anywhere; and no navy, however successful, was able to operate in wartime without risk. To exploit and maintain a dominant position required large numbers of frigates and smaller vessels, to serve as cruisers, scouts, convoy escorts and local patrols. It is significant that in proportion to their number of battleships, the British always built many more frigates than France or Spain, and the discrepancy increased in the course of the eighteenth century.

These smaller ships carried much of the burden of the war of attrition at sea, because most eighteenth-century naval battles were indecisive. The only possible fighting formation for ships mounting their main batteries on the broadside was the line ahead, but this was inherently a formation, like trench warfare, much stronger in the defensive than the offensive. Moreover it was difficult to form and hold a line of battle, and still more difficult to maneuver it, with ships of different size and performance. Captains and admirals needed long practice in handling their ships in company to fight effectively. Even then decisive results seldom followed unless one or another commander committed a gross blunder. Virtually all the decisive naval battles of the eighteenth century occurred when one fleet was heavily outnumbered, or failed to form a line of battle at all. Only in the 1790s were new tactical systems developed which broke the defensive superiority of the line of battle and made decisive results more accessible. Moreover the 25 years of almost continual warfare of the "great wars" against France bred a generation of British sea officers whose whole careers had been passed at sea, with no opportunities to forget their profession in peacetime. The result was a level of professional skill, and the development of professional doctrine in common to the whole navy, which had never been known before. For the first time it was possible to develop a regular system of choosing flag officers from the ablest captains and advancing them in regular progression as their experience increased. In previous wars the initial choice on the outbreak of war had always lain between admirals who had become too old and those who had not had sufficient experience, neither group being in practice. At the same time the French navy lost most of its officers and was obliged to replace them by wholesale promotions, and by borrowing from the merchant service. Villaret-Joyeuse, who commanded against Howe at the battle of the First of June in 1794, rose from lieutenant to vice-admiral in two years—and he was one of the most experienced and able senior officers available to France.

Throughout the eighteenth century, moreover, the signaling system conspired to make it extremely difficult for any admiral to control his squadron. The significance of the signal flags depended on which mast or yard they were hoisted on, which made it difficult to read them up and down a line at the best of times, and impossible when ships suffered damage aloft in action and smoke obscured the range. In all services the signals available referred only to a set list of commands, with no possibility of explanation or addition to meet particular circumstances. The British signal book consisted essentially of references to the *Fighting Instructions,* themselves a haphazard collection of orders, many of them obscure or ambiguous, reissued in constantly changing form by successive flag officers. The only method of sending any other message was to hoist out a boat and send an officer down the line to hail each ship in turn. In British practice, moreover, this was the only way to get a reply, as flagships alone were issued with a full set of signal flags. The first tentative steps at improving the British signal system were taken during the American War, but it was not until the introduction of Home Popham's "telegraphic" system in 1805 that it was possible for any ship to send virtually any message to anyone within sight.

By this year most of the decisive naval battles of the great wars had been won, and they were won by new tactical and professional methods which did not primarily rely on signaling. Older generations of admirals had found it both psychologically and practically difficult to confide in their captains, and some of them—notably Rodney—objected in principle to any subordinate, even a junior flag officer, using his initiative in any circumstances. Rodney's harsh discipline had some good effects, and he had the merit of thinking seriously and intelligently about tactical problems, but his uncompromising autocracy would have led battle tactics to a dead end even if he had had a better signal system with which to express his intentions. The most successful commanders in practice tended to be those, like Anson and Hawke, who had had the opportunity to build up a close relationship with their captains. Nevertheless Nelson's method of endlessly discussing with his captains what he wished them to do in any one of many possible situations was revolutionary, and it involved great practical difficulties and dangers. For captains to dine with the admiral at sea they had to hoist out their boats, but eighteenth-century ship's boats were not designed for the open sea and swamped easily. Before the introduction of boat davits in the 1790s they had to be hoisted out by yard tackles, and in the absence of the modern disengaging gear, slipping and hooking on in a seaway were very hazardous undertakings. To surmount these obstacles required determination and great practical skill; it was not a technique which came naturally. Nelson's reward for the effort was the crushing victory of the Nile, in which the critical early advantage was won by the initiative of Captain Foley of the *Goliath*, exploiting an opportunity which the admiral was too far away to see, in the manner which he knew would meet Nelson's wishes.

The "Nelson touch" was unique, but the successes of other British admirals of his generation owed a great deal to a combination of new tactical ideas and more flexible methods of command, exercised in a service whose professional standards were higher than ever before, and fighting an enemy critically short of experienced officers. These were obvious components of success, and for an older generation of naval historians they largely sufficed to explain British victory at sea. But naval warfare is a complex business, and there were many other influences, less obvious to the inexpert eye, but just as decisive. Among them was the long-standing French weakness in the technology of gunfounding. For much of the century the French navy had too few guns available to arm all its ships, and the suspect quality of French guns, liable to burst if overheated in action, acted as a powerful disincentive to French captains who wished to develop the rapid rates of fire so essential for success in action.

Equally important was the distinctive French tradition of warship design. French and Spanish ships of a given number of guns were almost always larger and longer than their British counterparts. British officers liked these big, handsome and comfortable ships, and extolled their merits (especially when, as captors, they were selling them to the Navy Board). But a larger ship for a given number of guns is a lightly armed ship of a given size, though this was in many cases offset by mounting guns of heavier calibers. French ships were also relatively lightly built. These long, lightly constructed and therefore highly stressed hulls were expensive to build and enjoyed short working lives. British officers liked them, but British naval administrators did not think them worth having unless they came free, as prizes. Moreover ships seldom sank in action, and defeat in battle was usually the result of heavy casualties. Thin scantlings, and the poorer timber which resulted from France's weaker credit and contacts in the timber trade, exposed French gun

crews to heavy casualties from splinters, while the British fought behind the protection of thicker timbers. Such factors were not obvious, but in battle they could be decisive.

Even more decisive in the long run were British resources in administration and maintenance. The superior quality and quantity of
British victuals made long cruises possible, while the greater resources of British dockyards, especially in dry docks, kept a greater
number of ships in repair at less cost. This last was particularly an
advantage in home waters, for no naval power possessed dry docks
in the Americas, and not least of the reasons why the Royal Navy
fought at a disadvantage during the American War of Independence
was that forces were concentrated in the West Indies, and therefore
lost the close support of the dockyards which they enjoyed in other
wars. In the East Indies, on the other hand, Hughes in his struggle
with Suffren enjoyed the inestimable advantage of three dry docks
at the East India Company's yard at Bombay, while his opponent
had to rely on the cumbersome and injurious method of careening.

All these and many other less obvious administrative and technical factors were crucial components of naval success, and it was necessary not only to excel in the individual skills, processes and resources, but to deploy the managerial competence ashore, and the
leadership and discipline at sea, to integrate all of them into an effective machine. Only then could victory be achieved, and only by analyzing all these factors can the historian hope to understand the nature of naval warfare in the eighteenth century.

NOTES

1. Daniel A. Baugh, *British Naval Administration in the Age of Warfare*.
(New Jersey: Princeton University Press, 1965).

2. David J. Starkey, "War and the Market for Seafarers in Britain,
1736–1792," in Lewis R. Fischer and Helge W. Nordvik, eds., *Shipping and
Trade, 1750–1950: Essays in International Maritime Economic History*.
(Pontefract, 1990), pp. 25–42.

SUGGESTIONS FOR FURTHER READING

P. W. Bamford, *Forests and French Seapower 1660–1789*. (Toronto,
    1956).

Daniel A. Baugh, *British Naval Administration in the Age of Wal-
    pole*. (Princeton, 1965).

Daniel A. Baugh, "Why did Britain lose command of the Sea during
    the War for America?," in Jeremy Black & Philip Woodfine, eds.,

The British Navy and the Use of Naval Power in the Eighteenth Century. (Leicester, 1988).

John Brewer,*The Sinews of Power: War, Money and the English State, 1688–1783*. (London, 1989).

John D. Byrn, *Crime and Punishment in the Royal Navy: Discipline on the Leeward Islands Station, 1784–1812*. (Aldershot, 1989).

Michael Duffy, *Soldiers, Sugar and Seapower*. (Oxford, 1987).

Michael Duffy, "The Establishment of the Western Squadron as the Linchpin of British Naval Strategy," in Duffy, *Parameters of British Naval Power, 1650–1850*. (Exeter, 1992), pp. 82–92.

Michael Duffy, "The Foundations of British Naval Power," in *The Military Revolution and the State, 1500–1800*. (Exeter, 1980).

J. R. Dull, *The French Navy and American Independence*. (Princeton, 1975).

John B. Hattendorf, et al., eds., *British Naval Documents 1204–1960*. Publications of the Navy Records Society, volume 130. (London, 1993).

Brian Lavery, et al., eds., *The Line of Battle: The Sailing Warship 1650–1840*. (London, 1992).

T. J. A. LeGoff, "Offre et productivité de la main-d'oeuvre dans les armements française au XVIIIème siècle," *Histoire Économie et Société*, II (1983), pp. 457–473.

J. R. McNeill, *Atlantic Empires of France and Spain: Louisbourg and Havana, 1700–1763*. (Chapel Hill, 1985).

R. A. Morriss, *The Royal Dockyards during the Revolutionary and Napoleonic Wars*. (Leicester, 1983).

James Pritchard, *Louis XV's Navy, 1748–62: A Study of Organization and Administration*. (Kingston & Montreal, 1987).

James C. Riley, *The Seven Years War and the Old Regime in France: The Economic and Financial Toll*. (Princeton, 1986).

N. A. M. Rodger, "The Continental Commitment in the Eighteenth Century," in Lawrence Freedman, Paul Hays & Robert O'Neill, eds. *War, Strategy and International Politics: Essays in Honour of Sir Michael Howard*. (Oxford, 1992) pp. 39–55.

N. A. M. Rodger, *The Wooden World: An Anatomy of the Georgian Navy*. (London, 1986).

A. N. Ryan, "The Royal Navy and the Blockade of Brest, 1689–1805: Theory and Practice," in Martine Acerra, José Merino and Jean Meyer, eds., *Les Marines de Guerre Européennes, XVII-XVIIIe siècles*. (Paris, 1985), pp. 175–194.

David J. Starkey, "War and the Market for Seafarers in Britain, 1736–1792," in Lewis R. Fischer & Helge W. Nordvik, eds.,

Shipping and Trade, 1750–1950: Essays in International Maritime Economic History. (Pontefract, 1990), pp. 25–42.

Nicholas Tracy, *Navies, Deterrence and American Independence* (Vancouver, 1988).

W. C. B. Tunstall, *Naval Warfare in the Age of Sail: Tactics in Battle,* edited by N. Tracy. (London, 1990).

Paul Webb, "Construction repair and maintenance in the battle fleet of the Royal Navy, 1793–1815," in Jeremy Black and Philip Woodfine, eds., *The British Navy and the Use of Naval Power in the Eighteenth Century.* (Leicester, 1988).

18

THE GLOBAL WARFARE OF BRITAIN AND FRANCE, 1739–1763: AIMS, STRATEGIES, RESULTS

Daniel A. Baugh

The first point to recognize when studying the pattern of armed conflict in the eighteenth century is that wars were an accepted a part of the natural order of international politics. War was regarded much as a lawsuit is today—a recourse whose pain, expense, and uncertainty of outcome ought to be avoided, but not always. As is well known, eighteenth-century wars may be regarded as "limited wars." The many reasons why they were limited cannot be taken up here, but it should be noted that their limited character is revealed not only in the conduct of operations, but also in the manner of their beginning and ending. Something will be said later on in the chapter about the manner of their ending, but for our purposes the manner of their beginning may be skipped. Tracing the maneuverings by which eighteenth-century wars began serves to reveal interesting features of diplomacy and domestic politics, but those matters are less important to the progress of Europe's global reach than aims, strategies, and results.

Aims. Phrases like "the struggle for empire" and "global warfare" imply that the primary objectives at stake in these wars lay outside Europe. Even if the view is confined to the western European powers this is essentially incorrect, and one must acknowledge the point straightaway because a focus on maritime and imperial history is bound to push the overseas aspects too hard. Yet the opposite view has also been pushed too hard. Some interpretations hold that the overseas aspects were small potatoes: it has been urged that these wars were really contentions for hegemony on the European continent or for its antidote, the preservation of the balance of power. As

far as France, Spain, and Great Britain were concerned, that interpretation is equally incorrect. It certainly does not describe the situation for the century as a whole. In fact, it rests more heavily than
its authors are inclined to recognize on the epochs of Louis XIV and
Napoleon, and covers only part of what was at stake even in those
epochs.

When one thinks about global aims in the eighteenth century one
must think first of the policy of Great Britain and begin by recog-
nizing that in the course of the "long eighteenth century" the emphasis of British policy shifted. In the quarter-century after 1689,
England was defending the "Glorious Revolution" and "Protestant
Succession," both of which were directly and explicitly threatened by
Louis XIV. The Grand Alliance, of which Britain's new king, William
III, was the greatest proponent, served to defend these things while
also serving the larger purpose of reducing the fearful power of
France on the continent (in other words, the balance of power). The
overseas aspects of the war of 1689–97 were indeed small potatoes.
The subsequent War of the Spanish Succession (1702–13) involved
similar aims, but now there was a significant maritime component.
For it should be noted that Britain's objection to the uniting of the
Spanish and French monarchies involved not only the balance of
power in Europe, but specific strategic and commercial concerns as
well: the fate of the Southern Netherlands, an area crucial to British
invasion defense; trade with Iberia, which was at that time important and lucrative; trade routes in the Mediterranean, which would
be easily dominated by a solid Franco-Spanish combination; and,
crucially, the trade of the Spanish Empire, which would be closed to
British and British-American traders if it came under the more
exacting supervision of France.

These specific strategic and maritime goals were carefully attended to by British negotiators of the Treaty of Utrecht, signed in
1714, a treaty that marked out a more maritime trajectory for
British policy. But in that same year, Queen Anne died and George,
Elector of Hanover, also became George I of Great Britain and Ireland. As a result, the security of Hanover was added to Britain's
other great continental concern, the independence of the Southern
Netherlands (which had been transferred from Spain to Austria by
the peace treaty). In fact, if one counts the independence of Portugal, British statesmen were aware of three specific territorial interests on the continent after 1714, and there was in addition a general
concern that the ports of Europe should not be closed to British exports. Clearly, British statesmen could not ignore the continent. Yet

it is to be remembered that there was no place in British policy for territorial annexation on the continent. Gibraltar was the only exception, and from a strategic viewpoint was effectively an island.

Public opinion was strongly oriented toward the sea. During the two decades of relative peace after 1714 the strength of the British fleet in reserve was kept at a high level even though France had virtually dismantled its fleet and Spain had scarcely begun to build one. Since Anglo-French relations were amicable until 1730, Britain's main rival in this period was Spain, and the Caribbean in particular became a focus of frictional disputes over contraband trade. In 1739 all this erupted in the War of Jenkins' Ear.

The following year, however, Prussia's invasion of Silesia threw Europe into a general turmoil which goes by the name of the War of the Austrian Succession, a war that stretched on until 1748. In reality, this war was an assemblage of particular wars for particular objects. The general effect on British policy was to give primacy to continental concerns: the defense of the Electorate of Hanover, of the Protestant Succession (in 1745–6 Britain had to prepare against an invasion threat in the south while a Jacobite army was on the loose in the north), and of the Southern Netherlands, which were nevertheless completely overrun by French armies by 1747. If this were all, one would have to say that the war of 1739–48 served to confirm the necessity of a continental accent in British policy, no matter how freely the popular press championed a maritime focus and reviled the Hanoverian connection.

This was not all, however. Although maritime objectives were submerged after 1740 by European events, even devoted Hanoverians were not prepared to deny the importance of naval and commercial supremacy. It had not escaped anyone's attention that the strength of Great Britain now lay in its navy and therefore upon shipping, mariners, naval stores, dockyards and bases; it was equally understood that Britain's capacity to engage militarily in Europe depended upon specie inflows (to compensate for military outflows) and commercial capital for financing the national debt. All of this depended greatly, as we have seen in earlier chapters, upon seaborne commerce. Independent members of parliament, whose patriotism was of a feverishly maritime and anti-Hanoverian character, were forever sounding off on this subject. Yet so long as the ingredients of maritime power were not under immediate threat, ministers of state saw no good case for favoring overseas objectives over European ones. That is why the capture of Louisbourg in 1745—inexpensively accomplished by New England soldiers and transports under the protection of the small British naval squadron already stationed there—was so important. Suddenly, France, whose army was handily conquering the Southern Netherlands, faced the prospect of losing of all of Canada. In 1746, a French fleet that was attempting to restore the position in North America was stricken by storms and shipboard diseases. On two occasions during 1747, French relief forces met with interception and defeat off Cape Finisterre. At the peace table in 1748, Louisbourg was exchanged for restoration of the Southern Netherlands to Austria and removal of the British navy's choking grip on France's trade and communication with her overseas possessions; thus Britain's maritime successes offset military failure in Europe.

It was not an expected outcome, and there is a strong case for arguing that it had a huge impact thereafter. After 1748, both countries' war aims shifted markedly toward the maritime sphere. French statesmen, who had taken satisfaction from the rapid growth of France's seaborne trade during the preceding two decades, now worried about its extreme vulnerability to British naval power, while British advocates of an aggressive maritime policy worried that French trade might resume its rapid growth. North America, which had until this time been considered far less important than the West Indies, now became a focus of these concerns. The stage was thus set for the Seven Years War. This was really two interconnected wars: a war in Central Europe that tested the survivability of Prussia, and an Anglo-French war for global maritime supremacy, which began officially in Europe in 1756 but in North America (as the French and Indian War) in 1754. The two were linked by a key element of France's grand strategy which envisioned military occupation of Hanover as the means of offsetting British successes overseas. Thanks to Prussia's military effectiveness and British intervention in western Germany, the strategy failed.

As British naval and overseas successes proliferated from 1758 onward, Britain's maritime war aims (under the influence of William Pitt the Elder) escalated accordingly. Notwithstanding the continental thrust of her strategy, France's principal aims in the Seven Years War were fundamentally maritime: the bolstering of her overseas colonies, trade, and fisheries. Her failure was all too obvious, and in the 1760s the French monarchy, under Choiseul's guidance, tried to rebuild a shattered navy. No one disputes that France's principal aim in the American Revolutionary War was to redress the balance of maritime and commercial power. It is therefore correct to conclude that from mid-century to the French Revolution not only British aims, but also French aims, strongly reflected a global "struggle for empire."

Naval Strategies. British naval strategy reflected the basic goal of command of the sea, that is to monopolize the use of the sea in wartime, and the ideal method would have been offensive: to destroy the enemy's warships at their moorings. In the eighteenth century this was almost impossible. Britain often attempted the next best thing, which was to prevent naval materials from flowing to the French dockyards; it was a poor second. In the realm of the practicable, the best strategic choice for the superior sea power had a defensive appearance. It called for bottling up the enemy's warships by superior forces while deploying cruisers at likely points of interception, thus making it impossible, or at least very dangerous, for enemy vessels of every kind— whether cruisers, privateers, troop transports, or traders—to put to sea. This may be loosely referred to as a "strategy of blockade."

The difficulties of this strategy are most easily understood by a comparison with land warfare. On land it is often not possible to avoid battle; even a fortress may be starved out unless it is rescued by a relieving army. In sea warfare, on the other hand, the inferior force simply stays in harbor and waits for the superior force to leave its station. Thus the superior force has to undertake the tedious task of standing off a port, or athwart its approaches, for as long as possible. When it leaves, the enemy ships may come out and the allegedly established "command of the sea" is thus in fact only temporary. For this reason, command of the sea requires not only combat superiority but also coverage and staying power (as explained at the end of Chapter 13). A second point emerges from a comparison with land warfare. On land it is seldom possible for any considerable force to escape by stealth and thereupon proceed to execute its mission or to ravage the enemy. In eighteenth-century sea warfare, thanks to the vicissitudes of wind and weather, a considerable force could do this. It happened quite often.

Nevertheless, given sufficient preponderance of force, the strategy of blockade was usually the best option for the British navy, regardless of whether a war's particular accent was on European or overseas campaigning. This has been widely recognized, but incautious treatments of the subject often refer to a "traditional" strategy of blockade as if it were applicable in all situations. In actuality, the strategy of blockade never became axiomatic in the eighteenth century. And if by "blockade" one means the close observation of French naval and commercial ports in order to stop all entry and exit, that was usually not possible.

To understand why these things were so, one must recognize not only the constraints imposed by wind, weather, and endurance, but also geography. Coping with the sea power of France (often allied with that of Spain) was much more difficult than coping with Dutch sea power had been the previous century. Consider the situation from north to south. The privateers of Dunkirk, protected from blockade by extensive sandbanks, had no difficulty slipping in and out. They wreaked havoc not only in the Channel but also the North Sea. Only Le Havre of all major French ports could easily be watched from English ports. In the Atlantic, the major French naval bases of Brest and Rochefort faced the open ocean, and Brest lay to windward of any English port except Falmouth. There was no easy or obvious way to blockade or even to watch these bases, and the same was true for the great commercial ports of Bordeaux, La Rochelle, Nantes and St. Malô. French naval and privateering forces, on the other hand, were well placed to intercept all shipping coming into the Western Approaches of the Channel, which is to say a very high percentage of British naval and commercial traffic.

One readily sees that, even if the lures and necessities of continental politics could have been set aside, France's maritime geography would have played a strong role in encouraging her to pursue the naval strategy that she did. French naval strategy mainly involved three sorts of enterprise. One was to send forth squadrons for the purpose of shepherding expeditions and trade; these naval squadrons, even when not inferior in strength to the British forces that were most likely to fall upon them, commonly practiced a strategy of avoidance. A second was to harass and capture British shipping. The third was invasion of the British Isles. Only the third required a measure of command of the sea for its execution. Again there was a geographical consideration: a decision to send a battle-fleet into the Channel was not to be undertaken lightly because contrary winds might easily prevent its withdrawal and there was no haven in which it could remain together yet safe from British attack. But the possibility of invasion was so frightening in England that this enterprise could be highly effective as a threat or feint—on occasions when the French government preferred not to commit itself to the expensive task of seriously preparing a true invasion army. As is well known, the French navy never aspired to a generalized command of the sea, and even the combined forces of the House of Bourbon at their height managed to operate on such a footing only fleetingly. All things considered, one might say that the main utility of French battle-fleets was to render the British navy's exercise of command of the sea more costly, difficult, and imperfect.

The most effective British response was something close to blockade, but not quite the same: the deployment of a Western Squadron, the name given to the strong fleet cruising in the Western Approaches. Although no one in the eighteenth century very clearly analyzed its advantages in writing, the placement of this squadron in principle allowed a single fleet of ships on one cruising station to fulfill several functions simultaneously. It was positioned mainly to watch Brest, but by deploying its own frigates to the southward, it could often gain notice of sailings by French convoys from the Biscay ports in time to catch up with them. (At the least, timely warning could be given to British forces overseas that a French squadron might be on the way.) It could cover the passage of British convoys in and out of the Channel. Finally it lay to windward of any possible invasion attempt. In the absence of an enemy naval base in the Channel, an invasion attempt had either to be made without the cover of a battle-fleet, in which case it could be dealt with by local forces, or the covering fleet would have to enter the Channel from the westward, in which case the Western Squadron might intercept it or track it down.

From the later 1740s for the next 80 years, the principle of a powerful Western Squadron was the focus of British naval strategy. Before then squadrons were sometimes deployed to the same location to watch, but they were not powerful enough nor did they remain long enough to deter a formidable French fleet. It took a while before the seaworthiness of British ships of the line, the growth of Plymouth dockyard, and improvements in victualling enabled the deployment of a powerful and durable cruising squadron. Within the basic strategic framework thus established, the actual practice was endlessly complex and difficult. No fleet could be everywhere at once, or cover a cruising ground stretching from Ireland to Spain, even with an ample allotment of frigates and good intelligence (both of which were often lacking). Circumstances might make it possible to divide the fleet to pursue different objectives, but there were obvious dangers in dividing one's forces when the enemy might rather easily achieve a concentration. To blockade Brest and the Biscay ports (a dead lee shore at all seasons of the year) was extremely hazardous. Yet, the alternative of positioning the fleet more safely and with less wear and tear in Torbay, or at Plymouth or Spithead, was too likely to allow the enemy to sail not only unopposed but unobserved. Different admirals had different ideas and applied them variously in changing circumstances.

The greatest defect of the strategy was its incompleteness. It could not encompass Toulon. France's second greatest naval base lay in the Mediterranean, remote from British surveillance. After 1708,

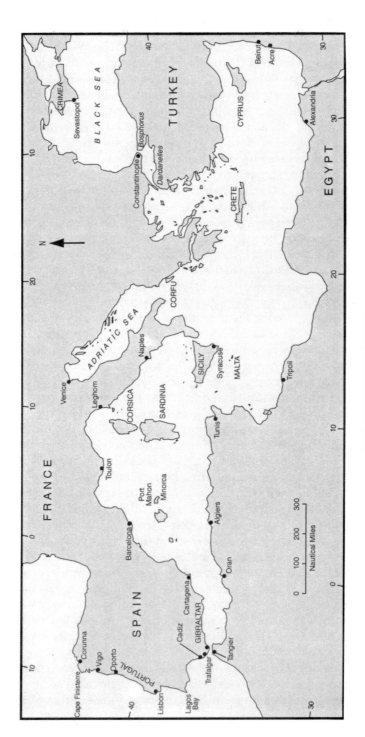

THE MEDITERRANEAN

the British occupied Minorca; its fine harbor at Port Mahon was supplied with stores for refitting, and a large battle squadron was sometimes based there. On a map, it would therefore appear that the
British navy could have easily blockaded Toulon, but in fact the prevailing winds made the task all but impossible. Because Toulon was
so difficult for the British to control, the Toulon squadron was a wild
card in naval strategy, free to intervene anywhere. Until it was neutralized, British naval operations everywhere in the world, including home waters, were not safe from interference. Toulon could not
be masked except by sending a squadron at least as far as Gibraltar,
but such a squadron was at risk of being caught between two fires
unless Brest could be very tightly watched, and that could not be
counted on. If Spain was or might suddenly become a French ally,
the problem was even greater. Thus Toulon posed grave difficulties,
and this led to British naval disgraces in the opening stages of three
wars: in 1756, 1778, and 1798. There were occasions, however, when
Toulon and the French Mediterranean forces could be conveniently
neutralized, usually when British assistance to allies called for a
strong fleet in the Mediterranean anyway. Toulon was at once
France's opportunity and her difficulty: because Brest and Toulon
lay so far apart by sea, France could never unite her fleets except by
a major operation and thus faced the risk of naval defeat in detail.

On the whole, the strategy of the Western Squadron could be, and
was, a fundamental factor in the rise of British naval supremacy. It
permitted the same fleet which often had to be kept in home waters
as a safeguard against invasion simultaneously to protect British
trade, interfere with the enemy's trade, and bring the enemy fleet to
battle if it put to sea. This economy of force left other forces free to
exploit the command of the sea which the Western Squadron obtained. So long as enemy battle-fleets lay close at hand in Western
Europe, dominance in European waters translated into dominance
in every other sea all over the world. One may not, therefore, deduce
British war aims from the locations where the heavy ships of war
were deployed. Even in the East Indies victory could be, and was, assured by the interception of reinforcements as they sailed from the
Biscay ports. Only in the twentieth century with the rise of naval
powers based outside European waters did the formula cease to
work.

Results. It is sufficiently obvious that sea control was the ultimate arbiter of military success in the global arena. Yet, when the
question of how eighteenth-century wars were won is considered the
military aspect in Europe cannot be ignored, even for wars that can

rightly be termed struggles for empire. After all, the British did have to give Louisbourg back in 1748, and probably would have had to give Canada back in 1763 if France had won the war in Germany. This is not the same as saying that eighteenth-century Britain was in danger of losing naval supremacy if France were not kept busy militarily on the continent. Nor does it say that the only real way to win a war was by fighting on the continent. This second point, however, is much at issue in current historical writings, some of which push an argument that British naval successes were irrelevant to winning: although they prevented Britain from losing and perhaps enabled Britain to enhance its wealth, wars against European powers had to be won in Europe, with armies. Only there and in that manner, one is told, could anything decisive be accomplished.

All this opens two interesting questions: one large, one a bit narrower. The large one is: how did wars end in the eighteenth century? The narrower one is: what role did decisive battles or campaigns have in bringing them to an end? Since the second is a way of approaching the first, let us begin with it. The focus will remain on Great Britain and France.

The Napoleonic era has established most of the paradigms of military history, and at the end of the Napoleonic wars, in 1813–15, there were two decisive battles, Leipzig and Waterloo. There had been "decisive" battles and campaigns earlier, most notably off Cape Trafalgar in 1805 and in Russia in 1812, but the former did not bring French naval operations to an end, even in the Mediterranean, nor did the Russian campaign cause Napoleon to bid a farewell to arms. Leipzig and Waterloo have provided the best models of war-ending battles.

Yet, where do these models apply? They certainly do not fit the eighteenth century as a whole. There was no decisive war-ending battle on land or at sea in the war of 1689–97. In the War of the Spanish Succession, Blenheim (1704) was a decisive battle, because by winning it Marlborough kept the war going on a far better footing for the allies than it would have been if Austria had been knocked out; the war continued, of course, for another nine years. Marlborough hoped that Malplaquet (1709), which in a formal sense he won, would cause France to quit the war, but it had no such effect. Despite the huge catalogue of British successes in the later years of the Seven Years War, one cannot identify a war-ending decisive battle or campaign. The year 1759 witnessed a cascade of British victories—Quebec, Lagos, Quiberon Bay, Minden, Guadeloupe—but a victorious termination was not achieved for another three years, by which time the ministry of Pitt and Newcastle, which had produced the victories, was no longer in office and Spain had entered on the Bourbon side (disastrously as it proved) to complicate the picture.

Two wars remain: 1739–48 and 1775–83. In the former, there were three campaigns that were decisive in that they contributed to ending the war: the capture of Louisbourg (1745), the British naval victories in the First and Second Battles of Cape Finisterre (May and October 1747), and the conquest of the Netherlands by French armies under Marshal Saxe, a conquest so thorough that it threatened the security of the Dutch republic, whose incapacity to fight had become plainly evident by the beginning of 1748. These were "decisive" in the sense that they created the circumstances under which the French and British (but not the Austrians) thought they must make peace; neither side won. In the American War, the decisive battles were: Saratoga (late 1777), which confirmed the French in their notion of escalating to open hostilities; Yorktown (late 1781), which tumbled the administration and brought in a British cabinet determined upon peace; and the British naval victory at the Saintes (May 1782), which reminded the ministry of Vergennes that France was well advised to come to terms. Thus, considering the whole period from 1689 to 1783, there were only two wars—1748 and 1783—whose termination was clearly shaped by decisive strategic events, and they happened to be wars that Britain drew or lost. In both of these wars, maritime victories salvaged British interests.

In addressing the question of how eighteenth-century wars ended, one must therefore recognize that victories did not often play a major role. There were many factors. In addition to irreparable losses (except by negotiation) of vital positions in Europe or overseas, or an impending danger of such losses, or serious curtailment of seaborne trade, there was the matter of exhaustion, especially in the financial sphere, where an acute shortage of specie or failure of administration might lead to collapse of public credit. Another quite common cause for a war's termination was an accidental change of dynasty which brought about a change in ministers and policy. In Britain, there were three occasions when a seismic political shift led to termination of hostilities: 1710, 1761, and 1782. In all three cases, the shift was war-related, though never entirely so. The political history of France offers similar instances. All these factors and others came together in different mixtures on different occasions. British and French armed forces fought to secure advantages; they were almost never in a position to deal a crushing blow and dictate terms.

The conclusion must be that it was never easy in the eighteenth century to predict how a war might end, what it would take to end it satisfactorily, or when the end might come. Under these circumstances, Britain, whose situation and resources were conducive to carrying on a war for a long time, enjoyed a considerable advantage. This enabled Britain to work for a moment of French exhaustion and thus to salvage vital interests in Europe as well as to maintain the most formidable foundations of seapower.

NOTE

The Naval Strategies section of this chapter has been contributed by N. A. M. Rodger.

SUGGESTIONS FOR FURTHER READING

M. S. Anderson, *The War of the Austrian Succession, 1740–1748.* (London, 1995).

Daniel A. Baugh, "Great Britain's 'Blue-Water' Policy, 1689–1815," *International History Review,* 10 (1988), pp. 33–58.

Michael Duffy, ed., *Parameters of British Naval Power, 1650–1850.* (Exeter, 1992).

Paul M. Kennedy, *The Rise and Fall of British Naval Mastery.* (New York, 1976).

Richard Pares, *War and Trade in the West Indies, 1739–1763.* (Oxford, 1936; repr. London, 1963).

Admiral Sir Herbert W. Richmond, *Statesmen and Sea Power.* Oxford, 1946.

N. A. M. Rodger, "The Continental Commitment in the Eighteenth Century," in Lawrence Freedman, Paul Hayes and Robert O'Neill, eds. *War, Strategy and International Politics: Essays in Honour of Sir Michael Howard.* (Oxford, 1992).

A. N. Ryan, "The Royal Navy and the Blockade of Brest, 1689–1805: Theory and Practice," in Martine Acerra, José Merino, and Jean Meyer, eds., *Les Marines de Guerre Européenes, XVII-XVIIIe siècles.* (Paris, 1985).

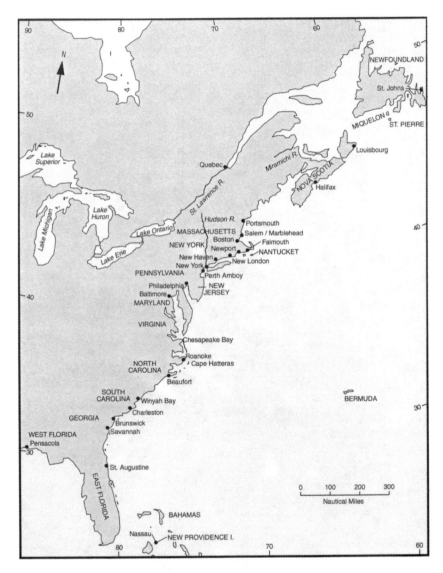

EAST COAST OF NORTH AMERICA

19

THE WAR FOR AMERICA, 1775-1783

Daniel A. Baugh and N. A. M. Rodger

The war of 1775–83 began as a war for America, but in 1778 it became a contest between Great Britain and France for global maritime predominance. At that point, it amounted to a renewal of the Anglo-French Seven Years War. The British public was therefore inclined to contrast its catalogue of naval failures with the naval successes that had marked the middle and closing years of the preceding war, and historians have done the same.

Yet despite such appearances the strategic character of this war was very different—in ways that put Great Britain under distinct disadvantages. One difference often cited by historians is that on this occasion there was no land war on the European continent and therefore no chance for Britain to hope that allied armies might divert France from maritime endeavors. In the war of 1778–83 France was free to concentrate her strategy and financial resources on her navy.

But by the same token so could Britain, and the absence of military activity on the European continent was in reality a less important factor in this war than is commonly supposed. Two other factors were of greater account: first, the difficulty and cost of the military effort to subdue the Americans; second, the fact that Spain, with its not inconsiderable fleet, became an active ally of France in spring 1779 (whereas during the Seven Years War Spain had remained neutral until almost the end). The Spanish contribution is most easily grasped by counting ships of the line (of 64-guns or more, not necessarily in active service). In the year 1780 there were 99 of these capital ships on the British navy list; France counted 67; Spain counted 54. Until the final year of the war British naval inadequacy influenced practically everything that was done and not done, both on land and sea.

Important as the capital-ship strength of the Bourbon navies was, it would nevertheless be a great mistake to attribute all the naval lapses in this war to that factor. Even before France entered the war, and notwithstanding the absence of an American fleet of capital ships (that is to say, the absence of a Mahanian sort of challenge), the British navy did not possess adequate control of the American seaboard. The underlying reason was that the American colonists were not merely a rural people "numerous and armed," but also a maritime people, long practiced in privateering and smuggling. American maritime resources were not to be ignored. As David Syrett has observed, "America in 1775 did not have a navy, but it did have a large merchant marine and well-developed shipbuilding industry." Approximately one-fourth of the shipping of the British Empire in 1775 was American-built. The combined tasks of subduing the rebellion on land and controlling the use of American waters posed a huge challenge to Great Britain and the challenge was not met.

The Opening Phase, 1775–1777. By what criteria may one justify the assertion that the British navy did not hold command of the sea on the American seaboard from 1775 to 1777? The task comprised four missions: first, to intercept American imports of guns and gunpowder, items which the American forces desperately needed from abroad, especially the latter; second, to prevent shipment of colonial exports, the commodities by which the Americans could pay for imported munitions; third, to prevent American raiders from getting to sea by imposition of an effective blockade; fourth, to protect British troop and supply transports from seizure. Since it was always more difficult to intercept inbound than outbound shipping and American imports of gunpowder were likely to come via the Caribbean (through disguised transhipments), the need for sizable cruising forces in that sea was clear. The fourth mission might be best served by convoy escorts. There is no question that Britain's war planners hoped to accomplish these missions, but the navy's watch of American ports, bays and estuaries was slow to commence and never became consistent or thorough. Not one of the missions was satisfactorily accomplished.

What accounts for this failure? Although the American seaboard extends for about 1,000 miles, that was not the main problem. The British navy overcame it in the War of 1812, and it could have been overcome in 1775. Except in New England, the Atlantic ports of the thirteen colonies were concentrated in particular locales—especially in the two large bays, Delaware and Chesapeake—and inland means of transportation from the smaller, more scattered ports was unsatisfactory. So the British task was not impossible. It did call for a large number of cruisers, but—and here lay a British advantage—there was no need to worry about interruption by a strong enemy naval concentration.

The urgent need for lots of cruisers should have been obvious in 1775, yet the buildup of the British cruiser force was wondrously slow. Even after allowing for other demands on the ship-repair and shipbuilding capacity of Great Britain at this time, a naval historian must remain puzzled by the British government's conservative, really lackadaisical, approach. Although it was standard Admiralty practice during the eighteenth century to order a half-dozen or more new cruisers to be built in merchants' yards immediately upon the outbreak of a war—they would usually be ready for service in about eight months—that was not done this time. Instead, every frigate in reserve, one after another in slow procession, was rehabilitated by dockyard workers who were already hard pressed by other tasks, such as inspecting and modifying vessels leased as troop transports. Cruiser deployment to American waters was in most cases further delayed by their being assigned as convoy for military expeditions.

This lack of any true sense of urgency with respect to the tasks of sea control is even more puzzling in the light of the reports that the Admiralty was receiving from its commander-chief in the American theater during the year 1775. The clear message was that very few of the cruisers already there could be devoted to sea control functions. Instead, they were desperately needed to answer emergencies created by the rebellion, such as providing refuge for royal governors and loyalists, conveying dispatches, and, above all, helping the army at Boston, which needed warships both for the defense of the city and for obtaining fuel, forage, and provisions now that local sources of supply were curtailed. The upshot was that nearly the whole North American squadron was devoted to services of this kind.

Even before Boston was evacuated (March 1776), it had been decided in London that a better situated base was needed. The choice was New York. Unfortunately, the huge expedition designed for the capture of New York was delayed by the difficulty in acquiring transports to carry 20,000 men across the Atlantic, an urgent need to strengthen the defense of Canada, and an ill-advised decision to support a body of loyalists in the Cape Fear River. In the event, the southern sideshow of spring 1776, which wound up attempting an attack on Charleston, had two adverse consequences. It employed warships that could have been assigned to the task of interdicting American imports of gunpowder, a commodity that had become practically nonexistent in the colonies by the end of 1775. It also delayed the main operation, for New York was to be taken not just to provide a naval base but as the place from which the great expeditionary army would march out and militarily knock the rebellion off its feet with "one decisive blow."

The fleet of Admiral Lord Howe arrived at Staten Island at about the same time the Declaration of Independence was signed in Philadelphia. By August 22nd, the Howe brothers (the army was commanded by General Sir William Howe) were ready to launch their assault. General George Washington's main force was unwisely, indeed dangerously, deployed on Long Island where it might have been cut off by the British navy and forced to surrender if the brothers had acted promptly to seal off the East River and the Sound. Except for that, the taking of New York, when it finally occurred, was a masterly combined operation, in which the navy (thanks to geography of New York harbor) played a continuing role. Half of the four dozen British warships in America were employed in the endeavor and it all took a very long time. These ships were not released for cruising until early December.

It is thus evident that, in the year 1776, the navy in North America was heavily employed in assisting military operations. Even Delaware Bay was left unattended. Throughout the year (until December) gunpowder poured into the rebellious colonies. From January to November 1776 the Americans acquired 2,150,000 pounds through importation while, notwithstanding the revolutionary government's emergency encouragements, internal production yielded a mere 115,000 pounds.

Still, Great Britain had deployed a huge army across the Atlantic Ocean—a remarkable logistical achievement by eighteenth-century standards. This army now controlled the best of all possible locations, both for military and naval purposes. From New York British forces soon extended their sway across the northern half of New Jersey, garnering declarations of loyalty from numerous inhabitants and cowing most of the rest into acquiescence. In New Jersey, the army could also acquire by local purchase a substantial share of its requirements for forage and provisions. Plans were drawn for it to move on to Philadelphia. Washington, it was imagined, would be compelled to pledge his army to the defense of the city and could be defeated once and for all. Moreover, Washington's army was in a desperate condition, short of everything and unable to get its soldiers to renew their enlistments. The Revolution's prospects on land looked bleak.

In early December 1776, the situation suddenly began to look equally bleak at sea as Lord Howe's cruisers began to take stations along the seaboard. Delaware Bay was blockaded; so was the Chesapeake. An expedition to capture Newport secured its objective within 10 days and Narragansett Bay was promptly closed. The exports of the middle colonies were totally stifled. From Philadelphia, Robert Morris wrote to Silas Deane, the American commercial representative in France, not only of the need to obtain massive credits but "a few Line of Battle Ships" too. It was the Revolution's darkest hour.

On Christmas Day, however, the situation was transformed by Washington's surprise attack across the Delaware River. Sir William Howe reacted by pulling back his garrisons, thereby reducing British occupation of New Jersey to the environs of New York. It was a fateful decision. The political repercussions of abandoning New Jersey loyalists were severe and permanent. Just as damaging were the logistical consequences; when loyalist support evaporated, so did the chance of peaceably provisioning the army. Provisioning parties had to go forth in strength as local militias harassed them in strength. Because the resounding success of Washington's brilliant attack had put spirit into the revolutionary cause, Howe's pull-back was perhaps unavoidable, yet whatever the case, the main British army now had to be fed from across the ocean, with all the expense, demands upon sea transport, and wastage that were thus entailed. This costly situation continued essentially for the rest of the war.

In early 1777, American prospects for overcoming the blockade also brightened. When the Delaware River thawed earlier than expected, the British cruisers were away refitting at Antigua. On the extremities the blockade was never well established. American trade between Charleston and the West Indies suffered a few losses, but neither Charleston nor Savannah was consistently watched. The most serious defects, however, were those in the arrangements for watching eastern New England, and in early 1777 a swarm of privateers headed from New England to the West Indies and Europe where they were given supplies in French and Dutch ports. British diplomats vehemently protested these blatant violations of neutrality, but the protests had little practical effect because the accused regimes well knew that Great Britain did not wish to add a French or a Dutch war to the American one. As for countering American shipping and privateering in the West Indies, the British cruiser squadrons based on Antigua and Jamaica were active but their numbers were woefully inadequate to the task.

It is well known that 1777 was the year when whatever chance there may of been of bringing the colonists to "a due subordination" by force of arms was lost, mainly because of General Howe's dilatory mode of taking Philadelphia and the disastrous predicament in which General John Burgoyne found himself at Saratoga in the autumn. It was also the year in which the war at sea against American privateers was lost. Initially the British situation at sea looked better. The watch on the American seaboard was somewhat improved over that of the previous year. In the spring of 1777 a considerable force (more than two dozen cruisers) plied the coasts of New England; they did not seal them off but made numerous captures. For the most part, the new warships commissioned by the state and continental navies were either contained or met and defeated. By summer, however, most of the cruisers assigned to the northern coasts were removed to serve with the expedition to Philadelphia, which went via the Chesapeake Bay; thus, once again, sea control was sacrificed to the needs of military operations.

American privateers got loose in large numbers. Their most damaging impact was in the West Indies, their most visible in European waters. The Royal Navy's ability to respond to them was quickly shown to be frail. In the West Indies the cruiser squadrons were far too small for the huge demands now thrown upon them. In home waters there were scarcely any cruisers left (finally the Admiralty ordered some built). The war against privateers in home waters had to be carried on mainly by lumbering ships of the line.

This odd development stemmed from the Admiralty's need to get ships of the line readied and manned as insurance against the increasingly obvious buildup of the French navy. All along, the First Lord of the Admiralty, the Earl of Sandwich, had kept a wary eye on the Bourbon navies. The government had permitted him to order the commissioning of a substantial Channel squadron in late October 1776 in response to disturbing intelligence of French preparations. At the end of August 1777 the British navy had 43 ships of the line in commission. Spain was reckoned to have 41 (she had mobilized for a North African quarrel); and France 23, with many more being readied. The volume of French shipments of gunpowder to the Americans—scarcely disguised anymore—signaled a French willingness for war. Thus, even before Saratoga, British authorities were forced to turn their attention anxiously to the emergent naval danger, which was both European and global. In March 1778, when France made overt its secret treaty arrangements with the American revolutionaries, everyone realized that the outbreak of a general maritime war was near at hand. Britain could only hope that Spain would remain neutral: against the combined fleets the inferiority of numbers was staggering. How had this situation come about?

Naval historians have commonly attributed it to prewar neglect, and it is broadly true that during the decade of peace after 1763 the British navy accepted a policy of stagnation, while the navy of France was vigorously rebuilt under the guidance of the duc de Choiseul. But this is not the whole story. First, France's fleet had had to recover from a level of extreme inferiority. Second, progress lapsed after the dismissal of Choiseul in 1770. Third, in the early 1770s some sweeping and ill-advised reforms introduced by Choiseul's successor threw the French dockyards into confusion. By 1775, the French navy had very plainly not made up enough ground to pose a serious challenge to Britain. The trouble was that a Bourbon alliance now seemed likely and Spain had been steadily augmenting its fleet of capital ships. To top it off, Sartine became France's new minister of marine in 1775; under his efficient management the dockyards were restocked with timber and stores, and the building program was quietly revitalized. All of this was approved, with suitable appropriations arranged, by the comte de Vergennes, the minister of state. Vergennes readily perceived that Britain's imperial civil war was offering France a maritime and imperial opportunity that "it would be a sublime effort of virtue to refuse."

The Global Maritime Contest, 1778–1783. During the opening phase, 1775–77, the British navy ordered practically no new ships of any kind. The government focused all its resources on trying to put down the American rebellion quickly. One sees the logic in this plan, but it was a gamble and it failed. Although the British began to build in 1778 and escalated the pace thereafter, progress toward closing the gap was agonizingly slow because the French yards were well stocked and continued to build. In fact, in 1780 the gap in total tonnage was wider than it had been in 1775. It required the utilization of practically every available building slip and shipwright in the realm for the British navy at last to overtake the Bourbon combination. Even then it never matched the Bourbon tonnage. But in the end it overmatched its enemies in terms of ships ready for action and skills of ships' companies. That was, however, a long way off in 1778. The next four years of naval inferiority posed excruciating strategic dilemmas and exacted humiliating defeats on Great Britain—in a now predominantly maritime war.

As noted, by the spring of 1778, war with France was clearly imminent, and war with Spain highly probable. In the face of so grave a threat, the British government decided to concentrate on home defense and the West Indies, and relegate the American struggle to a lower priority. In the circumstances, this was unquestionably a wise, indeed essential decision, but it was no sooner taken than the cabinet began to drift away from it. Germain, the colonial secretary, retained the king's confidence, and consistently argued for diverting resources away from what was now the main threat and back to the American theater for which he was responsible.

In that spring, though Spain was not yet in the war, the French had the opportunity of uniting their Brest and Toulon fleets to achieve near-parity in European waters. They chose instead to send the Toulon squadron to America, leaving the Brest fleet decisively weaker than the British, and this presented the British with an opportunity to strike a decisive blow, or at least to establish the Western Squadron with that early superiority which the experience of two wars had shown could in time become decisive. Instead, the cabinet yielded to Germain's demands and detached 20 ships of the line under Admiral Byron to pursue d'Estaing across the Atlantic.

The result was failure on all fronts. When the two home fleets, under Keppel and d'Orvilliers, met in a major engagement off Ushant on 27 July, they were equal in strength and the battle was indecisive. D'Estaing reached North America before Byron, but failed altogether to exploit his clear superiority there. He then moved on to the West Indies, where much the same thing happened. Byron in turn arrived in the islands in January 1779, and on 1 July he fought an indecisive action with d'Estaing. Both admirals brought their squadrons home about the end of the year, having spent a year and half cruising the Western Hemisphere to very little purpose.

Spain's entry into the war in June 1779 turned the strategic position sharply against Britain and the outlook was very quickly ominous. On 15 August a combined Franco-Spanish fleet of 63 sail entered the Channel, while 30,000 troops waited on the coast of France to invade. The British fleet under Sir Charles Hardy had only 39 ships of the line. What seemed to indicate an inevitable British disaster was averted by Hardy's skillful maneuvers, by the collapse of the health and victualling of the combined fleet, and by a large measure of luck, but from now on there was absolutely no margin of strength available for taking the initiative. Moreover, Britain's defensive commitments were much increased, notably by the need to defend Gibraltar, besieged by a Spanish army. Early in the new year Rodney sailed with a relief convoy; on 16 January he defeated a Spanish squadron off Cape St. Vincent, saw the transports safely into Gibraltar, and moved on to the West Indies. Soon after, a French squadron under de Guichen sailed for the same destination. The two squadrons fought an indecisive action off Martinique on 17 April, and met again in May with no clearer result. Some months earlier a great British amphibious expedition had sailed from New York to attack Charleston, which surrendered on 12 May.

In London the cabinet, unable to divine where the French meant to make their main effort, hesitated whither to send reinforcements. Having chosen, or allowed the enemy to choose, distant waters as main theaters of naval war, they were not in a position to learn what was going on in time to exercise any effective direction. For instance, when Rodney and his squadron left his station, without orders or permission, and turned up in New York on 13 September 1780, it was a complete (and unpleasant) surprise for the local admiral, and in due course for the cabinet. By abandoning his station and taking over another, Rodney also revealed the inadequacy of the traditional British system of naval "stations" with fixed boundaries to cope with the sort of war of movement over long distances which the transatlantic war had become. At sea, as on land earlier in the war, the cabinet failed to grasp the problems of command and control that were posed, and Britain's conduct of the war overseas suffered accordingly.

As the year 1781 clearly showed, only in European waters were distances short enough and communications fast enough to make it possible for the British to exploit intelligence and make usable plans. In March, the home fleet successfully relieved Gibraltar again, and on 5 August in the North Sea Hyde Parker fought the main Dutch fleet. (The British government, unyielding on the issue of Dutch shipments of naval stores for France, had acquired another adversary at sea.) In September, the Franco-Spanish combined fleet again appeared in the Channel, and again retreated with no harm done. But the British forces across the Atlantic were under poor direction. In the West Indies, Rodney failed to bring the French under de Grasse to action, and when Rodney set out for England in the autumn with six ships of the line he left Hood with only 10 to take to North America to reinforce the stationed squadron.

There, though Rodney did not know it, the crisis of the war in the colonies was approaching. The absence of clear direction from the cabinet, and the impossibility of controlling events thousands of miles away, left the naval command in the hands of a relatively junior officer, Rear-Admiral Graves, commanding a heterogeneous squadron, with inadequate information and no clear orders. He did not know that on land a trap was very slowly closing on Lord Cornwallis's army in Virginia, and that arrangements had been concerted between Washington and de Grasse for the French admiral to come from the West Indies to the Chesapeake Bay with his whole squadron. Hood, who became Graves's second-in-command in North America, informed him when he reached New York that a large French squadron was headed for the coast, but neither admiral knew exactly how big it was or where it intended to go. Their combined squadron numbered 19, de Grasse's from the West Indies 26. An indecisive action was fought off the mouth of the Chesapeake on 5 September. Not knowing the situation on land, Graves and Hood had no reason to think that their failure to engage more daringly and occupy the bay would prove decisive. Cornwallis himself did not greatly fear being surrounded; he expected to be embarked to safety by sea. But Graves's squadron, damaged and now heavily outnumbered (the French North American contingent from Newport joined up with de Grasse after the naval battle), was unable to come to his rescue. Though de Grasse remained in North America only a few weeks, for that period he had command of the sea, and Cornwallis was forced to surrender. That in turn brought about the collapse of Lord North's ministry in the spring of 1782, and its replacement by one pledged to make peace with the Americans.

Britain's struggle to prevent American independence was given up just as the tide of naval preponderance began to turn. Not only was the general balance of forces now more or less equal, but the British were reaping the reward of their risky decision of 1779, to fit the entire fleet with copper sheathing. There were unresolved technical problems which might have disabled, even caused the loss of, numerous ships had the war lasted much longer. But, as it happened, British ships were able to stay at sea for long periods without drydocking or careening, and British squadrons enjoyed a decisive advantage of speed. In the West Indies on 11 April 1782, Rodney at last won a clear victory over de Grasse, spoiling the Franco-Spanish plan to invade Jamaica. Though only seven men of war were taken prize, the moral effect of the battle of the Saintes was immense, and on both sides it was seen to have restored the superiority Britain had enjoyed at sea 20 years before. Ironically, the new ministry had already despatched Rodney's relief, who did nothing for the remainder of the war, though its failure to redeploy some of the troops in North America to the Caribbean deprived him of forces he might have put to use. Meanwhile, at home the Channel Fleet for the third time sailed southward and relieved Gibraltar. Far away in the East Indies, Sir Edward Hughes fought the great French admiral, Suffren, to a standstill and saved British India. On 28 June 1783, 21 months after the battle which won American independence, and 5 months after the preliminaries of peace between Britain and France had been signed, the last shot of the war was fired at Cuddalore in South India.

In the end, the British salvaged from the wreckage far more than their achievements at arms should logically have dictated—in fact, it occurred as much in spite of their strategy as because of it. In two wars they had earned rich dividends from concentrating in the Western Approaches until a decisive superiority had been won there, and in future wars they were to do the same again. Certainly there was in 1778 more at stake abroad than ever before, but there was more at risk at home too, and the harder the task, the more essential it became that no forces should be diverted from the critical point. There, in the waters near home, lay Britain's best chance of success. When Byron was ordered to sail for America, followed over the next four years by successive squadrons, this chance was thrown away, and with it probably Britain's only hope of frustrating the French naval effort and thus depriving the American cause of naval and financial support on which its war for independence had come so greatly to depend.

NOTE

1. Jan Glete, *Navies and Nations,* (Stockholm, 1993), volume I, pp. 278–80.

SUGGESTIONS FOR FURTHER READING

Daniel A. Baugh, "The Politics of British Naval Failure, 1775–1777," *The American Neptune,* 54 (1992), pp. 221–246.

Daniel A. Baugh, "Why did the Britain Lose Command of the Sea during the War for America?" in Jeremy Black and Philip Woodfine, eds., *The British Navy and the Use of Naval Power in the Eighteenth Century.* (Leicester, 1988).

Arthur Bowler, *Logistics and the Failure of the British Army in America, 1775–1783.* (Princeton, 1975).

Jonathan R. Dull, *The French Navy and American Independence: A Study of Arms and Diplomacy, 1775–1787.* (Princeton, 1975).

Piers Mackesy, *The War for America, 1775–1783.* (London, 1964).

Daniel A. Miller, *Sir Joseph Yorke and Anglo-Dutch Relations, 1774–1780.* (The Hague, 1970).

David Syrett, *The Royal Navy in American Waters, 1775–1783.* (Aldershot, 1989).

Part IV
The Maritime Legacy of Empire

Figure XXII. A print by Robert Dodd of the *Lady Juliana*, a larger merchantman of 379 tons, sailing in a convoy to Britain from the West Indies in 1782, being towed by a warship after the mainmast was struck by lightning. She had a remarkable and much-documented career, and was in every sort of trade and route continuously until the 1820s. *Courtesy of National Maritime Museum, London.*

20

THE ATLANTIC ECONOMIES BEFORE 1800

R. J. B. Knight

Cloths midling and superfine,
Figs, raisins,sugar-candy;
Sago and rice, pepper allspice,
Madeira wine and brandy.

Good corduroys for men and boys,
Excellent Irish linen;
Jeans and jeannets and velverets
And cloth of Joan's spinning.

Cloves, ginger, prunes and silver spoons,
Both wax and tallow candles;
Bottles and corks and knives and forks,
With horn and ivory handles.[1]

This advertising jingle of 1789, proclaiming some of the wares of a Philadelphia store in a local newspaper, was recalled by Samuel Kelly, one of those seamen who roamed the seas in merchant and naval ships in these years, and whose story will tell you more than any academic overview two hundred years later. It serves to show the variety of goods which an American citizen would take for granted at that time. Only slowly were those citizens beginning to produce such goods for themselves; in the main they came from the country from which they had just made themselves independent after a long war, though a curiosity of the 1780s is the speed of resumption and growth of trade between former enemies. Of course there is enormous impact from the war which began in 1793, but it is best to look at 10 years of peace and 10 years of war of the 1780s and 1790s as a continuum. The beginnings and ends of maritime wars do not provide the most satisfactory chronological framework when analyzing maritime trade.

The purpose of this chapter is to take the whole Atlantic, not only from an Anglo-American viewpoint, to begin to show how all the four main maritime countries of late eighteenth-century Europe—England, France, Spain and Portugal (the Dutch no longer being main players in the Atlantic) related to their overseas empires and, perhaps more important, to each other's empires. (Detailed consideration of the trade to the East has been excluded, and especially the British, French and Dutch East India Companies, but these trades do weave into this story). It is important to look at the Atlantic system as a whole, even though all these countries under eighteenth-century mercantilist principles tried to exclude the others from their own trade with their own colonies. Recent colonial historiography has tended to relate to countries which became countries after this period, and thus tend to stress the unique, rather than a common colonial background. Further, on the one hand there are the Anglo-American historians and on the other there are the Latin Americanists; both have tended to ignore the territory of the other. But this is far from how contemporaries saw it.

The period from the end of the American Revolution to the end of the eighteenth century is the nexus point of a great swirl of political, industrial and social upheaval, and this too has left its mark on the historiography of the period. Historians have grappled with the great growth of the Atlantic System broadly in two ways. The first is that of Robert Palmer and Jacques Godechot—the Atlantic Revolution—which provides a political and institutional link between the American and French Revolutions, welded by the Enlightenment as a progressive, democratic, political force. The economic interpretation (Marxist, but also classically Liberal) is the idea that it all started with the Industrial Revolution, the shift from commercial to industrial capitalism. "The Revolutions in America, both North and South, represent a shift from formal to informal domination, with the newly industrialized states—especially Great Britain—replacing the decaying bureaucratic and mercantilist empires of Spain and Portugal."[2] There is no doubt that the northern and southern economies of North and South America developed very differently; or to put it in Immanuel Wallerstein's terms, why did North America move from the periphery to the core of the world system, while Latin America remained peripheral?

Any initial stance in this argument must be dictated by a view of the Atlantic Ocean. Was it a barrier or a means of communication? Are the links or the differences more important? Some scholars are now viewing this rather philosophical point in a very pragmatic way.

Although it examines an earlier period, and only the communications of the North Atlantic, a most useful standard is set by Ian Steele's *The English Atlantic, 1675–1740; an exploration of communication and community*. He finds what he calls a "shrinking" Atlantic, which was traversed increasingly to service a North American population which grew five times in the first half of the century; packets and mails were regular, and took far less time than in the lifetime before 1740. The dangers were much reduced; there were better charts, lighthouses, breakwaters, port facilities. The English Atlantic he concluded "united that empire more than it divided . . . (and) was a functional economic, political and social universe."[3] Nor had anyone, he notes tellingly, while thousands crossed the sea, traversed the land of the American continent during this time.

Thus, when we take up our story in the 1780s, this was the period of great growth in the history of the whole Atlantic; the trade, population, wealth and influence in the ports of the Atlantic—not only those of the North Atlantic—Liverpool, Glasgow, Bristol; New York, Boston, Philadelphia, Salem; Bordeaux, Nantes, La Rochelle; but also Lisbon, Cadiz; and in South America, Buenos Aires, Santiago de Chile, Maracaibo, Bogota, and Guayaquil were prospering at the expense of the Andean highlands.

Let us look first at the thriving mercantilist commercial economy of central or the tropical Atlantic—the plantation economies of Central America and the West Indies.

The West Indies. These islands were, according to Abbe Reynal, "the principal cause of the rapid movement which stirs the universe;" the production in plantations of sugar, cotton and coffee, for which there was constant and rising demand, was the hub around which the whole of trade and shipping turned. The factors of production were not merely local land and capital, but capital and managerial labor from Europe. But the West Indies were the least self sufficient of economies; slaves were needed from Africa, diverse products such as Indian textiles were needed to trade for slaves, European cloth for plantation slaves, while every year New England provided tens of thousands of staves for the barrels required for shipping sugar.

These island economies were powerful, though the biggest stakeholder of all was Spain. The value of the commerce between Spanish America (including her islands) and Spain at this time was twice that of the British West Indies. One contemporary estimate valued France's domestic exports at just over 11¼ million pounds in 1787, whereas the export of its colonies to France averaged 8¼ million pounds between 1784 and 1790. Although it is difficult to comprehend now, the exports of Haiti in 1787 were more valuable than the total exports of the United States. Britain's islands produced less, being estimated between 1784–6 at 4 1/2 million pounds, at a time when the domestic exports were worth 14 million pounds. In fact, the West Indies contribution to British commerce had lost some of its vitality by the 1780s, partly because industrial growth in the rest of the economy made it relatively less important. Britain consumed almost all of its sugar, and the reexport of West Indies produce accounted for only 9% of all imports, whereas the reexport trade to the rest of Europe was very important for France and Portugal. France, between 1785 and 1789, reexported 69.4%. Other European countries had their islands, including the Dutch, the Danes and the Swedes. The sugar, cotton and coffee trades were still expanding, nor was their potential anything like reached by 1800.

As an index of these high-risk, hot-house economies, with their high level of conspicuous consumption, it is worth quoting from the journal of a lady traveler at the Dutch island of St. Eustatius, just before the American War, admittedly when times were very good:

> But never did I meet with such variety; here was a merchant vending his goods in Dutch, another in French, a third in Spanish etc. . . . From one end of the town of Eustatia to the other is a continued mart, where goods of the most different uses and qualities are displayed before the shop-doors. Here hang rich embroideries, painted silks, flowered Muslins, with all the Manufactures of the Indies. Just by hang Sailor's Jackets, trousers, shoes, hats etc. Next stall contains most exquisite silver plate, the most beautiful indeed I ever saw, and close by these iron-pots, kettles and shovels. Perhaps the next presents you with French and English Millinary-wares . . . I bought a quantity of excellent French gloves for fourteen pence a pair, also English thread-stockings cheaper than I could buy them at home. I was indeed surprised to find that the case of the British manufactures, but am told the merchants who export them have a large drawback.[4]

The consequence of all this growth and consumption was a very fragile economy and indeed, during the 1780s, the gilt had come off the gingerbread for the British West Indies, which had anyway suffered badly from the hurricanes of 1780 and 1781. Santo Domingo, which had all the geographical advantages—better soil, more economies of scale—did well. The life of a planter, however, on any of the islands, was a risky business. The price of sugar on the European markets was watched like a hawk, and visitors to the islands report that conversation was of little else. The yield of the sugar harvest was variable, and it was generally ready for shipment between early spring and late summer. Planters, shipowners and insurers were all anxious that ships should leave the islands before the first of August, the start of the hurricane season, so that ships had to leave England in the winter, before the state of the crops was known. Thus the supply of shipping was unrelated to demand. Freight rates were fixed locally by the planters together once various factors were known—the state of the crops, the number of ships available, war or peace, the state of the market (when known). For all these reasons, planters lived on a good deal of credit, and consigned their produce to agents or factors in Europe. If one adds the health problems to the uncertainty of life in the West Indies, it is not surprising that there were many absentee planters.

The Slave Trade. It is appropriate to contrast this picture of opulence with the slavery which was required to keep these economies going, for the islands, and mainland North and South America had an insatiable appetite for manpower. Sugar is a very labor intensive crop. Lacking an indigenous population, which largely had been wiped out by disease, the whole economic base required a continual stream of immigration. It has been estimated that between six and seven million slaves were taken across the Atlantic in the eighteenth century.

The whole issue of slavery is beyond moral judgment, but we must examine it as one of the chief engines of the Atlantic economies. Although the trade had been started by the Portuguese, who continued to be carriers in the South Atlantic, by the second half of the eighteenth century Britain and France were the most important carriers. The Americans entered the trade late and never gained a share equal to the Europeans. Spain, holder of the largest American empire, was a buyer of slaves from other carriers until the nineteenth century.

Particular ports specialized in the trade. Nantes was the leading French port; in England it was Liverpool and it is worth examining the scale of the trade in the late 1780s, which is seen by some as the peak volume of the trade.

SLAVE SHIP CLEARANCES FROM LIVERPOOL

YEAR	ANNUAL TONNAGE
1789	11,125
1790	18,183
1791	18,609
1792	24,401
1793	9,542
1794	21,623[5]

In 1787, Liverpool slavers estimated that British slavers exported 38,000 slaves, French 20,000, Portuguese 10,000, the Dutch 4,000, though all these may be low estimates.

Such a sensitive and difficult subject has more than its number of misconceptions, and merits comment on some of them. One over-simplification is in the buying of slaves, with the idea that slaves were kidnapped, or that there was unequal bartering "between cunning whites and naive blacks."[6] There were sophisticated systems, where black traders retained sovereignty over forts and factories, collected customs and organized systems of supply and marketing. Prices in Africa were susceptible to supply and demand, which could be affected by inland rainfall or by warfare (a chief would sell his captives). For instance, the impact of low rainfall in Angola in the 1780s led to severe famine which continued into the 1790s. In the 1780s, slave exports from the west central African region, to which Angola belongs, jumped to twice the level of the 1770s—even though the price rose only by 10% from one decade to the next. Where the region had once been a source of supply only for Portuguese slavers, French, British and Dutch slave traders now began operating on the coast north of the Congo River mouth. Political and climactic disasters had the effect of lowering the price. This activity was conducted alongside other trading. Though much of the trade took place on the decks of ships, there were factories, even though by this time the chartered companies had disappeared.

The Middle Passage, the voyage from Africa to the West Indies, is perhaps the most harrowing of the images—suffering, brutality and death. There was overcrowding, inadequate diet, shackles. At the same time economic self-interest must have played a part in providing an incentive for the safe delivery of healthy slaves. There is abundant evidence of precautions taken to ensure the health of slaves, and the death rate decreased during the century. Historians now point to the slaves' health at the time of embarkation as a significant factor in explaining mortality at sea. Finally, it was not enormously profitable, though it did well enough during the 1780s. Profits were estimated at 9.5% in the English trade and 6% for some French slavers.

Spain and Portugal. It is worth sketching in the essential differences between Spain and Portugal—and England. First, Spain and Portugal kept traditional division of nobles, clergy, commoners; there was a very small middle class—at most 6% of the population. The real power lay in the Crown and the nobility, and the Cortes had no power. The bourgeoisie thrived only in some ports, and all economic ideas and incentive had to come from government. Second, Spanish agriculture was far behind England and even France, although Catalonia should be excepted; there had been no such phenomenon as an agricultural revolution. Finally, New World bullion both drove and buoyed up the two economies. In particular, Brazilian gold held up the Portuguese economy, and at the same time had the effect of discouraging domestic industry; indeed, Portugal's wealth flowed out very quickly, mainly to England.

There is no doubt that the Spanish were worried throughout the eighteenth century about both British and French naval and economic depredations on their colonial empire. In the 1760s Charles III had tried to stem Spain's relative decline by allying himself to France and attempting to tighten up the exclusions on British trade. But he fought it on mercantilist principles. "Like Pombal, Charles III thought that British commercial dominance was due largely to greater monetary wealth and to favorable treaty provision, rather than, as it was, to superior capital, finance, technology, and resources, and to successful private and public cooperation in developing them."[7]

Nevertheless, there were some considerable reforms and advances. The old monopolistic trading connection of the Atlantic convoys from the Caribbean to Seville ended, and the trade diversified as a result. The Cadiz monopoly ended between 1765 and 1789. This made the Atlantic ports more important, increasing trade with Buenos Aires in salt beef, silver, hides, grains; with Caracas in cacao and hides; and with Cuba in sugar and slaves.

At the same time there were enormous leaks in the supposedly tight system, through the exploitation by all the nations of the "Asiento" (the Contract), negotiated after the Treaty of Utrecht in 1714. This illegal trade went through Jamaica. The Spanish exported mules, cattle, hides, wood, tobacco, much Peruvian and Mexican silver and Brazilian gold, particularly after the 1780s when it was discovered in large quantities in Minas Gerais in Brazil. In turn the British traded flour from North America, textiles and slaves. But much of this trade was carried on under license from factories of the English South Seas Company, which were established in Cuba, Vera Cruz, Campeche, Porto Bello, and Caracas, while in Buenos Aires the Company held a great deal of land. By the last 20 years of the century the Spanish were recognizing the inevitable. "English industrial development was generating products whose price and quality would permit them to penetrate most mercantilist barriers."[8]

In fact, however the Spanish changed the rules, the end was near. In the words of one Latin American historian:

> The . . . crisis at the century's end came with the conflict between England and Napoleonic France in large measure over seapower and trade with Spain's colonies. What defined these crises was Spain's monopoly of American silver production, its inability to develop a manufacturing industry to supply its colonies, and the competition between the two more developed economies over exploiting the Spanish empire in America.[9]

Peggy Liss goes further in her comment over the role of the United States:

> The new republic from 1783 to 1808 joined France and England in competing for commercial advantage in Latin America. The three nations and Spain played balance of power diplomacy, despatched agents, official and otherwise, to Latin America, and while watchful to make the most of every opportunity to further national interest, all were careful that it should not be a rival's profit. On this international situation depended to a great extent the fate of Spain and, more indirectly, of Portugal, still a British satellite, in America. And until 1810, Spain retained its American colonies, largely because other nations were cognizant that the advantages each might gain from Spanish independence could soon be offset by disadvantages arising should Spain's dependencies be controlled by a rival power stronger than Spain.[10]

We shall return to this theme in chapters 22 and 23.

The Postwar North Atlantic Trade. Let us now turn to the impact of American War on the previous thriving trade and the postwar debate on the resumption of trade. Fascinating and passionate debates took place in the House of Commons in 1783 on relations with the former colonies. Shelburne, the British Prime Minister negotiating for the peace, wanted to salvage as much as he could of the Anglo-American connection. He agreed to a peace treaty which recognized independence and, in the words of Charles Ritcheson, "made a cession of territory so extravagant that Vergennes blinked and Britons growled."[11] The second part of his plan, embodied in the American Intercourse Bill, aimed at keeping the former rebels economically within the empire by blending the interests of the two nations—the one manufacturer and carrier, the other customer and producer of raw materials. In other words, he was trying to loosen—formally—the mercantilist system, opening up British trade to another state. The debate, which went on through the 1780s and beyond, exposed the very heart of the principles of the British mercantilist system and it centered round three interests: the West Indian planters, who wanted their supplies of food and barrel staves to come from the new United States without duties or hindrance; a weak Canada which claimed that it could provide these essential supplies; and the shipping interest, which did not want to lose its protection, and those who saw mercantilism for what it was—economic nationalism.

The most celebrated diatribe against Shelburne's scheme (and he, never popular, fell from power very soon) was Lord Sheffield's *Observations on the Commerce of the American States*. His argument centered on three points: first, the bill was essentially a repeal of the Navigation Act; second, American proximity would dominate the economy and carrying trade of the British West Indies; third, Britain would lose a crucial nursery of seamen. Nor should this last be dismissed, for the West Indies carrying trade was more use in training sailors for the Royal Navy, as indeed it was argued, for the length of the voyage and size of the ships were more useful than the East Indies trade, where the voyages were too long, or the European coasting trade, in which the ships were too small.

As it turned out, the lobbying powers of the West Indies merchants at this time,were disappointing, and the argument for tightening the system prevailed. Shelburne's plans fell away, the United States was frozen out and suffered in the 1780s. Under the stress of war, the system had to be relaxed in the 1790s so that the United States could trade directly to the British West Indies. In a telling passage from a Canadian apologist (Hollingsworth, *The Present State of Nova Scotia*, 1787), while admitting that the West Indies planters and merchants should be listened to, wrote:

> but, if any measure tending to a relaxation of the navigation laws is the object of their wishes, they ought to remember, that such measures are sapping the very existence of the British naval power, and, by consequence, that which can alone protect the possessions, from whence their wealth and importance is derived; and not only so, but doing the same by all our other foreign dominions."[12]

At the same time, Canada, whose small population was now swelled with embittered loyalists, claimed the right and the potential to supply the West Indies. It was, of course, beyond their capacity, and part of Hollingsworth's book was arguing for a bounty (or subsidy) for lumber for the West Indies. Bryan Edwards, the lobbyist, member of Parliament and historian of the West Indies, was scathing when he wrote later in 1801:

an irrefragable proof that Canada had no surplus of either lumber or grain beyond her own consumption, or undoubtedly the Canadian market would have been resorted to, in preference to the United States. And thus vanished all the golden dreams and delusive promises of a sufficient supply from Canada and Nova Scotia to answer the wants of the West Indies; and the predictions of the planters and merchants have been verified and confirmed by the experience of years.[13]

Edwards was right on that question. Gerald Graham's judgment of 1941 was brisk: "The Maritime Provinces utterly failed to compete with the more mature economy of the United States, and lumbering remained an industry wherein losses became as common as profits."[14] The larger question of self-interest prevailed and the mercantilist system and the navigation laws were tightened. But it did raise the question again which had been asked since 1763: what was Canada for if it could not pay its way?

Britain's Industrial Growth. The 1780s was a period of rapid commercial and industrial growth throughout Europe. Spain and Portugal revived in the second half of the century. It was a time for prosperity for France, too, but its growth was relatively slow. There was real growth in the French West Indies trade, and these were great days for Bordeaux and Nantes (though not La Rochelle) both from colonial produce and from a growth in the slave trade. Nevertheless the French did not really have a substantial Atlantic outlet—only Santo Domingo, and dependence on that island was only emphasized when the revolt of 1791 knocked it out of the reckoning. As a result of this growth, the merchant fleets of Europe increased; by 1786 they totalled 3.4 million tons:

EUROPEAN MERCHANT FLEETS, 1786		
England	881,963	(26.1%)
France	729,340	(21.6%)
Denmark, Norway, Sweden	555,299	(16,3%)
Dutch	397,709	(11.8%)
Spain and Portugal	224,303	(6.6%)
Others: (Venice, Italy, German States)	569,785	(16.8%)[15]

However, when it came to economic growth in these 20 years, Britain was in a class of its own:

Figure XXIII. "A snow off the Mewstone, Plymouth Sound, 1803," print by Dominic Serres the Younger. The great majority of merchant ships were of this size, about 150 tons. She is designated a snow because of the small mast, just aft of the mainmast, carrying the fore and aft rigged mizzen sail. *Courtesy of National Maritime Museum, London.*

AVERAGE YEARLY GROWTH OF DOMESTIC
EXPORTS FOR ENGLAND AND WALES

1714–1744:	0.9%
1744–1760:	3.0%
1760–1783:	−1.4%
1783–1802:	5.9%[16]

COMPOSITION OF MANUFACTURED EXPORTS IN 1800

Woollens	28.5%	(1752–1754 = 61.9%; dropping sharply)
Linens	3.3%	(Same as mid-18th century)
Silks	1.2%	(Mid-century 2.5%; dropping sharply)
Cottons	24.1%	(Mid-century 1.3%; huge increase)
Metals	11.6%	(Mid century 9.2%; small increase)
Rest	32.3%	(Mid-century 21.7%)[17]

We should refer at this point to the long debate among economic historians on the importance of English overseas trade to the Industrial Revolution, though the importance of industrial growth to foreign trade is not at issue. Early writers took it for granted that the growth of overseas trade was central to industrial growth. However, the orthodoxy, until very recently, was opposed to this early view. The argument was that "the crucial demand for the products of British industries arose not from abroad but from increased domestic spending due to the progressive cheapening of food and the rise in the range of middle range incomes." Another argument which supported this point of view is that there was no direct investment in industry from the profits of overseas trade, and little introduction of new techniques from aboard, while industries directly dependent on trade—such as shipbuilding—were relatively small ones. Were exports a leading sector (or "engine of growth") or, alternatively, were sales overseas merely a response to the growing efficiency of British industry and agriculture, rooted in technical progress, superior commercial and industrial organization, and entrepreneurial vigor? It is a debate which still continues.

Cotton. Clearly cotton was the leader in this extraordinary growth, and one factor in the continued upward movement of this new industry was a flexible and elastic supply of cotton wool. The British West Indies could not supply enough, and the cotton manufacturers, always adept at lobbying, looked for alternative sources of supply. The result was the Free Ports Acts of the 1790s, which enabled cotton from French and Spanish colonies to be shipped to England through the British West Indies, especially through Jamaica, Grenada and Dominica. Between 1786 and 1790 imports of cotton from British West Indies increased by 50%, a good proportion of it foreign produce. Between January 1789 and January 1790 total imports equalled 32.6 million lb.; of this four million (an eighth of the whole) was brought into the free ports of the West Indies by foreign vessels. Alternative supplies came from India, Brazil through Portugal and a small amount from the United States. It was not until 1802 that the imports of cotton from America overtook those from the West Indies. Perhaps the most important fact is that the cotton trade was not halted or disrupted by the war, although there were fluctuations enough.

The Impact of War. There is no doubt that Britain's superior command of the sea hurt French commerce and trade considerably, and that the same thing happened to Spain at various points. The 1790s were bad years for the French western coast ports. As the continental markets began to close down, British trade turned to the Americas and it was a time of great prosperity for the New England merchants. Nevertheless, trading as a neutral had its risks, for the outbreak of war did not decrease the interdependence of nation upon nation. Take the example of the *Confederacy,* an unusually large New England trader of 459 tons. She sailed from New York in April 1795, with provisions and sugar for Le Havre, when two British frigates took her. Sent into Halifax, Nova Scotia, on the charge of carrying contraband in the provision casks, she was released by the Vice-Admiralty court and her captors had to pay the charges. Near the English Channel, she was again taken by an English frigate, and again released. The captain abandoned the Le Havre project, went to London, where the ship was sold to another New York firm which sent her to the East Indies. She sold her cargoes at the distant French colonies of the Isle de France and Bourbon, and by June was taking on a cotton cargo at Bombay. She sold the cotton at Canton, and loaded tea, cinnamon, sugar, chinaware, sailed for Hamburg by way of Cape Horn in January 1797. Just before the end of her voyage round the world, she was taken by a French privateer, and on the charge of not having a notarized crew list she was condemned as a prize at Nantes. The privateer's crew shared nearly $300,000 dollars at the forced sale.

If there is a larger theme to this chapter it is that the whole Atlantic system was interdependent; nor was it within the power of nations to enforce their own laws uniformly and efficiently, for the sea is a very large place. No one nation, nor colony, nor a single trade should be seen in isolation. It is better to think in terms, perhaps, of a couple of hypothetical voyages:

> A New England ship might sail to Jamaica with a cargo of barrel staves, horses and salt fish. These could be sold for bullion, derived in turn from smuggling slaves in South America—and Jamaica was the main entrepôt for that trade. In addition, the captain might buy a few slaves for sale on the North American mainland, but his "middle" passage would carry him only to Saint Dominique to complete his cargo with sugar and molasses, bought with bullion. On the way north, he could stop in the Chesapeake Bay to sell the slaves, then back to New England, where he would sell the molasses to be made into rum for the fur trade. The French sugar could then be relabelled "product of the British West Indies" for sale in Britain, where it and any leftover bullion could pay for British manufactures wanted in New England.
>
> Or a French ship might make the outward voyage to Africa, pick up a cargo of slaves, but sell it in Spanish America for bullion. The bullion in turn would find its way to the *Compagnie des Indies* for shipment to Southern India in return for indigo dies cloth of a kind much in demand in Senegal—not for slaves, but for gum and for Senegalese cloth in demand further down the coast in Dahomey. The Dahomean slaves would be sold, in turn, in the New World, and variants of the same cycle could be played out again.[18]

Summary. The most dominating feature of the whole Atlantic system in the 1780s and 1790s was the unprecedented growth of the British economy. Just at the time of the emphatic restatement of the Navigation Acts and mercantilist principles in the 1780s—perhaps their high point—an extraordinary industrial growth was underway which would be the main reason for the eventual abolition of the Navigation Acts in the 1840s. For the price and quality of British goods reintegrated the United States into the North Atlantic trade, in British ships, and resisted any French challenge; penetrated the Spanish and Portuguese markets; while the demand for raw cotton was beginning to demonstrate that national protected markets were in no one's interests.

Even those British politicians who were pushing the economic nationalism which closed out the United States were beginning to heed the writings of Adam Smith. They managed to combine economic liberation (free trade) with economic nationalism, in what has been called "neo-mercantilism."[19] They followed Adam Smith in making the government's encouragement of navigation an exception to a policy of freer trade. Each regulation and privilege for nationalist purposes had to be justified against the commercial advantage of freer trade. The enhancement of Britain's power as a nation, not the prosperity of her people, had priority in their recommendations for economic policy.

At this time there was a balance between the need for national control as against the natural liberalization of freer trade. It was tipped by the very real and continuing concern for the need for trained seamen; only when that was no longer an issue, as we shall see in Chapter 23, were the Navigation Acts abolished.

NOTES

1. C. Garstin, *Samuel Kelly.* (New York, 1925), pp. 170–171.
2. Kenneth Maxwell, "The Atlantic in the Eighteenth Century: a Southern Perspective on the Need to Return to the "Big Picture" *Transactions of the Royal Historical Society,* Sixth Series, 3 (1993), p. 212.
3. Ian Steele, *The English Atlantic.* (Oxford, 1987), p. 273; also pp. vii-ix.
4. E. W. Andrews, *Journal of a Lady of Quality.* (New Haven, 1921), pp. 136–138.
5. James A. Rawley, *The Trans-Atlantic Slave Trade.* (New York, 1981), p. 207.
6. Rawley, p. 432.
7. Peggy Liss, *Atlantic Empires.* (Baltimore, 1983), p. 61.
8. Maxwell, "Atlantic", p. 229.
9. Maxwell, "Atlantic", p. 225.
10. Liss, p. 108.
11. C. R. Ritcheson, *Aftermath of Revolution.* (Dallas, 1969), p. 5.
12. S. Hollingsworth, *The Present State of Nova Scotia etc.* 2nd ed. (London, 1787), p. 165.
13. Bryan Edwards, *The History Civil and Commercial of The British Colonies in the West Indies.* (London, 1801), p. 518.
14. Gerald Graham, *Seapower and British North America 1783–1820.* (New York, 1968), p. 44.
15. Richard W. Unger, "The Tonnage of Europe's Merchant Fleets, 1300–1800," *The American Neptune,* 52 (1992), p. 261.
16. Figures by François Crouzet, quoted in O'Brien and Engerman, "Exports and the Growth of the British Economy from the Glorious Revolution to the Peace of Amiens" in Barbara L. Solow, ed., *Slavery and the Rise of the Atlantic System.* (Cambridge and New York, 1991), p. 183.
17. O'Brien and Engerman, p. 184.
18. Both examples are from Philip D. Curtin, *The Tropical Atlantic in the Age of the Slave Trade.* (Washington, 1951), pp. 37–38.
19. John E. Crowley, "Neo-Mercantilism and the *Wealth of Nations;* Commercial Policy after the American Revolution," *Historical Journal,* 33 (1990), p. 342.

SUGGESTIONS FOR FURTHER READING

Contemporary Works

Evangeline Walker Andrews, in collaboration with Charles Maclean Andrews, eds., *Journal of a Lady of Quality, being the Narrative of a Journey from Scotland to the West Indies, North Carolina and Portugal, in the years 1774 to 1776.* (New Haven, 1921).

Tench Coxe, *A View of the United States of America.* (Philadelphia: 1794; New York, 1965).

Jarvis Cromwell, "Journal of a Trading Voyage around the World, 1805–1808," *The New York Historical Quarterly,* LXII (1978), pp. 87–137.

John C. Dann, ed., *The Nagle Journal: A Diary of the life of Jacob Nagle, Sailor, from the year 1775 to 1841.* (New York, 1988).

Bryan Edwards, *The History, Civil and Commercial, of the British Colonies in the West Indies.* (London, 1801).

C. Garstin, ed., *Samuel Kelly, an Eighteenth Century Seaman, whose days have been few and evil, to which is added remarks etc on places he visited during his pilgrimage in this Wilderness.* (New York, 1925).

S. Hollingsworth, *The Present State of Nova Scotia etc.* 2nd ed. (London, 1787).

John Baker Holroyd, Lord Sheffield, *Observations on the Commerce of the American States.* (London, 1783).

Abbé Guillaume Raynal, *A Philosophical and Political History of the Settlements and Trade of the Europeans in the East and West Indies.* 2nd. ed. (London, 1798).

Secondary Works

Robert Greenhalgh Albion and Jenny Barnes Pope, *Sea Lanes in Wartime: The American Experience, 1775–1945.* 2nd. ed. (Hamden, CT., 1968).

Roger Anstey, *The Atlantic Slave Trade and British Abolition 1760–1810.* (London, 1975; 2nd ed. Aldershot, 1992).

C. R. Boxer, *The Portuguese Seaborne Empire, 1415–1825.* (London, 1969; Carcanet, 1991).

Jaap R. Bruijn and Femme S. Gaastra, eds., *Ships, Sailors and Spices; East India Companies and their Shipping in the 16th, 17th and 18th Centuries.* (Amsterdam, 1993).

John G. Clark, *La Rochelle and the Atlantic Economy during the Eighteenth Century.* (Baltimore and London, 1981).

John E. Crowley, "Neo-Mercantilism and the *Wealth of Nations;* Commercial Policy after the American Revolution," *Historical Journal,* 33, 2, (1990), pp. 339–360.

Ann Currie, *Henleys of Wapping: a London shipowning family 1770–1830.* (Greenwich, 1988).

Philip D. Curtin, *The Tropical Atlantic in the age of the Slave Trade.* (Washington, 1951).

Ralph Davis, *The Rise of the English shipping Industry in the Seventeenth and Eighteenth Centuries.* (London, 1962).

Ralph Davis, *The Rise of the Atlantic Economies.* (London, 1973).

Ralph Davis, *The Industrial Revolution and British Overseas Trade.* (Leicester, 1979).

Michael Duffy, *Soldiers, Sugar and Seapower: the British Expeditions to the West Indies and the War Against Revolutionary France.* (Oxford, 1987).

Michael M. Edwards, *The Growth of the British Cotton Trade, 1780–1815.* (New York, 1967).

William M. Fowler, "Trye All Ports": the Port of Boston, 1783–1793" in Conrad Edick Wright, ed. *Massachusetts and the New Nation.* (Boston, 1992).

Jacques Godechot, *France and the Atlantic Revolution, 1770–1799.* (New York, 1965).

Norman A. Graebner, "New England and the World, 1783–1791" in Conrad Entick Wright, ed., *Massachusetts and the New Nation.* (Boston, 1992).

Gerald Graham, *Seapower and British North America 1783–1820: a study in British Colonial Policy.* (New York, 1968).

Vincent T. Harlow, *The Founding of the Second British Empire, 1763–1793.* Volume 1. (London and New York, 1952).

Richard Herr, *The Eighteenth Century Revolution in Spain.* (Princeton, 1958, 1973).

Peggy Liss, *Atlantic Empires: The Network of Trade and Revolution, 1713–1826.* (Baltimore and London, 1983).

John J. McCusker and Russell R. Menard, *The Economy of British America, 1607–1789.* (Chapel Hill and London, 1985, 1991).

Kenneth R. Maxwell, *Conflicts and Conspiracies: Brazil and Portugal, 1750–1808.* (Cambridge and New York, 1973).

Kenneth Maxwell, "The Atlantic in the Eighteenth Century: a Southern Perspective on the Need to Return to the "Big Picture"

Transactions of the Royal Historical Society, Sixth Series, 3 (1993), pp. 209–236.

P. K. O'Brien and S. L. Engerman, "Exports and the growth of the British Economy from the Glorious Revolution to the Peace of Amiens" in Barbara L. Solow, ed., *Slavery and the Rise of the Atlantic System.* (Cambridge and New York, 1991).

Alison Gilbert Olson, *Making the Empire Work: London and American Interest Groups, 1690–1790.* (Cambridge, Mass., 1992).

R. R. Palmer, *The Age of the Democratic Revolution. A Political History of Europe and America, 1760–1800.* 2 volumes. (Princeton, 1958, 1964).

James A. Rawley, *The Trans-Atlantic Slave Trade.* (New York, 1981).

Charles R. Ritcheson, *Aftermath of Revolution: British Policy towards the United States, 1783–1795.* (Dallas, 1969).

Ian Steele, *The English Atlantic, 1675–1740: An Exploration of Communication and Community.* (Oxford and New York, 1987).

Richard W. Unger, "The Tonnage of Europe's Merchant Fleets, 1300–1800," *The American Neptune,* 52 (1992), pp. 247–261.

Simon P. Ville, *English Shipowning during the Industrial Revolution: Michael Henley and Son, London shipowners, 1770–1830.* (Manchester, 1987).

Patrick Villiers, "The Slave and Colonial Trade in France just before the Revolution," in Barbara L. Solow, ed., *Slavery and the Rise of the Atlantic System.* (Cambridge and New York, 1991).

Immanuel Wallerstein, *The Modern World-System.* 2 volumes. (New York, 1974, 1980).

Figure XXIV. Plymouth Dockyard, 1798, by Nicholas Pocock, showing the remarkable size of the industrial establishments required to keep the British fleet at sea at this time. Portsmouth and Chatham yards were also the same size. *Courtesy of National Maritime Museum, London.*

21
CHANGING TECHNOLOGIES AND MATERIALS
R. J. B. Knight

Maritime technological advances in the last half of the eighteenth century were incremental and gradual. There were no great discontinuities, no great breakthroughs as there were to be in the next century, and it is ironic that when iron, which had the capacity to last much longer than wood, became the main shipbuilding material, regular technological advances made the life of iron ships shorter because of naval obsolescence or economic pressure, rather than the wear and tear and dry rot which wore out wooden ships. Nevertheless, in the half century before the coming of iron and steam, efficiencies were made, ships became steadily larger and far more numerous. One fact, however, should be remembered about the period before the coming of steam; the working of a wooden, sailing naval or merchant ship was far more dependent on a concentrated number of skilled men than it later became with iron and steam and what technological advances there were never overcame that dependency.

The other skill which maritime nations had to try to nurture was that of the shipwright and the other trades that were required to build ships and to maintain them. The industrial capacity of a nation to produce and maintain a fleet related very directly to its power at sea, and the one which had its fleet at sea earliest in a war had a strategic and tactical advantage which was very difficult to shake off. Every nation would argue, especially the main maritime players on the stage, Britain, France and Spain, that there were never enough shipwrights, and one of the key constraints of seapower throughout Europe in the late eighteenth century was lack of skilled shipbuilding labor.

Shipyards and Dockyards. From the time of the mid-century expansion of these rival navies, the infrastructure which went to support them grew continually, and because a ship needed continual maintenance, this task, undertaken by the dockyards, most tested the resources and administration of these states. The first industrial complexes of a twentieth-century scale came about because of the need to maintain seapower. Chatham, Portsmouth and Plymouth in England; Brest, Toulon and Rochefort in France; Cadiz, Ferrol and Cartagena in Spain were the main centers of maintenance and repair, but there were many others, including those of lesser powers, such as Amsterdam in the Netherlands, Copenhagen in Denmark, Karlskrona and Stockholm in Sweden and Kronstadt and St. Petersburg in Russia.

Each power ran the large workforces at these industrial sites on different principles. France and Spain had a long tradition of using convicts for unskilled work. When France abandoned her Mediterranean galleys in 1749, she sent her convicts to the dockyards. Britain also considered it and the measure came before the House of Commons in a parliamentary bill in 1752. In fact, this was very inefficient, for large bodies of unmotivated men, quite apart from the troops necessary to guard them, were not to be roused to great efforts when the need arose. In Britain, on the other hand, dockyard shipwrights had to be sought in the marketplace alongside those who worked in the thriving merchant yards, where wages were much higher, though job security was lower. As a result there were difficult labor relations problems in the English royal dockyards, and at the beginning of every eighteenth-century war there were strikes when the workforce held the whiphand. The task work strike of 1775 and unrest in 1801, for instance, were long, drawn out affairs, and of concern to statesmen and strategists as well as naval administrators. Britain's great strength, however, was the link of private and state capacity, for by the height of the Napoleonic wars 70% of the British navy was built in merchant yards, leaving the dockyards to maintain the fleets at sea.

The Humble Dry Dock. There was no more critical element of seapower than the humble dry dock, which in the preindustrial age represented an extraordinary amount of state investment. Expensive stone-faced docks were needed to stand up to wear and tear, and they began to be constructed by both the British and French from the 1680s. Other design improvements came about through the century—dock gates closing at an angle, curved gates built at Copenhagen and Karlskrona and caissons were invented. Pumping out the docks, needed particularly in the less tidal parts of Europe, was very slow and expensive; convicts were the motive power in France and Spain, using chain pumps, and later horse bucket pumps. At Karlskrona wind pumps were tried. Steam (atmospheric machines) was introduced into Spanish dockyards extraordinarily early, in 1774, and by the French in the 1780s, though it was slow to come in Britain, partly because of opposition from the well-established sawyers. However, as a notable exception, Brunel and Bentham between them designed and built the block mills at Portsmouth in 1798, the first continuous mechanized process in the world.

As the navies of the main powers expanded after the Seven Years War, they realized that in order to keep their investment in their fleet effective they would have to spend quite as much, if not more, on their shore facilities. As launching techniques improved and pressure on dry docks increased, in Britain in 1764 all 74 gun ships were ordered to be built and launched from slips, to keep the docks free for maintenance. Led by the ideas of the century's most admired surveyor of the navy, Sir Thomas Slade, British dockyards embarked on a sustained period of expanding all their facilities, and particularly their dry docks, which slowed only after 1815. Each period of peace resulted in enormous building activities in the dockyards, nor did it stop in wartime. And at the end of this dock-building "race," England had more dry docks than France and Spain combined, as well as more favorable tidal conditions in which to operate them. There was also spectacular new investment in the Baltic, where the Swedes were trying to resist Russian expansion. Both Karlskrona and Kronstadt expanded hugely in the 1780s, and there were grandiose plans by those who even saw such building as establishing a complete deterrent. One such plan at Kronstadt envisaged a spectacular graving dock installation of 10 or 12 docks, double, treble, or even quadruple, radiating out of a semicircular basin:

"an enormous reserve force, a means of dissuasion capable of launching in some ten days a fleet of the same size as that of Holland . . . The concentration of power without necessarily putting it at risk, to prepare a threat without ever having to unleash it: it was in fact a panoptic programme."[1]

However, while there was an appreciation of the strategic and technical value of these docks, there were none built where they would be most useful—far from home. Neither Britain, France nor Spain, in spite of repeated proposals, ever built one in the West Indies, where the strategic situation for the builder would have been transformed. Overseas bases there could undertake only superficial maintenance and ships had to sail home three thousand miles for a proper refit. By 1800, there were no dry docks outside Europe (except at Charlestown near Boston, where there was probably a dry dock at the end of seventeenth century, but it was short-lived); nor were there any in Italy nor Austria.

Timber and Naval Stores. To have an effective presence at sea, the eighteenth-century state which had pretensions to seapower had to have a reliable and consistent supply of good quality ship-building timber, both hard and softwood, hemp for rope and flax for sailcloth. By the end of our period this meant for Britain, essentially, a dangerous dependence on Russia, which had a virtual monopoly on the production of hemp, and controlled vast areas of pine and fir, necessary for masting ships. For the most of the last years of the eighteenth century, for instance, the Russians supplied 70% of all masts imported into Britain; in 1796 the total came to 17,659 which constituted 82%.[2] Russia also had an increasing hold on the supplies of oak, the most favored hardwood for the hulls, which became very scarce towards the end of the century. A parliamentary commission in England, set up to look at the problem in 1791, computed that the Navy consumed 50,000 loads (a "load" was slightly over a ton) a year and the country as a whole, 218,000 tons. Together with the ambitions of Catherine's Russia, the control of the supply of naval stores became a dominant factor in foreign policy in the Baltic, especially at the time of Napoleon's continental blockade. To ensure the continuance of the convoys from Russia, the British kept a fleet in the Baltic under Admiral Saumarez. Those supplies never stopped coming, partly because of Saumarez, but also because British merchants controlled the market, consistently paying higher prices and enjoying better credit than their French rivals. France, of course, had enormous resources of hardwoods in her own forests, but it was not to say that her navy could use them, for it always had to fight to be heard in French government circles. For this reason, France turned to the Adriatic for oak supplies, while she never developed the efficient network of merchants in the Baltic and ultimately became dependent upon Dutch carriers for her supplies of masts.

Although it was the most important, northern Europe was not the only source of naval stores. The tropical hardwoods in Central America under the control of the Spanish gave them a great advantage, and lead to some fine Spanish ships being built, primarily in Havana. From the Bounties Act of 1704, the British government had tried to encourage the timber trade from the North American colonies, but there were too many inherent economic disadvantages to the trade, not least the long Atlantic journey. Although the North America was an important supplement to the Baltic supplies, it never really became a viable alternative. The most important commodity was the very large masts transported from New England, though the elaborate argument built up in the pioneering work of R. G. Albion that the disruption of the mast supplies in the American War of Independence was a crucial factor in the defeat of the British navy should be questioned.[3]

Although there were those who feared, in several countries, real shortages of shipbuilding timber before the start of naval war in 1793, these seemed to be fears rather than reality. Certainly there were no price increases. But there were definite problems after 1800, when both Britain and France searched the Adriatic for fresh supplies of hardwood. British shipwrights were sent to search South Africa and even Australia. Eventually, the problem was eased by the end of the Napoleonic Wars by the British building ships in India of teak, while the French did the same in Burma.

Iron and Copper. It is tempting to relate these timber shortages very directly to the use of iron for building ships, and, indeed, there were early experiments. A report in a Birmingham newspaper appeared on 28 July 1787:

> A few day's ago a boat built of English iron, the *Trial,* by J. Wilkinson of Bradley Forge, came up our canal to this town, loaded with 22 tons 15 cwt of its own metal. It is of nearly equal dimensions with other boats employed on the canal being 70 ft long, 6' 8 1/2" wide, the thickness of the plates of which it is made is about 7/16th inches and it is put together with rivets like a fire engine boiler, but stem and stern posts are wood and the gunwale line is the same. The beams are of elm plank and the weight is about 8 tons. She will carry, in deep water, upwards of 32 tons and draws 8" or 9" when light.[4]

In fact, there was a good deal of distrust of iron by the shipwrights, and, although work remains to be done on this important question, one suspects that this distrust was justified. The brittleness of iron varied a great deal depending on the amount of phosphorous in the material, and it was especially prevalent in the British coke-smelted iron being produced at that time. Nevertheless, as the quality improved, attitudes began to change. The French had long used iron on their ships, especially for the vital knees and standards, which fixed the frame of the hull to the decks; but they had done so from a position of weakness, since their supplies of oak compass timber were less sure.

The brittleness of iron used for guns was also beginning to be understood and important reforms during the 1780s ensured that

British naval gunnery reached new peaks of effectiveness in the years to come. Again, these improvements were not the result of some break-through, but rather solid investment of time and money by Thomas Blomefield, Inspector of Artillery. It was through him that very large numbers of unreliable guns were condemned through extensive and thorough programs of "proofing" (that is, test firing), while he imposed new and higher standards of manufacture on the gunfounding con-tractors. Although more work on the subject is required, it does seem that in the coming wars British naval gunners had more confidence in their guns, with less fear of a gun burst, and were able to fire at a much faster rate than the French and Spanish. The adoption and develop-ment of the carronade, a short, recoilless gun of wide caliber, in the latter stages of the American War, changed close quarter tactics, for they were devastating at short range.

Copper, however, was the metal that made the most difference to naval warfare in this period, for the adoption of copper sheathing to protect ships from the worm, *teredo navalis,* and to keep hulls free of barnacles so that their sailing speed could be maintained, spread very quickly from the navy in the late 1780s to those parts of the merchant fleet, such as slave ships, which required speed. Experi-ments with copper sheathing had started in the 1760s and, in spite of some unsolved problems with the wasting away of iron bolts in the ship through electrolytic action, the decision to copper the fleet was taken at the height of the American war, when the British were out-numbered by the combined French and Spanish fleets. The naval ad-ministrators who made the decision, primarily Lord Sandwich, the First Lord of the Admiralty, and Charles Middleton, the Controller of the Navy, took a considerable risk. They were content with the in-sertion of tarred paper between the copper and the hull to prevent the electrolysis, which they knew was not a proven method. In an impressive burst of shipbuilding and administrative activity in the dockyards, the entire British fleet was coppered between 1779 and 1781, which brought a definite short-term advantage to a belea-guered navy. Ships sailed faster, the frequency of refitting and dock-ing was brought down and ships were turned round in port more quickly—effectively increasing the British fleet.

However, the protection against electrolysis did not work, and when four coppered ships of the line sank in a storm in 1782, it was clear that another solution had to be found. It was found by Thomas Williams, who had developed the copper mines in Anglesey in North Wales, and was the chief contractor to the navy for the supply of cop-per. By developing a bolt of copper alloy, hard enough to be driven

Figure XXV. A contemporary model of the *Bellona,* 74 guns, 1603 tons, built Chatham Dockyard and launched in 1760. She was one of the first to be given the new copper sheathing in 1778 during the American War, and it is said that this model was used when making the decision to go ahead with coppering the British fleet. *Courtesy of National Maritime Museum, London.*

into the hulls of ships, but with sufficient copper in it to neutralize the electrolysis, the problem was solved by 1786. The entire fleet therefore required rebolting, which put up the capital cost of a ship by an estimated 10 to 15%. Not every European state could afford this capital intensive form of warfare.

Conclusion. This period saw a technological race in slow motion. Ships increased slowly in size over the century. Whereas the largest ships of the line in the first half of the century averaged 1,100 tons, by the second half they had increased to 1,800 tons. The *Victory* of 100 guns is 2,000 tons. Design was to change but slowly; recent British research and writing has changed the view that French designs were superior; it is now accepted that, in general, British ships were designed for seakeeping and stability rather than speed, which suited the strategic and tactical uses to which they were put. This was a technology race which Britain led. The real edge was less in breakthroughs and risks, more in a superior infrastructure, of supply, of quality of timber and perhaps beyond everything, the sinews of power, superior finance. The first signs of radical changes in ship technology and materials can be seen in the 1780s and 1790s—the shortages of timber, the hesitant adoption of steam, the increasing use of iron, the overconfident adoption of copper for sheathing; but it is a race very much at the slower pace of the previous hundred years rather than enormous changes of the next hundred.

NOTES

1. José P. Merino, "Graving Docks in France and Spain before 1800," *The Mariner's Mirror,* 71 (1985), p. 48.
2. Arcadius Kahan, *The Plow, the Hammer and the Knout.* (Chicago, 1985), p. 210.
3. R. J. B. Knight, "New England Forests and British Seapower: Albion Revised," *The American Neptune,* XLVI (1986), pp. 221–229.
4. Quoted in D. K. Brown, *Before the Ironclad: Development of Ship Design, Propulsion and Armament in the Royal Navy, 1815–60.* (London, 1990), p. 73.

SUGGESTIONS FOR FURTHER READING

Martine Acerra and Jean Meyer, *Marines et Revolution.* (Rennes, 1988).

Robert G. Albion, *Forests and Seapower: the Timber Problem of the Royal Navy 1652–1862.* (Cambridge, Mass., 1926).

H. A. Baker, *The Crisis in Naval Ordnance.* (Greenwich, 1983).

Paul W. Bamford, *Forests and French Seapower.* (Toronto, 1956).

Jean Boudriot, *The Seventy-Four Gun Ship,* 4 volumes. (Paris, 1973; English translation, 1986).

D. K. Brown, *Before the Ironclad: Development of Ship Design, Propulsion and Armament in the Royal Navy, 1815–60.* (London, 1990).

Jonathan G. Coad, *The Royal Dockyards, 1690–1830*. (Aldershot, 1989).

Patricia K. Crimmin, "Hunting for Naval Timber in the Adriatic, 1802–1815," in *Français et Anglais en Mediteranne, 1789–1830*. (Paris, 1992), pp. 149–157.

Malcolm Crook, *Toulon in War and Revolution: from the Ancien Regime to the Restoration, 1750–1820*. (Manchester, 1991).

John Fincham, *A History of Naval Architecture*. (London: 1851; reprinted London, 1979).

Bess Glenn, "Cathcart's Journal and the Search for Naval Timbers," *The American Neptune,* III (1943), pp. 239–249.

Jan Glete, *Navies and Nations: Warships, Navies and State Building in Europe and America, 1500–1860*. 2 volumes. (Stockholm, 1993).

Joseph A. Goldenberg, *Shipbuilding in Colonial America*. (Charlottesville, 1976).

Gerald S. Graham, *Seapower and British North America 1783–1820*. (Cambridge, Mass., 1941; reprinted New York, 1965).

Raymond Grant, *The Royal Forests of England*. (Stroud, 1991).

J. R. Harris, *The Copper King: a biography of Thomas Williams of Llanidan*. (Liverpool, 1964).

J. R. Harris, "Copper and Shipping in the Eighteenth Century," *The Economic History Review,* XIX (1966), pp. 550–568.

A. J. Holland, *Ships of British Oak: the Rise and Decline of Wooden Shipbuilding in Hampshire*. (Newton Abbott, 1971).

Arcadius Kahan, *The Plow, the Hammer and the Knout: an Economic History of Eighteenth-Century Russia*. (Chicago, 1985).

R. J. B. Knight, "New England Forests and British Seapower: Albion Revised," *The American Neptune,* XLVI (1986), pp. 221–229.

R. J. B. Knight, "The Introduction of Copper Sheathing into the Royal Navy, 1779–1786," *The Mariner's Mirror,* 59(1973), pp. 299–309.

R. J. B. Knight, "The Building and Maintenance of the British fleet during the Anglo-French Wars, 1688–1815," in Martine Acerra, José Merino and Jean Meyer, eds., *Marines de Guerre Europeans XVII-XVIIIe siècles*. (Paris, 1985), pp. 35–50.

R. J. B. Knight, ed., *Shipbuilding Timber for the British Navy: Parliamentary Papers, 1729–1792*. (Delmar, NY, 1993).

Andrew Lambert, *The Last Sailing Battlefleet: Maintaining Naval Mastery, 1815–1850*. (London, 1991).

Brian Lavery, *The Ship of the Line: The Development of the Battle Fleet, 1650–1850*. 2 volumes. (London, 1983,1984).

José P. Merino, "Graving Docks in France and Spain before 1800," *The Mariner's Mirror,* 71 (1985), pp. 35–38.

José P. Merino Navarro, *La Armada Espagnola en el siglo XVIII.* (Madrid, 1981).

Roger Morriss, *The Royal Dockyards during the Revolutionary and Napoleonic Wars.* (Leicester, 1983).

J. J. Packard, "Sir Robert Seppings and the Timber Problem," *The Mariner's Mirror,* 64 (1978), pp. 145–156.

Richard Unger, *Dutch Shipbuilding before 1880: Ships and Guilds.* (Amsterdam, 1978).

Jenny West, *Gunpowder, Government and War in the Mid-Eighteenth Century.* (London, 1991).

Virginia Steele Wood, *Live Oaking: Southern Timber for Tall Ships* (Boston, 1981; reprinted Annapolis, 1994).

22

THE CONVULSION OF EUROPE: THE NAVAL CONFLICT DURING THE REVOLUTIONARY AND NAPOLEONIC WARS

R. J. B. Knight

It is a curious fact that there is no modern authoritative, all-embracing book which tells the remarkable story of the 23 years of naval war which began in 1793. For color and notably accurate details, the novelists who followed C. S. Forester's *Hornblower,* of whom the best today is Patrick O'Brian, have made the period a popular one. Historians still have to turn to large books written in the nineteenth century, such as those by William James and Laird Clowes, for operational details, although there are good smaller scale studies. Only a slim volume by Northcote Parkinson attempts to pull together the main themes, and although it falls short in many ways, it is a vigorous introduction to a complex period which set the European and the world agenda for the next century.

Peace 1783–1793. There was little sign of the convulsions of the 1790s when looked at from the previous decade. For five years after 1783, there was a recuperation period, when, as we have seen, there was a steep economic recovery throughout Europe. If there were any strains, they were on the edge of Europe, for diplomats worried about Poland and the further decline of the Ottoman Empire. Russia, under Catherine the Great, began to flex its muscles; it fought Sweden for more Baltic coastline between 1788 and 1790, and won, and it pushed down south to win its warm water port from Turkey at the same time. There was some Anglo-French antagonism through the Dutch crisis of 1787–8, where the pro-French "Patriot" party was forced out, mainly by invading Prussian troops, but also by English diplomatic and naval pressure. More significant, for our theme, was a classic diplomatic and colonial confrontation between Britain and Spain over Nootka Sound in 1790, when the Spanish reluctantly backed down in the face of an efficient British mobilization. The French would not—could not for financial reasons—back its former ally of the last war against British naval power.

This relative financial decline was not immediately obvious in the admiralties of Europe, which were observing a considerable arms race through these years. Great Britain launched 70,000 tons, though these new ships had largely been laid down before the end of the American War. It looked as though France and Spain were preparing for maritime war between 1786 and 1790, for France launched 95,000 tons of new warships, and Spain 60,000. By 1790, the French navy was 60% larger than in 1775 and in the following two years France and Spain had the largest navies that they would ever have in the sailing ship era. The combined Bourbon naval strength was 34% above the British (417,000 tons to 312,000). But this effort led to perilous financial weakness and the backdown over Nootka Sound. "The Bourbon quantitative superiority proved useless when tested. We are in fact facing a major political mystery— an enormous peacetime shipbuilding programme undertaken by an insolvent regime which faced political ruin."[1]

A number of matters were settled before the war began in 1793. The naval arms race reached a peak in 1790, when throughout Europe there was a total of 1.7 million tons of major warships, 1668 ships of the line requiring four hundred thousand men to man them. Not only that, but a further huge amount of money was spent in infrastructure and fortifications all over Europe, in particular large-scale dockyard works and fortifications at Cherbourg, Portsmouth, Plymouth, Kronstadt and Karlskrona.

In summary, three things were settled in the 10 years before 1793. First, there was the decline of French financial system by 1786, and her consequent diplomatic weakness; hinged on that was, second, the end of the Family Compact, signaled clearly by France failing to back Spain at Nootka Sound. Third, there was the emergence of Russia, which began to play a huge part in the geopolitical drama in Europe. Immediately, she worried France in the Mediterranean because of her important Levant trade; at the same time, British naval power was increasingly dependent upon Russian naval building timber, both hard and softwoods, as well as hemp and pitch.

The Nature of the War. The war which started in 1793 was unlike any conflict which had gone before. At first Great Britain, though not the other European powers, welcomed the overthrow of the absolutist monarchy which it had opposed since the days of Louis XIV; but by 1792, with military success on the continent, France was beginning to export revolution. One ideological system was fighting a completely opposing system. It thus became a total war, one which we can easily recognize from this century.

The British aim was the overthrow of the French regime by the armies of the continental allies and replacement by a government acceptable to the allies. Successive revolutionary governments had shown themselves to have been incapable of negotiation, mostly because of their own internal instability; only the restoration of the monarchy could give internal stability on which the peace of Europe depended; and when Napoleon restored stability within France, he was perceived as a permanent threat to the balance of power in Europe, for after the Peace of Amiens no one trusted him. It became increasingly clear from the turn of the century, and especially after Trafalgar, at the peak of Napoleon's power in Europe, that England's maritime strength was unsafe, for he could obtain the maritime resources to challenge Britain's empire.

It thus developed into an unprecedented war of attrition. To some degree, all eighteenth-century wars were wars of financial attrition and as happened in those wars, Britain's financial strength paid to keep the armies of Prussia, Austria and Russia in the field. But there was a totality about these 22 years which have more in common with the wars of the twentieth century than those which immediately preceded it.

British Strategy. One might think, with the French navy in revolutionary chaos in 1793, and with the British navy at a high peak of efficiency after the successful mobilization of 1790, that there would have been startling British success in the first years. Was a completely maritime strategy—keeping off the continent—a possibility? It was not, however, possible to avoid the old British strategic dilemma of commitment to the continent or to the colonial empire, for the almost total success of the French armies on the continent gave the British a great problem. Holland was overrun and the Prussians declared a zone of neutrality in North Germany; any British army would therefore have no bases. With the exception of Portugal, the whole of the continental coastline from Gibraltar to Denmark was denied to them. For the Revolutionary War, it was going to be amphibious expeditions which were the only way to get at France.

In spite of the ebb and flow of war throughout these years, there were some strategic constants. The first was the British need to control the Channel and the Western Approaches. Fear of French control of the Low Countries, with the deepwater ports of Antwerp and the Scheldt, ideally positioned for mounting an invasion, was the initial reason for war in the first place. The British hold on the Western Approaches was never easily maintained, but it held. Until 1805 it was maintained by remarkable feats of blockade on the French coast. There was great British concern about a French naval renaissance in 1810, but in spite of challenges by single ships and privateers making inroads into British merchant ships, British control did not waver. For this reason, the real weight of the British fleet was kept in home waters. After 1782, with the exception of the dash across the Atlantic by Villeneuve and Nelson, no battlefleet ever again ventured outside European waters, until the twentieth century.

Second, the Mediterranean assumed central strategic importance for the first time since the seventeenth century. For some time, with the British share of the Levant trade declining, it had not been seen as a priority in relation to the West Indies, but for much of this war, it was vital to support Austria against Napoleon, as well as to keep the Kingdom of the Two Sicilies fighting against Napoleon.

Third, there was constant economic warfare against wealth creation by both the French and the British. A very contentious push was made by Pitt, Grenville and Dundas, who ran British strategy in the 1790s, against the French West Indies, and these expeditions sustained heavy troop losses, mainly from sickness. For long this has been heavily criticized, but a recent spirited defense of these decisions concludes, "the Caribbean . . . had served its purpose in helping to establish a decisive British maritime and commercial supremacy over France. Not until 1825 did French foreign trade exceed its 1788 level again, and by then it was largely reorientated towards mainland Europe: not until the middle of the nineteenth century did French merchant shipping tonnage regain its 1788 level."[2] Henry Dundas, more than anyone, was conscious of the need for the wartime financial support from colonial trade: "I have no hesitation in saying that I would much rather hear that 15,000 men were landed in Ireland or even Great Britain, than hear that the same number were landed in Jamaica with a fleet there superior to ours."[3]

For most of the Revolutionary War, there was thus the classic stalemate between land and seapower; or to use a contemporary saying, the "whale" had never before felt so much in the power of the "elephant." British control of sea routes could not destroy the French; Napoleon's military might could not reduce England. Britain fought a maritime defensive strategy with limited offensives, which went throught three phases: first, emergency operations to weaken the French battlefleets and remove neutral fleets from his grasp; second, securing overseas bases and denying them to the French— the Cape of Good Hope, Ceylon, Malta, Madeira; third, limited offensives against enemy colonies and forces overseas.

But unquestionably, in *strategic terms,* by the time of the Peace of Amiens in 1801 Britain had lost the Revolutionary War. Further, she very nearly lost the economic battle in the 1790s. British credit nearly gave way, for Britain was borrowing at such a rate that it had to stop; and while the working economy was in good shape, the financial system was running hot. Reform of the financial system was needed and the introduction of income tax provided much needed government income. Pitt tried very hard and nearly succeeded in suing for peace in 1796. The news of the British victory at St. Vincent in 1797 was of immense psychological importance in restoring political and financial morale.

Certainly, Britain and Ireland had been defended successfully, for the French attempts at invasion of Ireland and the West Coast of England came to nothing. India had been made safe by Nelson's overwhelming victory at the Nile, while the attempt to form a Northern Alliance against England had been foiled. There were plenty of British colonial maritime successes, but these conquests were given back at the Peace of Amiens, except Ceylon, Trinidad and parts of India, while Malta was to be neutralized. But all these British victories had been purely defensive: not one of them put France in any danger, while she had defeated every combination of continental power during the campaigns of the Second Coalition. British objectives had been to prevent France from being dominant in Europe and above all in a position of dominance over the Rhine estuary—to keep France out of what is now Belgium and Holland. And to restore the monarchy.

The Invasion Threat and Trafalgar. The Peace of Amiens in 1801–2 was never likely to last long, and distrust of Napoleon's intentions led to continued hostilities. British merchants found that trade with the continent was discouraged, while large-scale French warship building caused the British government, now under Addington, to refuse to release Malta from British control as was agreed at the peace. Napoleon, rather in the manner of his bold stroke to Eygpt in 1798, tried to break the deadlock with a concentrated effort on

Figure XXVI. The battle of Trafalgar, evening, by William John Huggins, demonstrating the heavy damage wrought by both sides, as well as the lowering skies which signalled the start of the prolonged gale which the battered ships had to endure for four days afterwards. *Courtesy of National Maritime Museum, London.*

invasion. The invasion flotilla which gathered in Boulogne, Etaples and Wimereux was capable of transporting 167,000 men of the Grand Army, three times as large as the defenders and much more experienced. Because of the rejuvenation of the French navy, swelled with captured ships, and the fact that at this point the Spanish were allies, meant that the British were at a disadvantage. Nevertheless, the French could not get the local superiority for their invasion barges. It led, as we know, to Villeneuve's feint across the Atlantic, with Nelson in pursuit, and then to Trafalgar, and to one of the most famous judgments in naval history:

> The world has never seen a more impressive demonstration of the influence of seapower upon its history. Those far distant, storm-beaten ships, upon which the Grand Army never looked, stood between it and the dominion of the world.[4]

In fact, Trafalgar did not prevent invasion, for Napoleon had already given up before the battle was fought; but it was a real turning point in the naval balance. At Trafalgar, France and Spain lost 23 battleships, measuring almost 70,000 tons. Before the battle Britain had 330,000 tons, which was the equivalent of France, Spain and the Netherlands; by the end of 1805 Britain had the advantage of 570,000 to 350,000 tons.[5] For the next 10 years, Britain's control over European waters was firm. Its ability to protect trade and support land warfare against the French, wherever that might be, was now assured. And yet, from 1805 to 1807, Napoleon had his greatest run of land battles—Ulm, Austerlitz, Preisburg, Jena-Auerstadt, Eylau and Friedland—leaving him in firm control of the continent of Europe. Land and seapower stood deadlocked.

The Continental Blockade. Unable to settle matters by the sword, Napoleon tried to go for Britain's other great weapon, credit and the trade that supported it. He was now able to order all of Europe, except Sweden, to exclude all British trade, which he did by the Berlin Decrees; the British retaliated by the Orders-in-Council:

> Whereas, certain orders, establishing an unprecedented system of warfare against this kingdom, and aimed at the destruction of its commerce and resources, were some time since, issued by the government of France, by which "The British Islands were declared to be in a state of blockade" thereby subjecting to capture and condemnation all vessels, with their cargoes, which should continue to trade with His Majesty's Dominions . . . [6]

Britain was unquestionably very vulnerable and came near at times to crisis, in 1808 and between 1811 and 1812. There were vast stocks of colonial goods in British warehouses, unemployment, unrest in the counties, at the same time as an enormous rise in the national debt. Relations with the United States worsened, and with the application of the U.S. embargo, pressures became intense. However, military events conspired to break the hold of Napoleon. His invasion of Portugal in 1807 freed up Portuguese Brazil to British merchants while the revolution in Spain in the next year enabled British goods to pour in there. Russia's break with Napoleon brought relief to the 1811–12 slump. And the system leaked; as we have seen before, officials could be bribed and goods could be smuggled; French officials could issue false licenses. Trade also developed in those parts unaffected by the continental system or by the American "Nonintercourse" policy—in Asia, the West Indies, Latin America and the Near East. As before, the war destroyed the commerce of her rivals as the war spread to Holland and Denmark; British conquest continued and her far markets expanded. Nevertheless, British merchants had to be very responsive to the market; there was much boom and bust as each new country fell.

So in spite of everything, British exports constantly increased. Between 1794–1796, £21.7 million; 1804–1806, £37.5 million; 1814–1816, £44.4 million. War stimulated armaments, iron, metals, coal, timber. Pig-iron production in 1788 was 68,000 tons; in 1806, 244,000; in 1811, 325,000 tons—up nearly five times in 20 or so years. Cotton, as we have seen, was by 1815 the greatest export. This new wealth had to be taxed to pay for the war. In 1793 customs and excise receipts were £13.5 million a year; by 1815 they were £44.8 million. The new income tax and property tax raised £1.67 million in 1799; by 1815 it was £14.6 million. In fact, between 1793 and 1815 the British government secured the staggering sum of £1,217 million from direct and indirect taxes, and proceeded to raise a further £440 million in loans from the money markets without exhausting its credit. At the critical point in the middle years of the conflict, the economy saw Britain through its worst years:

Between 1799 and 1808 the government's income doubled. Without this increasing revenue the government would never have been able to borrow as heavily as it did to maintain a fleet of nearly a hundred ships of the line, an army (including militia) numbering on paper over 350,000 men in 1814 and to subsidise her allies to the tune of about thirty-five million between 1810 and 1815.[7]

This economic effort outlasted France. French economic growth was still slow, in spite of having the whole of Europe within its system; its agriculture never went through the revolution that was experienced in England. British control of the seas made the economy turn inwards, away from the Atlantic economy. French credit was never far away from a crisis, and while this had less effect on the army, the capital-intensive navy suffered. Napoleon, of course, fed his armies outside France, and supplied the country through the plunder of conquered lands through indemnities, confiscations and spoils. As long as the army was successful, and kept going, then the system worked. But even at its most successful, it took its losses and experienced troops started to become scarce. There was, perhaps, a final contradiction: a nation which proclaimed liberty, fraternity and liberty spread those messages by conquest, and in the end the conquered non-French population threw it off. Perhaps Napoleon had to have unending war to survive.

The War on Trade. Between 1793 and 1815 almost eleven thousand merchant vessels were captured by French warships and privateers. To put this very high figure in perspective, it should be seen against the entries and departures of ships to and from London, which carried on more than half the commerce of the country, which recorded between thirteen and fourteen thousand *annually*. Nevertheless, there was real pressure. Marine insurance rates rose dramatically, there was press criticism of the Admiralty. In 1800, after Napoleon had pounced on British shipping in the Baltic and total shipping losses reached their highest ever in a single year (619), the Committee of Lloyds was formally censured by its members. French privateering was particularly effective between 1797 and 1802 in the Western Approaches, as French trade collapsed and southwest France declined commercially and industrially; seafaring communities put their effort into the risky business of taking British shipping. Ships from Dunkirk, Saint-Malo, Nantes and Bordeaux went after different trades and different prizes—slaves, whalers, Newfoundland fisheries. In the east, Mauritius was a hotbed, until taken in 1810.

It is difficult to know exactly how much of a dent this made in British trade. British financial confidence, as we have seen, was maintained at a high level, except for the period 1796 to 1797. The tactical answer, as for every eighteenth-century and subsequent war, was the adoption of convoys. The Convoy Acts of 1793, 1798 and 1803 were imposed on reluctant shipowners; only the large ships of the East India and Hudson Bay Companies were exempt from having to join a convoy. Extraordinary steps were taken for the safe passage of the Baltic convoys. Ships of the line were stationed at each end of the Belt (the main passage into the Baltic) and at intervals long it. Convoys of five hundred ships would gather at Spithead.

The End of the Wars. Napoleon's immense military strength was not to be dislodged until Wellington had prized open Portugal and Spain, and failure in Russia had weakened the Grand Army. The final act only lasted from 1813 to 1815, and up to that time Britain had operated a successful blue-water policy. "While other European parties emerged from wars weakened economically," Daniel Baugh has observed, "Britain was financially stronger than ever. If the true geopolitical object of a nation's external policy is to ensure a relatively favourable post-war outcome, blue-water policy served the purpose remarkably well."[8] British naval strength at sea was now of a superpower standard, directly analagous to the situation of the United States in the early 1990s. In 1790 its share of world naval tonnage was 30%; by 1810 it was 50%. It was the only time in the history of wooden navies that a single country owned half the world's battlefleet.

NOTES

1. Jan Glete, *Navies and Nations.* (Stockholm, 1993), volume 1, pp. 276–277.

2. Michael Duffy, *Soldiers, Sugar and Seapower; the British Expeditions to the West Indies and the War against Revolutionary France.* (Oxford, 1987), pp. 389–390.

3. John B. Hattendorf, et al., eds., *British Naval Documents.* (London, 1993), p. 342.

4. John B. Hattendorf, ed., *Mahan on Naval Strategy: Selections from the Writings of Rear Admiral Alfred Thayer Mahan.* (Annapolis, 1991), p. xxviii.

5. Glete, *Navies and Nations,* I, p. 378.

6. Hattendorf, et al., *British Naval Documents,* p. 351.

7. David French, *The British Way of Warfare, 1688–2000.* (London, 1990), pp. 106–107.

8. Daniel A. Baugh, "Great Britain's 'Blue Water' Policy," *The International History Review,* X (1988), p. 58.

SUGGESTIONS FOR FURTHER READING

Martine Accera and Jean Meyer, *Marines et Revolution.* (Rennes, 1988).

Daniel A. Baugh, "Great Britain's 'Blue Water' Policy," *The International History Review,* X (1988), pp. 33–58.

Sir W. Laird Clowes, *The Royal Navy: A History from the earliest times to the death of Queen Victoria.* 7 volumes. (London, 1897–1903).

Malcolm Crook, *Toulon in War and Revolution; From the Ancien Regime to the Restoration, 1750–1820.* (Manchester, 1991).

Patrick Crowhurst, *The French War on Trade; Privateering, 1793–1815.* (Aldershot, 1989).

Michael Duffy, *Soldiers, Sugar and Seapower; the British Expeditions to the West Indies and the War against Revolutionary France.* (Oxford, 1987).

Michael Duffy, "The Establishment of the Western Squadron as the Linchpin of British Naval Strategy," in Duffy, ed., *Parameters of British Naval Power, 1650–1850.* (Exeter, 1992), pp. 60–81.

David French, *The British Way of Warfare, 1688–2000.* (London, 1990).

Jan Glete, *Navies and Nations: Warships, Navies, and State Building in Europe and America, 1500–1860.* (Stockholm, 1993).

Richard Glover, *Britain at Bay; Defence against Bonaparte, 1803–14.* (London, 1973).

Christopher D. Hall, *British Strategy in the Napoleonic War, 1803–1815.* (Manchester, 1992).

Christopher Hall, "The Royal Navy and the Peninsular War," *The Mariner's Mirror,* 79 (1993), pp. 403–418.

John B. Hattendorf, ed., *Mahan on Naval Strategy: Selections from the Writings of Rear Admiral Alfred Thayer Mahan.* (Annapolis, 1991).

John B. Hattendorf, R. J. B. Knight, A. W. H. Pearsall, N. A. M. Rodger, and Geoffrey Till, eds., *British Naval Documents, 1204–1960.* Publications of the Navy Records Society, volume 131. (London, 1993).

William James, *The Naval History of Great Britain, 1793–1827.* (London, 1822; editions of 1837, 1878, 1886 and 1902).

Paul M. Kennedy, *The Rise and Fall of British Naval Mastery.* (London, 1976).

Paul M. Kennedy, *The Rise and Fall of the Great Powers: Economic Change and Military Conflict from 1500–2000.* (New York, 1987).

Piers Mackesy, *The Strategy of Overthrow, 1798–1799.* (London, 1974).

Piers Mackesy, "Problems of an Amphibious Power: Britain against

France, 1793–1815," *Naval War College Review,* 30 (1978), pp. 16–25.

Piers Mackesy, *War without Victory; the Downfall of Pitt, 1799–1802.* (Oxford, 1984).

Roger Morriss, *The Royal Dockyards during the Revolutionary and Napoleonic Wars.* (Leicester, 1983).

C. Northcote Parkinson, *Britannia Rules: the Classic Age of Naval History, 1793–1815.* (London, 1977; reprinted Gloucester, 1987).

A. N. Ryan, "The Royal Navy and the Blockade of Brest, 1689–1805: Theory and Practice," in Martine Accera, José Merino and Jean Meyer, eds., *Les Marines de Guerre Europeenes XVII-XVIIIe siècles.* (Paris, 1985), pp. 175–193.

Paul Webb, "Construction, repair and maintenance in the battle fleet of the Royal Navy, 1793–1815," in Jeremy Black and Philip Woodfine, eds., *The British Navy and the Uses of Naval Power in the Eighteenth Century.* (Leicester, 1988), pp. 203–219.

Paul Webb, "The Frigate Situation of the Royal Navy, 1793–1815," *The Mariner's Mirror,* 82 (1996), pp. 28–40.

London Docks.   Published by Henry Moses March 1 1825

Figure XXVII. London Docks, print by Henry Moses, 1825. With the expansion of trade through the wars, there had been huge investment in docks. This is a view of the ships, lighters and warehouses, part of a "wet dock" or basin with gates that ensured that ships floated at all states of the tide. *Courtesy of National Maritime Museum, London.*

23

THE LAST YEARS OF SAIL

R. J. B. Knight

Unlike the two great wars of this century, in 1815 Britain emerged as not only the naval and military victor, but with unprecedented economic advantages. It was the most efficient industrial market economy in Europe and, though the government consisted of aristocrats and landowners, came the nearest to a "businessman's government" of its day. Yet it was a state which had spent an extraordinary amount on military expenditure, and it is worth looking back at the whole question of war, credit and the state in Hanoverian England; and, at the same time, to bring together the main themes of war and trade and their interdependence.

From the time of the Glorious Revolution of 1688 until the battle of Waterloo, Britain had declared war against foreign powers no less than eight times and mobilized its troops and sailors for about half those years. In real terms normal or "peacetime" expenditure on goods and expenditures climbed three times from the mid-1680s to the mid-1780s: wartime expenditures grew from four million pounds a year in the 1690s to nearly seventeen million a year in 1790s: and by a factor of five if we compare national expenditures during the Nine Years' War, 1689–97, with the War against Napoleon, 1803–15. Taxation rose in real terms by a factor of 16 between the reigns of James II and George IV. Yet the state spent very little (estimated 0.5% of GNP) on social overheads; little on law, though it was strong on authority; and all its infrastructure, canals, navigable rivers, roads, were paid for by private capital. At the same time as these wars took place, there was long-term development of the economy.

The overwhelming preoccupation of the Hanoverian State was with funding and directing foreign, strategic and commercial policies. The startling fact is that 83% of all public money spent on goods and services between 1688 and 1815 was military in origin and purpose. Further, almost all British eighteenth-century wars were waged largely on borrowed money. In 1688 the national debt was less than two million pounds—less than 5% of GNP; in 1816 it was 834 millions—twice the GNP. Broadly, by creating the Bank of England in 1689, subjecting governmental expenditure to the control of the Treasury and the review of Parliament, Britain demonstrated a degree of financial probity that encouraged capitalists to lend very large sums of money over long periods at reasonable rates of interest. The French state did not achieve such credit-worthiness until the 1830s and Imperial Russia never did. In fact, the City of London as the only international capital market, attracted foreign capital to finance its wars, and over this hundred years the costs of borrowing fell dramatically. In the wars of Louis XIV it was between 8 and 9%; against Napoleon it was less than 5%.

Sixty percent of all these revenues went on the navy. Otherwise, substantial armies were sent to the continent only three times (1689–97, 1702–13 and 1808–15), or the revenues supported direct subsidies to continental powers or hiring German troops (Hessians, Hanoverians, or Swiss).

On balance, this huge amount of money seems to have been well-spent. The Royal Navy remained in command of the Channel and the North Sea, and largely in control of the Atlantic trade routes. More than that, there was no invasion between 1688 and 1815 to waste the domestic economy. Britain preserved her island security, capital assets and agriculture. There was no ransacking of grain or destruction of capital equipment or industrial raw materials. The share of English artisans drafted into the army and navy remained small, because troops were raised from overseas, or from among the unskilled, colonial and Celtic fringes; there were many foreign seamen in her naval and merchant ships; and because Britain concentrated the bulk of military investment into capital intensive (i.e., *naval*) campaigns rather than labor intensive (i.e., *army*) campaigns to secure her national objectives.

Before 1805, no great power emerged on the mainland of Europe capable of obstructing Britain's trade with the continent. Foreign aggression against British commerce and territories overseas declined into insignificance. As we have seen, after independence in 1783, the United States was reincorporated into the Atlantic economy with Britain at its hub, and on Britain's terms. At the same time, diplomacy backed by military force had compelled the rival empires of Portugal, Spain and Holland in the South Americas and Asia and the Mughals in India to concede entry to British trade and ships. British privateering, as well as Royal Navy blockades and assaults upon the merchant ships of Holland, France and Spain (together with the vulnerability of Amsterdam and Frankfurt to invading armies on the continent) led to the domination of the international markets of the City of London.

During that long (but still by historical standards rapid transition), Hanoverian statesmen entertained no illusions about the international order their businessmen had to operate within. For more than a century, when the British economy was on its way to maturity as the workshop of the world, its governments were not particularly liberal nor wedded ideologically to laissez faire. Like the proverbial hedgehog of Aeschylus, the Hanoverian governments knew some big things, namely that security, trade, Empire and military power really mattered. In fruitful (if uneasy) partnership with bourgeois merchants and industrialists they poured millions into strategic objectives which we can see (with hindsight) formed preconditions for the market economy and night-watchman state of Victorian England, as well as the liberal world order which flourished under British hegemony from 1846 to 1914.[1]

Spain and Portugal. If this was a period of consolidation and even domination for Britain, what was happening to Spain and Portugal? These two empires were also locked in a life and death struggle with Napoleon.

Between 1810 and 1825 the crown of Spain lost control of one of the largest and richest empires in world history. Thirteen immense territories were lost—Argentina, Chile, Peru, Ecuador, Bolivia, Venezuela, Colombia, Mexico, Central America, Paraguay, Uruguay, Santo Domingo and Florida. It collapsed virtually without a fight, although in 1829 there was one half-hearted attempt to retake America with the dispatch of three thousand troops to Mexico, but it was decisively defeated on the Mexican coast. Recognition of independence by the homeland had to wait until the 1830s. Over 16 million people, more than half the total population of the empire, wrested political control of their homelands. Sixteen individual republics would eventually come into existence. By 1825, the map of the world was radically changed, and Spain held on only to the Philippines, Cuba and Puerto Rico, until these were eventually lost in 1898. The commercial and economic consequences were immense, with Spain immediately plunged into the second or third rank of European powers. The total value of gold and silver imported into Cadiz from 1797 to 1821 was 183 million pesos. In 1809, the remission of wealth from America in Cadiz had been 43 million pesos and it fell gradually over the ensuing war years until it dried up completely.

The story of the loss of the Portuguese Atlantic Empire, by which we mean Brazil, follows much on the same lines, though with some important variations; it was very much linked with British economic progress and expansion. Nor should this be seen entirely as a one-sided economic relationship, for Britain depended very much upon Brazilian raw cotton, directly shipped or reimported through Portugal. Between 1785 and 1790, the balance of trade between England and Portugal had been brought into equilibrium and from 1791 to 1795, for the first time in the eighteenth century, Portuguese exports to England showed a surplus over British exports to Portugal. By the first decade of the nineteenth century about a quarter of Lancashire's cotton wool imports came from Brazil. There was pressure on politicians from industrialists to recognize its importance. Indeed, as early as 1801, Lord Hawkesbury instructed the British minister in Lisbon to let it be known that:

> in the case of invasion, the British envoy was authorised to recommend that the court of Portugal embark for Brazil . . . and the [British] were ready for their part to guarantee the security of the expedition and to combine with [the Portuguese government] the most efficacious ways to extend and consolidate [their] dominions in South America.[2]

That invasion came in 1807, when the Prince Regent finally rejected Napoleon's demands that Portugal should join the continental blockade against Great Britain. It led to flight of the Royal family to Brazil (under British naval protection) where it stayed until 1821. From 1807, when he arrived in Brazil, the Prince Regent decreed that all Brazilian ports should be opened to friendly powers, which meant effectively the British alone until the end of the Napoleonic wars. Brazil was elevated to being a separate kingdom in 1815. King John VI (as he became in 1816) showed no great enthusiasm to return to Portugal and when he did eventually leave in 1821, he left his son there as Regent. The break came in the same year, when the Cortes (the Parliament) insisted that Brazil be brought under full Portuguese military control; the Prince Regent threw in his lot with the Brazilians in 1822. After some fighting—the remaining Portuguese troops were thrown out by a scratch expedition led by Lord Cochrane—the Portuguese eventually recognized independence in 1825.

The economic consequences of opening the Brazilian ports to Britain hit promising Portuguese industry, unable to keep up with British productivity. The country had few of the ingredients for industrial takeoff—no coalfields, canals, good roads or adequate means of transportation. It also paved the way for three decades of political turmoil and unrest, which developed into civil war at times between liberals and absolutists. The liberals tried to dismantle the close connection between church and state and came up against the innately conservative outlook of what was largely a peasant agricultural community. Moreover, the liberals concentrated on political, constitutional and administrative changes—rather than economic, social and technological ones.

British commercial and industrial strength, combined with their naval strength and control of the Atlantic, played a large part in unraveling the Portuguese and Spanish Empires. For Britain, the acquisition of the South American markets had long been at the center of their thinking. Henry Dundas, secretary for war, in a remarkable cabinet memorandum of 1800, put it succinctly:

> The acquisition of the South American market is a more extensive consideration . . . my plan is not one of additional aggrandisement by extensive conquest, or the acquisition of colonial dominion: for although I am satisfied that the sovereignity of Spain over that extensive empire is in its last extremity, I am not urging you to yield to the temptation which such circumstances may seem to present. If ever we interfere to aid or to regulate the establishment of any one or more forms of government which may be built on the total ruins of Spanish power in South America, let that interference arise out of the feelings of goodwill, friendship and cordiality which the habits of commercial intercourse will naturally produce. No other connection with them can be attainable or durable. But on the other hand we should in my judgement be culpable if we neglected to embrace at the present moment the means which are in our power to possess ourselves of such stations on the coast of South America, as may secure to us under every probable circumstance an unbounded market in that extensive empire for the various produce of the industry and commercial enterprise of this country. I need not remark, because it is obvious, that the present strength and pre-eminence of this country is owing to the extent of its resources arising from its commerce, and its naval power, which are inseparably connected. They must stand and fall together. In proportion as our commerce is flourishing beyond example, exactly in the same proportion it is the duty of the government of this country to omit no probable or rational means of extending our commercial markets.[3]

In the words of a perceptive modern scholar: "One cannot help thinking that it would have been better for the French if they had left Iberia alone when, after the victories of Nelson, they could not challenge British naval superiority in the Atlantic Ocean."[4] That invasion, quite apart from allowing British armies a safe foothold when successful invasion came, was an attack on the two empires of the Southern Atlantic and it was England's commerce and credit—those engines of war—which reaped the benefit.

The character and speed of the Latin American revolutions differed considerably from that of North America. The Spanish Empire was too large and too fragmented to be united. By the time they occurred, the French Revolution, with its excesses, had also taken place, which induced caution; and from the view of tropical America, with its plantation economies and slave economies, the great slave revolt in Haiti in 1792 had a major impact, equal to the American and French Revolutions. While it brought caution to the elites of Spanish America, it also brought greater caution to the governments of Europe. For Britain, in particular, there was nothing to be gained if rebellion was to bring instability and violence which would destroy the very wealth that attracted British traders in the first place. Sir John Barrow, Secretary to the Admiralty, traveller and shrewd commentator, wrote in 1806:

> Revolutions in states where each individual has some interest in their welfare are not effected without the most serious calamities. What, then, must be the consequences in a country where the number of slaves exceeds the proprietors of the soil? In promoting revolutions, I trust England will never be concerned, being fully convinced that however much South America might gain from a quiet change of masters, she will be soon thrown back into a state of barbarianism by revolutions.[5]

The End of Slavery. The Haitian revolt of 1792 was the first significant step in the dismantling of slavery, and Haiti managed to get itself recognized as an independent state by 1804. In 1794 the French Revolution formally emancipated all slaves within the French Empire. Napoleon reinstituted slavery elsewhere, but the first steps nevertheless had been taken. The abolition of the slave trade was the critical step, since in most places the plantation complex depended on a continuous flow of fresh slaves from Africa to make up for the difference between births and deaths. Denmark and the Netherlands led the way in abolishing their own diminished slave trades in the 1790s, but the first serious blow came with the British and American abolition acts in 1808. On 25 March 1807, after a lengthy and bitter struggle inside and outside the British Parliament, it was declared illegal for British subjects (and at this point during the Napoleonic Wars at least half the trade was in British hands) to trade in slaves after 1 May 1808. "Encouraged by this success the British abolitionist movement brought pressure to bear on the British government to go further in expiating Britain's own guilt by using all the means at their command to persuade 'morally inferior' nations to follow Britain's lead."[6] There were, of course, clear economic reasons why Britain should pursue this policy. The British West Indies were now deprived of their cheap labor; it was important that their rivals, especially those in Cuba and Brazil who already enjoyed many advantages over them, should be put on an equal footing. The effect of the abolition of the slave trade on the economy of the United States was neutral because the American South already had a slave population that could increase by natural growth. As a result, the demand for slaves in the United States was comparatively small compared to developing sugar colonies like Cuba, British Guiana or Trinidad. Although there have been scholars who have doubted this, the British act did do its trading economy harm—it has been called "econocide"—the destruction of a hitherto successful economic order in the name of moral principle.

For the next 50 years after Britain herself abolished the slave trade, successive British governments strove to achieve the international abolition of the transatlantic slave trade by persuading or coercing those states which had an interest in the trade to enter into abolitionist agreements with Britain, or to introduce and enforce their own antislave trade legislation. There was much service by British frigates and sloops on the West and East African coasts in trying to prevent the trade. This was resented, for few other nations shared Britain's abolitionist views. By the late 1830s the slave trade had been prohibited by all the major European and American states, while the emancipation of slaves in the British Caribbean colonies took place in 1834, followed by the French in 1848, the Dutch colonies a little later and the United States in 1865.

But there was a long way to go until the end of the trade, which for centuries had been the chief source of labor for the Atlantic economy and underpinning powerful interests in Europe, Africa and the Americas; it was not to be readily suppressed. Though the volume is difficult to measure, during the 1840s the trade probably reached an all-time peak. Two of the most important branches—the Brazilian (illegal since 1830) and the Cuban (illegal since 1820) continued into the second half of the nineteenth century. The Brazilian slave trade was finally suppressed in 1850–1, although a few isolated landings of slaves from Africa occurred as late as 1855; the trade to Cuba was finally brought to an end in 1865. Brazil and the last of the Spanish

Empire eventually emancipated their slaves in the late 1880s, while the last British slavery patrols on the East African coast took place in 1890.

*　*　*　*　*　*

ENDGAME

The final part of this book is called "The Maritime Legacy of Empire" and there are enough discontinuities between 1815 and 1850 to see it as the end of an era. As usual, none of them ends simply and a clear date is not easy to discern.

Sail to Steam. The most obvious one is the end of sail and the beginning of steam, but for both the naval and merchant fleets of the world this was a very gradual process. "The popular idea that steam made sailing ships obsolete overnight is based on a telescoping of invention and successful application."[7] In fact, the first successful iron and steam battleship, *Le Napoleon,* was launched as late as 1850; only then was it possible to create an effective balance of sailing qualities which included a steam plant. Perhaps 1812 is the other significant date, when the first steamboat in Britain to be put to commercial use went into service on the Clyde. The process developed slowly, moving in stages from rivers, to cross-Channel, to the near-sea business in the 1830s and across the Atlantic only in the 1840s, though the *Sirius* and the *Great Western* crossed the Atlantic in 1838. Engine efficiency was the key to everything on the longer routes and the proportion of coal bunkers to cargo space was a critical ratio. But it was not until the 1850s, with the adoption of screw propulsion and iron hulls, that the steamship presented a genuine alternative to the sailing ship.

Additionally, the steamship business grew up alongside rather than taking over from the traditional sailing routes. High capital and running costs, as much as the speed and regularity of the service, dictated frequent operation over defined advertised routes. From the late 1830s, some of these lines were artificially supported by mail contracts (P&O, Cunard, Royal Mail etc.). If there were no contracts, a sufficient volume of business was necessary to bear higher freight rates, which would allow frequent voyages to be undertaken. Steam therefore proved suitable to the carriage of passengers, livestock and perishable goods, but these were new shipping markets created by speedy and for the most part reliable steam service. Thus for instance, a founder of the P&O Steam Ship Company explained in 1844:

Figure XXVIII. An aquatint of the SS *Elise*, a very early French steamship arriving in Paris, 29 March 1816; the early stage of development can be seen, and she would not have navigated more than the River Seine. *Courtesy of National Maritime Museum, London.*

With regard to the coasting trade, I do not think that steam navigation has at all materially interfered with that trade; much of the conveyance now by coasting in steam vessels has taken existence from steam navigation, such as whole cargoes of cattle and dead meat, which never came by sailing vessels. All the main articles conveyed coastwise are still left untouched to the sailing coasting vessels, such as iron, copper, lead, stone, lime, coals, timber.[8]

Sail was very far from dead; indeed the last commercial sailing ships did not die out until after the Second World War.

It is worth seeing how the British navy, the arbiter of the seas in this period, adapted to the new technology. There are a number of misconceptions—that nothing much happened; that there was no international friction; that governments and admiralties did not understand the possibilities of steam and were slow to react; that sea power was exercised by Britain in a hundred gunboat wars, where she upheld her formal and informal empire before, in the second half of the century, all of Europe and the United States scrambled for the rest of the world.

In fact there was a good deal of friction, with Britain trying to maintain the status quo against France and Russia in particular, and it was in her interests to ensure that they did not come together. Keeping French influence out of the Low Countries for defensive reasons and Russia out of the Mediterranean for geopolitical and trading reasons, were the twin thrusts of British diplomatic policy. France was unstable in the decades after the Congress of Vienna, and had five regimes, all of which were aggressive at one time or another, principally in 1840 in the Syrian crisis, when the mobilization of the British fleet settled matters. But there were also challenges to British interests in Greece, Belgium, the Ottoman Empire, North America, the Caribbean, Persia, China and Scandinavia. British naval strength prevented European intervention in the new Latin American republics and, in spite of worries on both sides, after the War of 1812 both the United States and Britain realized that any conflict between them would inflict damage without either side being able to deliver a mortal blow. It was in Britain's interests to keep the world as it was shaped in 1815 at the Congress of Vienna; and broadly, that is what happened.

Up to the middle of the century, this was ensured not by a technological race, but by further developments on the old eighteenth-century themes: secure finance and the economic strength which backed it, sound design, the battle against decay to make sure the reserve fleets were effective. And again they were maintained bet-

ter than any rivals. This is not to deny that there were very significant technological developments, and by the 1830s things were
beginning to move—the invention of the condenser so that boilers
did not have to use salt water, was critical. The United States was
foremost in the search for steam power in the development of the
Fulton, used for coastal defense, while Britain was not slow to
adopt it for its gunboat role, for instance, in the Opium Wars of the
1840s.

Rather than these new technological developments, it was careful
development of wooden technology upon which British naval power
was founded. Ships increased dramatically in size. Sir Robert Seppings introduced diagonal bracing in the hull which enabled ships to
treble in size: the largest wooden battleship ever built was the *Howe*
of 1859: she was 7,000 tons, compared to the *Victory* of just over 2,000
tons. Perhaps more important than size was real progress with the
problem of timber decay. Largely through pragmatic observation, the
use of building sheds and seasoning on the stocks and the use of hardwoods from the East, this problem was, in effect, solved by 1830. The
pre-1815 ships were repaired, while those built subsequently were
constructed with more attention to the seasoning requirements of
oak, or the use of teak which required far less special handling. The
use of tropical hardwoods helped to banish the specter of dry rot, but
careful seasoning and slow construction were the only effective preventive measures; anything else was only an attempt to stop infes-
tation already firmly established and as such unlikely to succeed.
"The battlefleet of 1850 was far superior to that of 1815, as the later
career of so many large units was to demonstrate."[9] (Two frigates, the
Trincomalee and *Unicorn* are still afloat today, while many lasted
until well into this century as training ships or in other capacities:
*Vernon, Implacable, Conway, Worcester, Howe, Daedalus, Foudroy-
ant, St. Vincent.* The *Victory* is now mostly built of teak).

Thus the battlefleet of the British navy became, in sailing terms,
modernized, utilizing an improved understanding of ship structures
and timber seasoning and improvements in managing seamen.
Though there was heavy political pressure to keep costs down, the
cost of the navy was never a major political issue and there was
cross-party consensus on the issue. "The only time when money was
wasted was in the premature rush into iron and aspects of the early
screw ships."[10] These wooden ships were the strongest ever made
and those that were built before 1815 were brought up to the new
standard. The real maritime power, and the strength of deterrence,
lay not in the small squadrons which made the headlines in small

Figure XXIX. H.M.S. *Prince,* 110 guns, pictured by E. W. Cooke in July 1828 with a reduced rig in Portsmouth harbor. The life of this ship spanned the period of the last four chapters. The keel was laid in 1782; she was launched as a 90-gun ship in 1788. In 1796, she was lengthened 17 feet 6 inches for an increase in tonnage to 2,088 tons. She was put to harbor service in 1816 and broken up in 1827. Though she is floating high in the water, Cooke captures the size and bulk of a smaller example of the last generation of wooden fighting ships. *Courtesy of National Maritime Museum, London.*

foreign wars, but was apparent to those who saw the long lines of reserve ships lying at Portsmouth, Plymouth and Sheerness.

Free Trade and the End of the Navigation Laws. The second
major discontinuity at this time is the beginnings of free trade and
the end of mercantilism. The repeal of the Navigation Acts brought
an to end more than two centuries of protective legislation for
British shipping, a major change in commercial policy. Yet it has
tended to be seen as a postscript to the repeal of the Corn Laws and
the beginnings of free trade, and nineteenth-century historians have
seen it as insignificant, in spite of the fact that there was protracted
political struggle between the shipping interests (the protectionists)
and those who thought that the Navigation Acts strangled British
trade. After 1 January 1850 foreign vessels were free to do business
in Britain's colonial trades and to carry goods from anywhere in the
world into British ports, though it left untouched the considerable
British coasting trade.

The central reason for this change was that British shipping had
failed to match the expansion of British business. In 1848 foreign-
owned vessels accounted for just under 29% of the total tonnage entering and clearing British ports with cargo. In 1850, the first year
when they were allowed access to colonial and indirect trades, their
share was 33% and by the late 1850s it was averaging almost 40%.
Not all countries accepted reciprocity agreements. France, Spain
and Portugal denied British ships access to their colonies, while
their vessels freely entered British colonial ports. Nor did the United
States come to a reciprocity agreement, though the Civil War dealt
a tremendous blow to American competitiveness. In fact, the 10
years that followed the repeal of the Navigation Laws was a pros-
perous time for British shipping because of expansion which was
happening in any case, but probably not directly related to the repeal of the Acts.

One prop on which the Navigation Laws could no longer rely was
the "nursery for seaman" argument, held so dearly up to 1815, by
which the merchant marine provided the main source of manpower
for the navy. However, the Victorian navy needed far fewer men because far fewer ships were at sea and because with steam there was
less need for manpower per ship; in 1815 there were 120,000 seamen
in the Royal Navy, in 1818 23,000 and for much of the 1830s under
30,0000. It was by now employing much more enlightened recruitment, training and discipline policies. The contribution of Sir James
Graham, the reforming First Lord of the Admiralty in the 1830s,
who spoke for the government in the abolition debates, is revealing.

Noting that he regarded the navy as the "arch of our power," he asked: "Will the repeal of the Navigation Laws injure that commercial marine which is the mainstay of the Royal Navy? If I could bring myself to entertain this belief, I should not vote for this bill." The bill, he believed, would lead to a lowering of freights, which would increase imports and exports, so stimulating trade and consumption, and hence, as he said, "will inevitably lead to an increase in the number of our seamen and our ships."[11]

"The End of the Columbian Era?" The third justification for ending the story of Europe, the Americas and the Atlantic at this point in history is the issue of continental land power versus sea power which was being debated at the end of the nineteenth century. In the debate, the principal proponent of land power postulated that the world had come to the end of the long era which had started with the discovery of the Americas by Columbus. The origins of this debate go back to the "Blue-water/Continental" issue which began in the early eighteenth century.

The foremost sea power prophet was Alfred Thayer Mahan, whose influence was at its height at the end of the nineteenth century, when he argued the case of sea power on historical grounds in a number of books, the most important being *The Influence of Seapower upon History, 1660–1783* (1890). He claimed that "the key to much of history as well as of the policy of nations bordering the sea" would be found by a study of the naval conflicts of the seventeenth and eighteenth centuries, and he proceeded to illustrate by historical examples, with a certainty which only the Victorian era could muster, how particular immutable conditions (the geographical position and physical conformation of a country; the extent of national territory to be defended or extended; the size and character of its population; the nature and wisdom of its government) were the real reasons for the steady rise to world power of the British Empire at that time and for the relative decline of those states such as Spain, the Netherlands and France.

The opposing thesis, put forward by Halford Mackinder in 1904, was that it was the land that mattered. The Columbian epoch—four centuries of overseas exploration and conquest by the European powers—was now coming to an end. Britain's naval power would no longer remain supreme when other nations with greater resources and manpower overhauled her industrial lead—and that sea power itself was waning in relation to land power.

With very little of the world left to conquer, "every explosion of social forces" would take place in a much more enclosed environment and would no longer be dissipated into unknown regions; efficiency and internal development would replace expansionism as the main aim of modern states. He saw central Russia as the great strategical pivot area of the world. That vast region, once the source of the many invading armies which had for centuries poured into Europe and the Middle East, had been outflanked and neutralized and much reduced in importance by the seamen of the Columbian Era. For four hundred years the world's trade had developed on the sea, its population had on the whole lived near the sea, political and military changes had been primarily influenced by sea power. Now, with industrialization, massive investments, railways, new agriculture and mining techniques, central Asia was poised to regain its former importance. One of his admirers, Leo Amery, wrote soon after:

> seapower alone, if it is not based on great industry, and has a great population behind it, is too weak for offence to really maintain itself in the world struggle . . . both the sea and the railway are going in the future . . . to be supplemented by the air as a means of locomotion, and when we come to that . . . the successful powers will be those who have the greatest industrial base. It will not matter whether they are in the centre of a continent or on an island; those people who have the industrial power and the power of invention and science will be able to defeat all others.[12]

Much of this argument was based on the impact of the railways which from the beginning of the second half of the century were crisscrossing Europe and the Americas. The transport of goods, which had for centuries been cheaper and faster by water, now became easier by land, a tendency which was to increase with motorized transport. The Columbian epoch, when most trade and populations had remained close to the sea, was slowly ending as continental countries were slowly freed from physical restriction. People could be transported much faster—and railroads were used brilliantly by the Prussians in 1866 during the war against the Danes and, in 1870, against the French. India, previously reached only by sea, was now vulnerable to Russian railway building; Canada could no longer be defended. Railways had now neutralized large-scale sea blockade. Also the new inventions of the mine, the torpedo, the submarine and long-range coastal ordnance were making operational application of close blockade very difficult. It is an argument which still goes on.

By 1850, in the last days of sail, the British navy presided over a world with free trade. It is not that British warships were everywhere, but that there were no other warships in significant concentrations. British command of the sea was command in a vacuum, maintained by a small fleet and in large measure by bluff, though those well-preserved reserves were always there in the background. There was no serious threat to British power, trade and influence. Of the other countries that had played in the great struggle, Spain, disillusioned with empire, failed to support a king who wanted the Indies back and slipped down the rankings; the Portuguese Empire survived, in a decayed form; the French, unstable at times at home, were in an irritated frustration; the Dutch surprisingly recovered most of their colonial empire, and kept an uneasy understanding with the British in the East; this left the United States, a formidable commercial competitor, at the start of her rise to world power. But that is another story.

NOTES

1. Patrick K. O'Brien, *Power with Profit: the State and the Economy, 1688–1815.* (London, 1991), p. 33.
2. Kenneth Maxwell, "The Atlantic in the Eighteenth Century: a Southern Perspective on the Need to Return to the "Big Picture," *Transactions of the Royal Historical Society,* Sixth Series, 3 (1993), p. 230.
3. John B. Hattendorf, et al., eds., *British Naval Documents, 1204–1960.* (London, 1993), p. 346.
4. Maxwell, "Atlantic," p. 231.
5. Quoted in Maxwell, "Atlantic," p. 235.
6. Bethell, *Abolition of the Brazilian Slave Trade,* p. ix; the next paragraphs are based directly on Bethell's preface.
7. Andrew Lambert, *The Last Sailing Battlefleet: Maintaining Naval Mastery 1815–1850.* (London, 1991), p. 188.
8. Sarah Palmer, *Politics, Shipping and the Repeal of the Navigation Laws.* (Manchester and New York, 1990), pp. 8–9.
9. Lambert, p. 123.
10. Lambert, p. 16.
11. Palmer, p. 155.
12. Quoted in Kennedy, *Naval Mastery,* p. 184.

SUGGESTIONS FOR FURTHER READING

Timothy E. Anna, *Spain and the Loss of America.* (Lincoln and London, 1983).

C. J. Bartlett, *Great Britain and Sea Power, 1815–1853.* (Oxford, 1963; reprinted Aldershot, 1993).

Leslie Bethell, *The Abolition of the Brazilian Slave Trade.* (Cambridge, 1970).

C. R. Boxer, *The Portuguese Seaborne Empire, 1415–1825.* (London, 1969).

Philip D. Curtin, *The Tropical Atlantic in the age of the Slave Trade.* (Washington, 1951).

James A. Field, *America and the Mediterranean World, 1776–1882.* (Princeton, 1969).

Jan Glete, *Navies and Nations: Warships, Navies and State Building in Europe and America, 1500–1860.* 2 volumes (Stockholm, 1993).

Gerald Graham, *Sea Power and British North America, 1783–1820: a study in British Colonial Policy.* (New York, 1968).

Raymond C. Howell, *The Royal Navy and the Slave Trade.* (London, 1987).

Paul Johnson, *The Birth of the Modern World Society, 1815–1830.* (London, 1991).

Andrew Lambert, *The Last Sailing Battlefleet: Maintaining Naval Mastery 1815–1850.* (London, 1991).

Christopher Lloyd, *The Navy and the Slave Trade.* (London, 1949).

Kenneth Maxwell, "The Atlantic in the Eighteenth Century: a Southern Perspective on the Need to Return to the "Big Picture," *Transactions of the Royal Historical Society,* Sixth Series, 3 (1993), pp. 209–236.

Kenneth R. Maxwell, *Conflicts and Conspiracies: Brazil and Portugal, 1750–1808.* (Cambridge and New York, 1973).

Patrick K. O'Brien, *Power with Profit: the State and the Economy, 1688–1815.* (London, 1991).

Sarah Palmer, *Politics, Shipping and the Repeal of the Navigation Laws.* (Manchester and New York, 1990).

J. H. Parry, *Trade and Dominion: the European Overseas Empires in the Eighteenth Century.* (New York and Washington, 1971).

Figure XXX. The sublime ocean of romanticism: "The Red Rover and the Bristol Trader," engraved by J. D. Thompson from a painting by James Hamilton. *Courtesy of Thomas Philbrick.*

24

ROMANTICISM AND THE LITERATURE OF THE SEA

Thomas Philbrick

Anyone who undertakes a course of reading in the literature of the sea is confronted with certain puzzling questions when it comes to British and American writing of the eighteenth and nineteenth centuries: why is it that in Great Britain, unquestionably the dominant sea power of the era, the maritime literature of those same centuries is a marginal affair, largely a matter of sketches of naval life like those of Tobias Smollett and Frederick Marryat and the sea songs of Charles Dibdin? Why is it that the one great writer of the sea in British literature was the Polish Joseph Conrad, and why is it that an artist of Conrad's stature did not emerge until well after the heyday of British maritime activity?

On the other hand, why is it that in the first half of the nineteenth century American writers achieved what their British contemporaries did not, the creation of a varied and vigorous body of literature that associated maritime experience with the central concerns of life and gave it expression in an idiom that spoke to the nineteenth-century imagination? So obvious was it that such was indeed the case that as early as 1856 a writer in the *Dublin University Magazine* structured an entire essay on the paradox that however surely Britannia ruled the waves, the sea in literature was the dominion of the Americans Cooper, Dana, and Melville.

The existence of that apparent anomaly reminds us that the relation of history and literature, of experience and the imagination, is not as simple or direct as one might hope. Certain activities and environments can be of enormous importance to a society and yet those activities and environments will not find widespread expression or reflection in its art. One thinks, for example, of the difficulty the arts, both visual and literary, had in coming to terms with the industrialism that increasingly pervaded life in the West over the last two centuries. Apparently a way of imagining reality has to be found which will lend it meaning and value. New forms, new conventions, new styles, new systems of value must be evolved before a mode of life or an environment that has not been a traditional subject of art can find artistic expression.

Perhaps this assumption gives us a way of understanding the comparative poverty of maritime literature in Great Britain during the century that culminated in Nelson's victory at Trafalgar in 1805, with the destruction of the last remaining threat to British control of the ocean. After that time, the focus of British energy and interest would be on colonial and industrial development, and maritime experience would become more and more a matter of nostalgic recollection, as it is, say in Turner's great painting of the line-of-battle-ship *Téméraire* being towed by a steam tug to the wrecker's yard. But in the eighteenth century, the sea was at the very center of British life, the arena of her long struggle with France for colonial empire, and the avenue to the commercial wealth that made her the most energetic and progressive power in Europe. The sea was important not only to the politicians of empire, careerist naval officers, and mercantile nabobs. It was involved in the lives and deaths of the hundreds of thousands of sailors who manned the wooden walls and the Indiamen and the colliers and the whole vast apparatus that defended and enriched the island-nation. It was the very basis of existence in the commercial ports, naval bases, and fishing villages that lined the British coast. Yet all of this goes almost without notice, with scarcely an echo in eighteenth-century English literature. We remember, perhaps, the seaborne wanderings of Crusoe or Gulliver, the horrific naval episodes in *Roderick Random,* or the pathos of a sailor's parting in songs like John Gay's "Black-ey'd Susan." That, however, is very much on the margins of the text. The text itself concerns the doings of London or Bath or the inland villages of the squirearchy. The reality that it conceives is overwhelmingly a social reality, one in which the focus is kept unrelentingly on human relationships, familial, financial, sexual, or hierarchical, and in which the natural world functions, when it is present at all, only anthropomorphically, as an amplifier of the feelings of the human beings for whom it serves as backdrop. Think how it is in Richardson, or Fielding, or Goldsmith.

In such a scheme of things, maritime settings and maritime experience have little place. Gardens and farms are admissible, but the wilderness of forest, mountain, or ocean—the features of primitive nature—are more apt to be the objects of abhorrence than of wonder and delight. That quintessential inhabitant of the eighteenth-century, Samuel Johnson, said it best: "A ship," he told Boswell in 1776, "is worse than a gaol. There is in a gaol, better air, better company, better conveniency of every kind; and a ship has the additional disadvantage of being in danger. When men come to like a sea-life, they are not fit to live on land." In this view, the ocean becomes a scene of monotony, relieved only by occasional intervals of panic. The sailor becomes a grotesque figure, a person who by choice or necessity has become separated from that social world which contains all significance and all value and so has become something less than human. He may be funny, perhaps, or simply disgusting, but he can scarcely be regarded as having either the sensibility or the dignity that would equip him to be the hero of a fiction.

If English writers never fully succeeded in breaking this eighteenth-century mold and creating a literature in which maritime experience has a bearing on universal experience, they did, in the early nineteenth century, provide an indication of how it might be done. The basis of that achievement was the new set of attitudes and values which have come to be called romanticism and which, in the last decades of the eighteenth century and the first ones of the nineteenth, became a major force in British culture, in all its aspects, from landscape gardening to poetry. In the complex of ideas that the movement involved, two were to prove essential to the development of maritime literature. One was a new interpretation of primitive nature, by which wilderness took on the value of sublimity; the romantic sensibility was thereby encouraged to bring to forest, mountain, and ocean the awe, the ecstatic absorption, and the humbling sense of the insufficiency of mankind and its works which had customarily been responses to the contemplation of God. The other crucial concept of romanticism, closely linked with the first, offered a new interpretation of the individual, who was no longer to be defined in relation to society but as a self, autonomous in everything but its dealings with nature, for in this view nature fosters and influences the sensibilities and moral perceptions of those who live their lives in her company.

Two writers in particular, Byron and Walter Scott, pointed the way by which the ideology of romanticism could lead to the development of a new maritime literature. Byron's contribution is the more recognized and recognizable. In the so-called "Address to the Ocean" in Canto Four of *Childe Harold's Pilgrimage,* Byron in 1818 established the formula that would ever after invest the sea in sublimity. Let me quote a few lines, something that would have been entirely superfluous 150 years ago, when every American schoolchild was made to memorize them as an essential part of the cultural inheritance:

Roll on, thou deep and dark blue Ocean, roll!
Ten thousand fleets sweep over thee in vain; . . .
Thou glorious mirror, where the Almighty's form
Glasses itself in tempests; in all time,
Calm or convulsed—in breeze, or gale, or storm,
Icing the pole, or in the torrid clime
Dark-heaving;—boundless, endless, and sublime—
The image of Eternity—the throne
of the Invisible;—. . .

To Byron too, the nineteenth century was indebted for its vision of the sea as the scene of illimitable freedom, of wild adventure, and of self-realization. The opening lines of his poem *The Corsair* of 1814, a sort of pirates' chorus, provide a full-voiced celebration of those values:

'O'er the glad waters of the dark blue sea,
Our thoughts as boundless and our souls as free,
Far as the breeze can bear, the billows foam,
Survey our empire and behold our home! . . .'

These lines of Byron are echoed everywhere in American maritime literature—in the mottoes that head Cooper's chapters; in the preface to Dana's *Two Years before the Mast,* and again and again within the texture of Melville's allusive prose. And this is to say nothing of their reverberation through that vast substrata of maritime writing in the magazines, giftbooks, and dime novels of the American nineteenth century.

Scott's contribution is harder to define and document than Byron's. Nevertheless, I wish to credit Scott with creating the novel of place, or better, the novel of environment, the great innovation that led in one generation to Cooper, in another to Hardy, and in still another to Faulkner. It is sad that Scott, who is generally blamed for the invention of the costume romance, is not widely celebrated as the novelist who first developed a vital connection between human life and the setting in which that life is led. In his fictions and for the first time in a significant way the natural environment of landscape and weather and the cultural environment of folkways and traditions are seen as shapers, if not determinants, of character and experience. And those environments are particularized and differentiated in time and space, having various consequences in various regions and eras. In Scott's great novels, like *The Heart of the Midlothian* and *Old Mortality,* we are at the opposite pole from Jane

Austen's eternal village, where the only nature is human nature. In Austen bad weather can make for dirty walking; in Scott it can kill.

It is true that Scott's single attempt at anything like a sea novel, *The Pirate* of 1822, is weak as a novel and was written, as Cooper observed, by one who knew little of the sea, but it is significant that he, and he alone, made the attempt. And without his vision of environment as the matrix of individual experience, nothing like the true sea novel could emerge.

Scott's effort, like the example that Byron provided, had little effect on maritime writing in his own nation. For the most part Captain Marryat and the small armada of others in England who, in the late 1820s and 1830s took up their pens in response to the American Cooper's successful creation of the sea novel, missed the grand romantic point—that the natural world and the individual consciousness are significant and related—and largely contented themselves with exploring the intricacies of that most intricate of all British social institutions, the Royal Navy.

In the United States, the situation was very different and for a number of reasons. I would argue that, in the first place, the impact of romanticism on American culture was still more pervasive and far more stimulating than it was on British culture. For the inhabitant of a highly developed and institutionalized society like England's, the romantic doctrine that society was at best a distraction and at worst a source of corruption and error was scarcely bracing news; it was, on the contrary, considered subversive (Lord Byron's infamous reputation was not entirely owing to his sexual behavior) and productive of self-questioning and doubt. In the New Republic, by contrast, that same doctrine was a source of immense encouragement and reassurance. To be told that urban civilization was a curse and that an authentic life in nature was the highest good could be nothing but heartening to a young man or woman living three thousand miles or more from the nearest major library, great cathedral, or significant collection of paintings. At once all the sources of American discontent and inferiority were turned into assets and advantages: our provincial isolation was the basis of our simplicity, our innocence, our virtue; our fever-ridden backwoods were the true temples, the perfect setting for what William Cullen Bryant called a "forest hymn"; if we lacked Chartres and Versailles, we had Niagara and the Natural Bridge; if we lacked a past, we had a glorious future; if we lacked sophistication, we were, above all, sincere.

Surely here are the springs of that outpouring of cultural energy to which F. O. Matthiessen gave the name "the American Renaissance," and which might better be called simply American Romanticism. The rise of American maritime literature is coincident with that larger movement and is, indeed, a component of it.

But I do not mean to suggest that romanticism in itself was sufficient to engender a significant body of maritime literature in the United States, any more than it was in Great Britain. The catalyst, it would seem, was the emergence during the War of 1812 and in the decade immediately following it of a new spirit of nationalism in this country, surely a local manifestation of the great tide of nationalism that was rising in Europe as a consequence of the Napoleonic conquests. Just think of how many of the icons of American nationalism, the slogans and emblems and songs, spring from this period. The curious thing is that in so many of its expressions this new effort to define an American identity fixed on the sea as the arena of national power and of individual opportunity. The country was still essentially a seaboard society, one whose chief triumphs in its two involvements in the great wars of Europe, first against France and then against Great Britain, had been on the ocean, where American frigates had won those victories that keep us still maintaining "Old Ironsides" as a national shrine. To many observers, Cooper among them, England offered the obvious model for the United States to follow. The continent stretching to our west should not distract us from the development of urban centers of commerce and industry along the seaboard, the creation of a vast merchant marine, and, to defend it all and assert our position as a great power, the building of a large and efficient navy, one capable of forming a line of battle and fighting in fleets.

The program of the maritime nationalists came close to realization. In the next few decades American maritime enterprise did displace Great Britain in area after area, from the transatlantic packet service to the Pacific whale fishery. The United States launched an exploring expedition, thus entering the competition for national prestige and commercial supremacy that was the nineteenth-century equivalent of the space race. American shipbuilders perfected the wooden sailing vessel as an instrument of commerce, an effort that culminated in the evolution of the clipper ship. By the middle of the century the navy had no less then eleven ships-of-the-line, as well as five of the far more useful steam frigates, and was ready to impose the will of the United States on what one contemporary work called that "jealous and secluded people," the Japanese.

More to my point, American popular culture came increasingly to reflect and amplify this interest in all things maritime. The American stage was populated with nautical pieces, from the compounds of patriotic tableaux and songs concocted to commemorate the naval victories of the War of 1812 to the dramatizations of Cooper's early sea romances—*The Red Rover* alone was honored with three different adaptations for the stage in this country. That newly devised medium of entertainment and edification the panorama treated its audiences to elaborate depictions of great naval battles or the workings of the American sperm whale fishery. Booksellers in the new railroad stations offered their customers anthologies of maritime disaster—shipwrecks, mutinies, explosions and fires, cannibalism and piracy. Long before Deadwood Dick found his way onto the pages of American pulp fiction, Wharton the Whale Killer and Ramon the Rover of Cuba were there in all their glory.

The buzz of maritime activity and excitement, then, pervaded the atmosphere in the years from 1824 to 1851 when Cooper, Dana, and Melville created the body of writing that was to test and expand the possibilities of the literature of the sea. Before that time, the sea had played a part in American writing roughly equivalent to that it had in Great Britain. The scale was smaller, of course, but a few prose writers had inserted brief nautical episodes into their Smollett-like tales of picaresque adventure or into their Richardson-like sentimental romances. Only one author, Philip Freneau, a poet and, like all successful writers of the sea, a sailor himself, had brought to maritime experience a power and depth of representation that has made his work survive as something more than a historical document. Freneau's sea poems, the best of which were written in the closing decades of the eighteenth century, are less a Byronic celebration of natural sublimity and wild freedom than a Homeric depiction of the voyage as an ordeal, in which human ingenuity, skill, and courage are apt to be overwhelmed by the forces of nature and from which the voyager returns, if he returns at all, a chastened man, at last content with the security and comfort of a life on land. Moving as Freneau's themes are, they were not consistent with the great expectations that Americans attached to the sea in the first half of the nineteenth century, a time when Freneau was remembered only as the scurrilous journalist and political propagandist who had served as Jefferson's hatchet-man.

It was left to James Fenimore Cooper to devise a representation of maritime experience that would fully meet the requirements of the nineteenth-century imagination. Significantly, he chose as his medium not verse but the dominant literary form of the century, the novel, the standard three-decker that he had received from the hands of

Scott. But the substance with which Cooper filled that form was something that struck his readers as entirely new. His first three sea novels—*The Pilot* of 1824, *The Red Rover* of 1827, and *The Water-Witch* of 1830—were met with an excitement and admiration that our literary histories, in their exclusive focus on Cooper as the author of the Leather-Stocking Tales, have forgotten. Praised and imitated not only in the United States but in Europe, where Cooper was coming to be regarded as, along with Goethe and Scott, a founding father of romanticism, the three books rocked the literary world. Here, for example, is Mary Russell Mitford, England's leading woman of letters, writing to a friend in March of 1824, just after the first appearance of *The Pilot:*

> Mr. Cooper . . . has opened fresh ground . . . (if one may say so of the sea). No one but Smollett has ever attempted to delineate the naval character; and then *he* is so coarse and hard. Now *this* has the same truth and power, with a deep grand feeling. I must not overpraise it, for fear of producing the reaction which such injudicious enthusiasm is calculated to induce; but I must request you to read it. Only read it. Imagine the author's boldness in taking Paul Jones for a hero, and his power in making one care for him! I envy the Americans their Mr. Cooper. Tell me how you like 'The Pilot.'

Romances, all of them, *The Pilot, The Red Rover,* and *The Water-Witch* each center on an ambiguous figure, a superb seaman who has detached himself from his society and its norms and now pursues a career devoted exclusively to his peculiar needs and values in defiance of all conventions and restraints. In that figure one can discern the outlines of, at one end of the scale, Melville's Ahab, and, at the other, the swashbuckler played by Errol Flynn and John Payne in the pirate movies of the 1930s and 1940s. Cooper invented the pirate as a literary subject; but much more than that, in these three books, he invented the sea novel as a literary genre. His great disciple, Joseph Conrad, put it best: "In Cooper's sea tales, the sea interpenetrates with life; it is, in a subtle way, a factor in the problem of existence." That creation of a fictional world in which the maritime environment becomes the ground of existence is, I should think, the essential defining characteristic of the sea novel and before Cooper it had not been achieved.

The aura of glamour and romance in which Cooper had clothed his first three explorations of the fictional possibilities of maritime experience began to give way to a more sober and realistic mode in his maritime writing of the 1830s and early 1840s. In part the change

seems to be a result of his own internal development as his art ma-
tured and his view of the world darkened; surely the trend was reinforced by his absorption in what was by far his most demanding
maritime work of the 1830s, his carefully researched and authoritative *History of the Navy,* which appeared in 1839.

External influences contributed to the shift from romance toward
realism. When Cooper began to write in the 1820s, his chief competitor was Sir Walter Scott. Now, in the 1840s, it was Charles Dick-
ens. The difference between the two British novelists epitomizes the
whole tendency of romanticism in those decades as it turned from
the remote and exotic to the familiar and the commonplace, turned
to what Emerson called in his great phrase in "The American
Scholar" of 1837 "the meal in the firkin; the milk in the pan."

In maritime literature the decisive manifestation of this new climate was Richard Henry Dana's *Two Years before the Mast,* which
first appeared in 1840. Not a fiction at all, the new book was a lit-
eral account of its author's own first and only voyage as a foremast
hand from Boston to the California coast and back again with
cowhides for the shoe factories of Lynn. As Dana announced in his
preface, his aim was to demystify maritime experience by portray-
ing it as it really was, "the light and the dark together." Now the
grimy life of the forecastle, not the quarterdeck, became the focus of
attention. Here the emphasis was not on freedom and mobility but
on confinement, brutal discipline, and numbing physical labor. But
I do not mean to suggest that Dana returned his readers to Dr. Johnson's view of the ship as a prison. Along with the rotten food and the
flogging come celebrations of the sublimity of the ocean and the dignity, indeed nobility, of the common seaman that are beyond the ken
of Johnson and his century. In other words, we are still inhabiting a
fundamentally romantic vision of maritime experience, much though
the tone and emphases have changed.

It is hard to overstate the impact of Dana's book. Before its appearance American maritime literature had been preoccupied with
pirates and smugglers, and their wicked-looking long, low black
schooners, as it followed with a rigidity bordering on caricature the
course that Cooper had charted in his three early sea romances. Although the sea romance never did expire, it was now overshadowed
by a succession of works that attempted, or at least pretended, to
carry out Dana's program of depicting the reality of maritime life. A
procession of tars, young and old, offered American readers factual
accounts of their experience at sea, some of which, like Nicholas
Isaacs's *Twenty Years before the Mast,* far outdid Dana's in length of

Figure XXXI. The seaman as romantic hero: An illustration drawn by F. O. C. Darley and engraved by Thomas Phillibrown. *Courtesy of Thomas Philbrick.*

service, if not in literary skill and intelligence. There were good books in the lot, however, like Ross Browne's *Etchings of a Whaling Cruise* of 1846 and Cooper's contribution to the genre in 1843, a book called *Ned Myers,* the life story of one of the writer's shipmates on his own boyhood voyage before the mast.

The influence of Dana, however, was not limited to these factual narratives of life at sea. At its furthest, it would seem to have been the chief stimulus for the emergence of what I should think is the characteristic form of nineteenth-century American literary art, the young man's first-person narrative of exploration and discovery. We have inland versions of the pattern in books like Francis Parkman's *The Oregon Trail,* localized versions of it in Thoreau's *Walden* ("I have travelled widely in Concord"), allegorical versions of it in Melville's *Mardi,* even colloquial versions of it in Twain's *Adventures of Huckleberry Finn.*

More to our point, the example of Dana gave direction specifically to American sea fiction over the crucial decade that followed the publication of *Two Years before the Mast.* Consider, for instance, Cooper's *Afloat and Ashore,* published in 1844. This huge novel, twice the size of Cooper's other books, is, unlike any of the author's previous sea fiction, narrated in the first person. The narrator is Miles Wallingford, a man in his sixties who recalls the voyages he made as a youth in the era of the Napoleonic wars. Although born into a respectable family, Miles, like Dana and like Cooper himself, first ships before the mast. Sailing out of New York on board a succession of merchant vessels, he follows virtually every trading route known to American commerce in the period. Surviving the hardships of the forecastle, Miles rises in his profession to the point that, still in his early twenties, he both owns and commands a vessel. That vessel, however, along with its cargo is wrecked and lost, and Miles ends his nautical career a ruined man, imprisoned for debt almost as soon as sets foot once more in New York.

All of this is narrated in a subdued and matter-of-fact manner that has nothing to do with the glamour, mystery, and heroic posturing of Cooper's early sea romances. Here the emphasis falls on the technology of ship-handling and navigation and on the details of trade. And the maritime materials of *Afloat and Ashore* are integrated with its land sequences in one long and ranging examination of the economic aspects of human experience, as Cooper explores the bases of wealth, the rights and obligations of ownership, the pecuniary consequences of sex and race, and a whole bundle of related issues. The book firmly embeds sea fiction in the ordinary concerns of life, in the familiar and the commonplace. It is unmistakably a post-Dana work.

So too, in its sometimes quite different way is the sea fiction of Herman Melville. Melville's literary career began squarely in the wake of Dana as he set about working up in *Typee* a heightened version of his own adventures as a fugitive whaleman in Polynesia. Here again, then, was a genteelly reared young man's account of experience in the rough-and-tumble world of the foremast hand, more shaped and colored as a fiction than Dana's book, it is true, but sharing many characteristics with it nonetheless, not the least of which is its reformist tone.

Neither *Typee* nor *Omoo* and *Mardi,* its successors in the Polynesian triptych which launched Melville's career, are in any essential sense works of sea fiction. In them maritime materials are incidental, in the first two, to the depiction of the distinction between civilization and savagery, a contrast so complex that its two terms often exchange values, and in the third to the rather awkward adaptation of the motif of Pacific voyaging to an allegorical quest for the ideal. Melville's achievement as a writer of the sea resides almost entirely in his second trio of books, *Redburn* of 1849, *White-Jacket* of 1850, and *Moby-Dick* of 1851.

The three books are very closely related. Together they encompass the three great sectors of American maritime activity at the mid-century, the merchant marine, the navy, and the whale fishery. All three have a strong autobiographical basis, for those three sectors of maritime activity, of course, are the very ones into which Melville's own service in the merchantman *St. Lawrence,* the whaler *Acushnet,* and the frigate *United States* had carried him. Read in the sequence of their composition, the three seem to participate in an accumulating tendency toward wider and deeper statement. We begin with the relative simplicity and straightforwardness of *Redburn,* the account of a boy's first voyage in which nearly all issues and concerns center on the needs and anxieties of the individual, here the green hand thrust into the bewildering world of the ship and the disillusioning world of adult hypocrisy and corruption. In *White-Jacket* the horizon expands beyond the self to take in the community of mankind, here examined and criticized as a social and political entity. In *Redburn* the ship had functioned primarily as the arena of initiatory experience, an arena in which the narrator had been the protagonist. In *White-Jacket,* by contrast, the ship has become a microcosm; the densely crowded frigate with its occupational diversity and elaborate hierarchies presents to us, as the subtitle of the book announces, "the world in a man-of-war." And here the role of the narrator in the action of the book is significantly diminished, as he steps aside to report and comment on the thick and complex world he inhabits.

In *Moby-Dick,* these tendencies reach their climax. The central concerns of the book are neither personal nor social but metaphysical. The ship has become a vehicle for the exploration of responses to ultimate reality, its crew less an assemblage of seamen than a collection of carefully graduated and differentiated consciousnesses.

The narrator, much to the puzzlement of some of Melville's critics, virtually vanishes from the scene, absorbed into the thoughts and passions of others, or, better, becoming the mind that encloses and contains them all, making the fundamental action of the book that of his own meditation.

Seen in this way, the three books form a progression, one built upon another, as Melville probes and enlarges the possibilities of sea fiction as the medium of meaning, a process that would seem to be a precise reflection of the sense of rapid artistic and intellectual growth, at once exhilarating and terrifying, of which he speaks so movingly in his letters to Hawthorne. The outcome of that process in *Moby-Dick* is the most brilliantly successful fusion of the physical world of maritime experience and the abstract world of ideas that we possess. It makes all previous and all later attempts at the same thing look skeletal, amateurish, and contrived, not excluding Melville's own effort in *Mardi*.

As we have seen, *Moby-Dick* was not written in a vacuum. It draws not only upon its two immediate predecessors in the Melville canon, but it and they as well grow out of the whole body of maritime writing that Cooper and Dana and their followers had created. Indeed, whole books have been written about Melville's sources—one thinks particularly of Howard Vincent's *The Trying-Out of Moby-Dick*. I have in mind now not those writers from whom Melville borrowed his technical and anecdotal detail and his stylistic mannerisms, but what I think is a more significant and more interesting matter, those writers who persuaded Melville that maritime literature was not an inappropriate vehicle for an artist who aspired to the scope and power of Shakespeare, the same writers who, just as importantly, had created an audience prepared to find in sea fiction something more than mere adventure.

From this point of view, the central figures are beyond question Cooper and Dana once again. As previously noted, it was Cooper who had first transformed maritime experience into the materials of nineteenth-century fiction, an achievement without which the very existence of Melville's three marine novels is inconceivable. But Cooper's contribution to Melville's art would seem to have taken more specific forms as well. If Melville's acquaintance with Cooper's books began, as he tells us, in boyhood and produced "a vivid and awakening power" upon his mind, the contact continued at least until the year before he undertook the composition of *Moby-Dick*. In that year, 1849, he reviewed Cooper's latest novel, *The Sea Lions*, for Evert Duyckinck's magazine *Literary World*. Even at this late date in his career, only two years before his death, Cooper was still experimenting with the possibilities of the sea novel as a vehicle of meaning, experimentation that in *The Sea Lions* produced an extraordinary linkage between a realistic portrayal of the Antarctic seal fishery and an allegorical and symbolic representation of the experience of religious conversion. It is a book at once fascinating in the boldness and resourcefulness of its artistic attempt and infuriating in the dogmatism of its ideology. But surely amid the welter of reading that went into the making of *Moby-Dick, The Sea Lions* played its part, indicating the path by which the humble materials of the American maritime economy might be transformed into the vehicles of intellectual and spiritual discovery.

With Dana the association is still more direct. Members of the same generation and sharing the great common experience of an extended immersion in the life of the forecastle, Melville and Dana inevitably came in contact. Melville had read *Two Years before the Mast* in the interval between his own first voyage in the *St. Lawrence* and his embarkation for the Pacific in the *Acushnet*. The two writers became acquainted in 1847 and corresponded over the next three years, exchanging literary ideas. Indeed it may be, as Leon Howard has speculated, that Dana was responsible for the inception of *Moby-Dick* by suggesting that the younger writer do for the whale fishery what he, Dana, had done for the merchant service. Of course Melville in *Redburn* had himself dealt with the merchant service, and in a way that was thoroughly consistent with Dana's tone and stance. In *White-Jacket,* too, Melville followed the course laid down by what he called in that book "my friend Dana's unmatchable *Two Years before the Mast.*"

Of Melville's three books, *Moby-Dick* least depends upon the example of Dana. There the reformist zeal is most muted, and the book quickly outgrows the simple narrative of personal experience upon which Dana's work was constructed. Perhaps more important, *Moby-Dick* bursts the bonds of realism that Dana had imposed upon maritime writing and exploits the full tonal range of previous literary uses of the sea, from Homer's epic sweep to Smollett's bawdy humor, from the solemnity of the Bible to the gorgeous thunder and lightning of Byron. Ancient myth and modern Gothicism mingle with the operations of the whale fishery and produce a voyage beyond Dana's wildest imaginings—though perhaps not those of Cooper, who died a month before *Moby-Dick* was published.

With Melville's great book, American maritime literature reached its apogee. New times would produce new modes, as Bert Bender's fine study of American sea fiction after Melville, *Sea-Brothers,* richly demonstrates, but there is little that movements like literary naturalism or modernism could do that was not already anticipated and, in a strange way superseded, by *Moby-Dick.* I don't mean to attribute the achievement of that book to Melville's genius alone, although perhaps we have lost sight of just how extraordinary individual attainment can be. But the two great motives of the rise of American sea fiction, romanticism and maritime nationalism, at full flood in *Moby-Dick,* would never after find such confident expression. For *Moby-Dick* is the supreme manifestation of romanticism in America, entirely given over to its twin explorations of the nature of nature and the nature of the self. The book is the last of Melville's works to draw upon the hopeful vision of American manifest destiny that animates his earlier works, a vision that here is most apparent in the ringing celebration of the Nantucket whalemen in Chapter 14, "these naked Nantucketers, these sea hermits, issuing from their ant-hill in the sea, [who have] overrun and conquered the watery world like so many Alexanders."

For Melville, the path ahead was to lead from the vastnesses of the Pacific to the cramped law offices in which Bartleby lives his shrunken life; from the huge figure of Ahab, self-proclaimed co-equal of the gods, to the frail figure of Hunilla, widowed, raped and abandoned on her Galápagos island; from the rich abundance of Melvillean prose to the tight-lipped precision of Melvillean poetry. And for Americans as a whole the path was to lead inland to the confusion and disillusionment of the Civil War—"What like a bullet to undeceive," wrote Herman Melville in his gnomic verse—and then to the land-rushes and industrial imperialism of the last decades of the century.

To a country dedicated to the exploitation of the continent and to the creation of Pittsburghs and Chicagos, the sea was a swiftly fading memory. On the shipping lanes, the new age of steam power and iron hulls belonged to the British, as Americans forsook the maritime frontier for the continental one. In our popular culture, the image of the sea was overwhelmed by the outpouring of tales of Western adventure. It was now that the king of pulp fiction, E. Z. C. Judson turned from cranking out the nautical exploits of Ned Buntline to the invention of Buffalo Bill, even to the point of fitting out a flesh and blood person, William Cody, to assume the role. It was a paradox, to be sure, for nearly all of us as immigrants had the ocean in our background and very few of us ever knew the cutting edge of the continental frontier, but from this time forward the national imagination became fixated on a 20-year span of American history and a territory known chiefly to a few young roughnecks and drifters, an imagination obsessively and endlessly cherishing the icons of the West, the six-shooter and the ten-gallon hat, as if they, and not the Pittsburghs and Chicagos, contained the essence of the national life.

Some writers, like Crane and O'Neill and Hemingway, and painters like Winslow Homer, continued to associate their art with the sea, but even with them maritime experience increasingly became attached to the nostalgic recollection of the age of sail or to the lives of people more simple and more natural than either the artists or their audiences. For most Americans, the life of the sea had become an irrelevance.

The existence of maritime museums and semesters at sea, of tall ships and wooden boat regattas, of waterfront restoration and the new green awareness of the oceanic environment, may be a sign that the times are changing, and that the American maritime past is being recovered. But as one who has spent a good deal of his life trying in vain to persuade his colleagues that the Cooper of the sea novels is at least as interesting as the Cooper of the twig-snappers, I am not optimistic. The Leather-Stocking Tales still reign supreme, even to the point of sending Daniel Day-Lewis bare-chested through the North Carolina woods, as a two-gun, Miami-vicious version of poor Cooper's illiterate and tobacco-chewing scout. Whole sectors of American culture and whole reaches of the American past still lie neglected, not the least of which are those that begin at the water's edge.

SUGGESTIONS FOR FURTHER READING

Chronological List of British Literary Works

Daniel Defoe, *Robinson Crusoe.* (1719).
Tobias Smollett, *Roderick Random.* (1748).
William Falconer, *The Shipwreck.* (1762).
George Gordon, Lord Byron, *The Corsair.* (1814).
George Gordon, Lord Byron, *Childe Harold,* Canto iv. (1818).
Sir Walter Scott, *The Pirate.* (1822).
Frederick Marryat, *Peter Simple.* (1834).
Frederick Marryat, *Midshipman Easy.* (1836).

Chronological List of American Literary Works

Philip Freneau, *Poems.* (1786).
James Fenimore Cooper, *The Red Rover.* (1827).

James Fenimore Cooper, *Afloat and Ashore*. (1844).
James Fenimore Cooper, *The Sea Lions*. (1849).
Edgar Allan Poe, *The Narrative of Arthur Gordon Pym*. (1838).
Richard Henry Dana, *Two Years before the Mast*. (1840).
Herman Melville, *Redburn*. (1849).
Herman Melville, *White-Jacket*. (1850).
Herman Melville, *Moby-Dick*. (1851).
Walt Whitman, "As I Ebb'd with the Ocean of Life" and "The World below the Brine" (1860).

Anthologies, Histories, Criticism, Bibliography

W. H. Auden, *The Enchafèd Flood or the Romantic Iconography of the Sea*. (New York, 1950).
Bert Bender, *Sea-Brothers: The Tradition of American Sea Fiction from Moby-Dick to the Present*. (Philadelphia, 1988).
Patricia Ann Carlson, ed., *Literature and Lore of the Sea*. (Amsterdam, 1986).
Charles Lee Lewis, *Books of the Sea: An Introduction to Nautical Literature*. (Annapolis, 1943; reprinted Westport, Conn:, 1972).
C. Northcote Parkinson, *Portsmouth Point: The Navy in Fiction, 1793–1815*. (London, 1948).
Thomas Philbrick, *James Fenimore Cooper and the Development of American Sea Fiction*. (Cambridge, Mass., 1961).
Jonathan Raban, ed., *The Oxford Book of the Sea*. (Oxford, 1992).
Charles N. Robinson, *The British Tar in Fact and Fiction*. (New York, 1909; reprinted Detroit, 1968).
Jeanne-Marie Santraud, *La mer et le roman américain dans la première moité du dix-neuvième siècle*. (Paris, 1972).
Myron J. Smith, Jr., and Robert C. Weller, *Sea Fiction Guide*. (Metuchen, N.J., 1976).
Harold Francis Watson, *The Sailor in English Fiction and Drama: 1500–1800*. (New York, 1931).
Donald P. Wharton, ed., *In the Trough of the Sea: Selected Sea-Deliverance Narratives, 1610–1766*. (Westport, Conn., 1979).

INDEX